AUSTIN PRESBYTERIAN THEOLOGICAL SEMINARY

A Seventy-fifth Anniversary History

AUSTIN PRESBYTERIAN THEOLOGICAL SEMINARY

A Seventy-fifth Anniversary History

By Thomas White Currie, Jr.

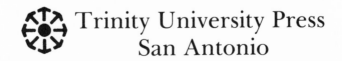 Trinity University Press
San Antonio

Chapel Reredos
Matthew: Why doth the pelican pierce her own breast with her bill?
Prudence: To nourish her young ones with her blood and thereby to show
   that Christ the blessed so loveth His young (His people) as to save them
   from death by His blood.
From John Bunyan, *The Pilgrim's Progress* (New York, Chicago, Toronto:
   Fleming H. Revell Company, 1903), pp. 240, 241.

*On the basis of the contents of this volume the author was invited by
the faculty to deliver the 1978 Thomas White Currie Lectures at
Austin Presbyterian Theological Seminary, Austin, Texas.*

Dedicated
to the
Memory
of
Thomas White Currie
Stuart Dickson Currie
and in
gratitude for the lives
of
David Mitchell Currie
Elizabeth Jeannette Currie
Thomas White Currie, III
and
James Stuart Currie
whose homes have been inseparable
from the light that shines forth
through
Austin Presbyterian Theological Seminary
Austin, Texas

Acknowledgments

This history of Austin Presbyterian Theological Seminary owed its inspiration, in the first instance, to Dr. Ernest Trice Thompson, for many years professor at Union Theological Seminary, Richmond, Virginia. He suggested the subject as appropriate for a Th.D. dissertation, and much of the data for the early period was obtained in connection with that effort. More recently Dr. Prescott H. Williams, Jr., former President of Austin Presbyterian Theological Seminary, wrote to inquire whether the author would be interested in bringing the study up to date in connection with the celebration of the seventy-fifth anniversary of the opening of Austin Seminary. It was hoped that the distribution of the story of the Seminary might kindle new interest on the part of candidates for the Gospel Ministry and on the part of those who might pray for it and give to it.

The board, the faculty, and the staff have given permission for access to records and have at all points been gracious and helpful. Gratitude is especially due to Dr. David L. Stitt, Dr. Prescott H. Williams, Jr., Dr. Jack Martin Maxwell, without whose support and aid the necessary information could hardly have been assembled. John Smiley, Herman Harren, Cathy (Mrs. Marvin) Sautter and Sara (Mrs. S. D.) Currie supplied items of special interest. Librarians, Norman Dow and Calvin Klemt, arranged free access to the archives. A word of special gratitude is owed Brian Holt for careful research into matters relating to early property transactions.

The response of alumni, board, and faculty members to appeals to delve into the treasury of vivid recollections of Seminary-related events and personalities has given this volume a unique flavor.

The arduous task of typing the dissertation was a gift from Alice (Mrs. H. J.) Belleville. The similar kindness for this volume came from the hands of Barbara (Mrs. Don) Chaney.

The time given to this work was with the gracious consent of the Sessions of St. Paul Presbyterian Church, Houston, Texas, and of Oak Cliff Presbyterian Church, Dallas, Texas.

The enabling donation to Austin Seminary which put this study into form available to many throughout the Southwest and beyond was made by Mr. and Mrs. Thomas Flint Williams, Jr. of Houston, Texas, to whom heartfelt thanks are tendered.

For careful research, manuscript examination and correction, for unfailing encouragement, unbounded gratitude is due Alison (Mrs. T. W., Jr.) Currie to whose love the author can never pay sufficient tribute.

The committee having particular responsibility for this history was composed of Dr. David Vigness, Chairman, and Rev. William H. Tiemann from the board, of Dean Edward D. Junkin for the faculty, and of Rev. Jerry R. Tompkins from the staff. Having given helpful guidelines, the committee allowed the author liberty as the work progressed. While the committee may rightly receive credit for any usefulness accruing from the book, it cannot be charged with errors or blunders that may have crept in.

If this study of the Seminary appears unfairly to obscure the warts, to hide the record of student drop-outs or other serious faults and failures, such imbalance may be laid to the writer's bias. The author loves the school, and connections with the Seminary through parents, brothers, children, and friends make dispassionate appraisal unlikely. A sense of what the Seminary has been and what it can be in the Kingdom of God in the Southwest and far beyond, has been a motive to give evidence of its advantages.

Thomas White Currie, Jr.
Dallas, Texas

Foreword

A framed parchment now in the Office of the President of Austin
Presbyterian Theological Seminary bears this inscription:

THE THOMAS WHITE CURRIE TEACHERS
MEMORIAL FUND
On December 24, 1950, the Tom Currie Men's Bible Class of
the Highland Park Presbyterian Church established. . .
THE THOMAS WHITE CURRIE
TEACHERS MEMORIAL FUND
in order that the spirit of Thomas White Currie, the founder
and former teacher of the Class, may live forever, and to honor
all the teachers, past, present and future, of the Class.

The purpose of the Fund is to sponsor the series of lectures,
now being held annually at The Austin Presbyterian Theological Seminary at Austin, Texas, which will be named *The
Thomas White Currie Lectures*. These Lectures were established to improve and inspire ministers of all denominations
and the students of the Seminary, which its former President
loved so devotedly.

These Lectures can be continued as *The Thomas White Currie Lectures* from year to year only if the Class and the individual members thereof dedicate themselves to perpetuate it. This
is written and placed here as a constant reminder that to this
great project the members of the class are forever committed.

It is a "great project" to which the members of that class—undoubtedly some of whom did not know Thomas White Currie, but
who have nevertheless been caught up in the spirit of that man—
have indeed remained faithful. It is also a project from which Austin
Seminary and the entire scholarly community have derived not a
little benefit. Even a partial list of the previous lecturers in this
series and the volumes which resulted from their research indicates
its significance: George S. Hendry, *The Holy Spirit in Christian
Theology*; John A. Mackay, *Christian Reality and Appearance*;

John Dillenberger, *Protestant Thought and Natural Science*; James Hastings Nichols, *Romanticism in American Theology*; Paul Lehmann, *Ethics in a Christian Context*; James Barr, *Old and New in Interpretation*; Dietrich Ritschl, *Memory and Hope*; Robert McAfee Brown, *Frontiers for the Church Today*.

Although the nature and intent of this volume are different in certain respects from its predecessors in the series, it is extraordinarily fitting that Thomas White Currie, Jr. write the history of Austin Presbyterian Theological Seminary, that the substance of his research be presented as The Thomas White Currie Lectures, and that those lectures be featured during the Seventy-fifth Anniversary of the Seminary.

Dr. Currie brings to this engaging study not only his keen intellect and perceptive insights into theological education, but also a love for and knowledge of Austin Seminary. His tutor, after all, was none other than Thomas White Currie, Sr., for twenty-two years the Seminary's distinguished president.

To confess that this study is not a dispassionate, "objective" history takes nothing away from its value. It is a family history, intimately and lovingly told. And yet this chronicle is also an important chapter in that much larger volume which rehearses how the Church trains its leadership.

In these pages the reader will encounter an institution with a corporate personality, committed, despite what seemed at times to be overwhelming obstacles, to train men and women principally for the parish ministry. That has always been the distinctiveness of Austin Seminary. Although many of its graduates may be found among the ranks of distinguished scholars, seminary presidents, and judicatory staff, their service to the Church is enriched because of the character and quality of their education at APTS.

With a keen sense of that legacy documented here, I heartily commend this volume.

Jack Martin Maxwell, President
Austin Presbyterian Theological Seminary

Contents

Acknowledgments · vii
Foreword · ix

1   Roots of the Seminary · 1
2   Beginnings of the Infant Institution · 15
3   A New Location and Some Teachers · 29
4   Financial Troubles · 47
5   The Faculty: 1921–1930 · 57
6   The Period of the Thirties · 71
7   Through the Eyes of a Student · 81
8   Other Impressions · 93
9   Outside the Regular Curriculum · 109
10 The Beginning of the Chapel and the End
    of an Era · 119
11 The Seminary and University Relations · 131
12 David Leander Stitt Becomes President · 139
13 Additions to the Facilities · 151
14 The Faculty: 1945–1970 · 161
15 Beyond the Classroom: Lectures and
    Publications · 177
16 The Board of Trustees · 191
17 Alumni Recollections · 199
18 Field Education · 229
19 Development of the Curriculum and a
    New President · 233
20 Into the Last Quarter of the Twentieth
    Century · 241
    Epilogue: A Look Ahead · 247

Appendices
   The Faculty · 253
   Roster of Members of the Board of Trustees · 259
   Present Campus and Housing properties, listed chronologically · 264
Bibliography · 267
Index · 277

List of Illustrations

Chapel Reredos · iv
Robert Lewis Dabney · 2
Richmond Kelley Smoot · 3
Stuart Seminary · 11
Samuel Blair Campbell · 13
Thornton Rogers Sampson · 16
Sarah C. (Mrs. George) Ball · 18
John Leighton Read and Charles Frederick Hancock · 24
William Hayne Leavell · 30
Sampson Hall and Lubbock Hall · 31
Robert Ernest Vinson · 40
Arthur Gray Jones · 49
Charles Henry Hardin Branch · 56
Thomas White Currie · 61
John Walker Vinson · 75
The Chapel · 122
Charles Turner Caldwell · 123
Interior of the Chapel · 124
Bertram Oliver Wood · 132
Aerial view of The University of Texas and Austin
  Seminary · 134
David Leander Stitt · 141
The "Leper Colony" · 152
Growth in Assets Chart · 153
The Library · 154
Married Students' Apartments · 155
The Campus · 156
Single Students' Dormitory · 157
Trull Administration Building · 158
McMillan Classroom Building · 159
Charles Leonidas King · 192
Shirley Caperton Guthrie · 194
John William Lancaster · 197
L. Frank Moore · 234
William Speight McLean · 235
Prescott Harrison Williams · 237
Jack Martin Maxwell · 242
Arch McD. Tolbert · 244
Seminary Chapel · 246

AUSTIN PRESBYTERIAN THEOLOGICAL SEMINARY

A Seventy-fifth Anniversary History

Roots of the Seminary 1

Austin Presbyterian Theological Seminary, Austin, Texas, opened its doors October 1, 1902 under the aegis of the Synod of Texas of the Presbyterian Church in the United States, but the idea for formal Presbyterian theological education had arisen some years before. In the charter issued November 22, 1849 for Austin College (now at Sherman, Texas), there is evidence that Daniel Baker and others collaborating with him in the beginning of the college saw the need for theological education west of the Mississippi. "A Theological Professorship" was mentioned as a possibility.[1] Indeed, a significant element in the effort to establish Austin College was the passion to supply pastors and evangelists for the Southwest. In the biography of his father, William M. Baker remarks,

> Yes, let it be forever remembered by the Church in Texas—let it be distinctly impressed upon the minds of the Trustees and members of the Faculty of Austin College in all succeeding generations—the one idea of its founders, that for which they wept, and prayed, and toiled, and gave their means, was that it might be an institution wherein there might be raised up for Texas, generation after generation, a native ministry.[2]

Although Austin College trained many who, after further study elsewhere, were ordained to the Gospel ministry, formal Presbyterian theological education in the Southwest found its beginnings in the center which had become the capital of Texas, Austin. Two ministers of that city, Dr. Robert Lewis Dabney and the Rev. Richmond Kelley Smoot, D.D., were concerned that the developing Southwest should have a means of training young men who were called to the ministry.

Dr. Dabney was a member of the initial faculty of The University

---

[1] William Stuart Red, *A History of the Presbyterian Church in Texas* (Austin, Texas: The Steck Company, 1936), p. 237.

[2] William M. Baker, *The Life and Labours of the Rev. Daniel Baker, D.D., Pastor and Evangelist* (Philadelphia: William S. & Alfred Martien, 1858), p. 412.

Robert Lewis Dabney, Professor of Theology, The Austin
School of Theology 1884–1895

of Texas in 1883. He was Professor of Mental and Moral Philosophy.
Dr. Dabney came to Austin from Hampden-Sydney, Virginia, where
he had taught in Union Theological Seminary since 1853 and where
he had served as pastor of the college church 1858–1874. He had
served for a time in 1862 as chief of staff to Stonewall Jackson and
chaplain to the Stonewall Brigade. In 1869 he had presented to the
General Assembly of the Presbyterian Church in the United States a
paper concerning theological education, and in 1870 he had been
elected Moderator of the General Assembly. At this time Dr. Smoot
was pastor of Austin's Free (now First Southern) Presbyterian
Church. He had been pastor since 1876 and was Moderator of the
General Assembly 1882–1883.

2

Richmond Kelley Smoot, Professor of Church History, The
Austin School of Theology 1884–1895; Professor of Church
History, Polity, APTS, 1802–1905; Board of Trustees, 1899–
1904

The Southwestern states were indeed growing as the following
census figures indicate:[3]

	Arkansas	Louisiana	Oklahoma	Texas
1840	97,574	352,411		
1850	209,897	517,762		212,592
1860	435,450	708,002		604,215
1870	484,471	726,915		818,579
1880	802,525	939,946		1,591,749
1890	1,128,211	1,118,518	258,657	2,235,527
1900	1,311,564	1,381,625	790,391	3,048,710
1910	1,574,449	1,656,388	1,657,155	3,896,542

3 *1973 Edition The World Almanac and Book of Facts* (New York, N.Y.: The
World Almanac, 230 Park Avenue, 10017), pp. 134–135.

3

In 1840 the center of population in the United States was 16 miles south of Clarksburg, West Virginia. By 1910 it was in the city of Bloomington, Indiana. The population of the State of Texas trebled during the final quarter of the nineteenth century.

John M. Ireland succeeded Oran M. Roberts in the office of Governor of the state January 16, 1883. Barbed wire, introduced into Texas about 1879, had been used by landowners to enclose their property, but this led to conflict with the cattlemen who were jealous of the open range. So bitter were the feuds arising out of fencing and fence cutting that in 1884 Ireland called a special session of the Texas legislature to seek some solution. Fencing unowned land and fence cutting were both made felonies. A gate was required for every three miles of fence.[4]

A group of stone masons from Scotland were employed in the erection of the capitol building in Austin.[5] They knew how to work the pink granite quarried near Marble Falls, Texas. The cornerstone of the building was laid on Texas Independence Day, March 2, 1885. The building continued to rise during the drought of '87 and was completed and occupied May 16, 1888, at a cost of 3,025,000 acres of land.[6]

During these years there were three branches of the Presbyterian Church at work in Texas. The following table shows both their relative strength and also in part the effect of the Cumberland merger with the Presbyterian Church of the United States of America in 1906.[7]

	1880	1890	1900	1910
Cumberland Presbyterian Church	13,994	21,956	28,859	10,707
Presbyterian Church, U. S. A.	1,103	2,357	3,099	23,480
Presbyterian Church, U. S.	5,206	10,036	17,749	27,496

In 1890 the Presbyterian Church, U. S. had about 100 ministers in Texas, and by 1900, 167; however, there were 200 more congregations than preachers. Of course, many ministers served two or more congregations, but the vacant pulpits were evidence both of the growth of the church and of the need for more clergymen.

Sensing the need for ministers trained in the Southwest who

---

[4] *Texas Almanac and State Industrial Guide*, 1974–1975 (Dallas, Texas, A. H. Belo Corporation), p. 581.

[5] Norman Kotker, ed., *Texas*, introduction by Lon Tinkle (New York, N.Y.: Chas. Scribners & Sons, n.d.), pp. 42–43.

[6] *Texas Almanac, op. cit.*, p. 620.

[7] See relevant copies of the Minutes of the General Assemblies of the three churches.

4

would stay in the Southwest, the development of the Austin School of Theology was an effort within the Presbytery of Central Texas to help meet this situation. Having in its membership two such able men as Dabney and Smoot might not have been enough, but when The Presbytery of Central Texas discovered that these two would offer their services without remuneration, the task began to assume manageable proportions. What money could be raised would be used to employ a young assistant who would teach Hebrew and Greek, and further appeal would be made to supply a building for classes and for a library.

The idea of such a school had been the subject of a conversation between Dabney and Smoot following a mid-week prayer meeting in the spring of 1884.[8] The plan was that Smoot would be titular head of the school and teach Church History, Government, and Pastoral Theology, while Dabney would teach Systematic Theology. The candidates could take other courses toward the completion of their college work at The University of Texas. A recent graduate of Union or of some other seminary would be enlisted on a teaching fellowship to instruct in languages. The teaching fellow might also study in the graduate school at The University.

About half the ministers of the Presbytery of Central Texas at a camp meeting in Belton in July of 1884 endorsed the plan. The presbytery itself in Georgetown on October 27, 1884 voted that it

> does now establish A SCHOOL OF THEOLOGY AT AUSTIN, TEXAS, recommending that students desiring to do so, may matriculate in The University of Texas, and thereby secure to themselves Dr. Dabney's lectures on Natural Theology and Moral Philosophy, also Classical Greek, as well as private instruction from Dr. Dabney . . .
>
> This Presbytery hereby overtures the Synod of Texas to take control of the school and provide for its future needs.[9]

The Presbyteries of Eastern Texas and Western Texas gave their approvals October 24 and 25 respectively, as did the Synod in Belton October 30.

Smoot and Dabney assumed personal responsibility for the first year's expenses. Classes met in the First Southern Presbyterian Church for the convenience of Dr. Smoot and in the study of Dr.

---

8 Thomas Cary Johnson, *The Life and Letters of Robert Lewis Dabney* (Richmond, Virginia: The Presbyterian Committee of Publication, 1903) , p. 264.

9 Malcolm Black, "The Austin School of Theology, Austin, Texas" (no place, no publisher, no date) .

Dabney at 507 West 23rd Street. George L. Bitzer, a licentiate, became the teaching fellow. Alonzo Rice Cocke was a post graduate student, Bitzer and William G. McDonald were seniors, C. M. Staples, a middler, and W. Stafford and Stonewall Jackson McMurry, the juniors.

The school grew, and in the fall of 1889 a lecture room and library building was erected two blocks west of The University campus, the money having come from Texas and Virginia and from "some excellent Presbyterian ladies of Baltimore."[10] The first large gift of books was about 1,000 volumes from the Rev. R. E. Sherrill. The school had now several distinguished teachers, some able students, a building, a library. Furthermore, it was debt free and had begun the effort to endow the position of teaching fellow. But difficult days were ahead.

Dr. Daniel A. Penick who for many years was a professor at The University of Texas and a member of The University Presbyterian Church has written

> I often heard my sister speak about Dr. Dabney whom she walked with and read to. (Never use a preposition to end a sentence with.) She was a great pet with Dr. D., especially after he became blind. I did have the benefit of his lectures in class for three years and admired him very much in spite of his views on the civil war and the Negro question, etc. He had trouble keeping up with progress: e.g., when tracks were being laid for trolley cars, it is reported that he would feel for the tracks with his cane so as to avoid stepping on the rails lest he be electrocuted. I do not give this as a fact. He had a master mind. He was a real thinker. I shall never forget his course on the history of Philosophy. His method was to set up every man's theory so that it looked to be perfect and then knock the props from under it and establish the correct philosophy which was always built on Christ and his principles.
>
> Dabney and Smoot, mostly Dabney, were responsible for the early days of the Seminary without any encouragement from Central Texas Pres., or the Synod of Texas. He put up the little one room house where he taught the boys and when forced to give up the task sold it to our church (Highland, now University Presbyterian) for its first building on Nueces St. then known as August St. Both D. and S. were violently opposed to union with the USA (Church) and bitterly opposed it. Dr. Smoot went so far as to have his church incorporated as the Free

---

[10] Black, *ibid.*, p. 6.

Pres. Church. . . . Both men were very strong minded and often disagreed. Dr. D. insisted that Faith precedes works, Dr. S. says that works are the basis of faith. Regardless of their disagreements they did a wonderful job without pay and without appreciation and the present seminary is based on that foundation, tho not officially so regarded. They turned out some fine men, such as McMurry, McLeod, J. P. Robertson, J. A. Montgomery, J. M. Purcell, *et al.* They had the vision which our Synod finally woke up to. Both men had fine minds of a very different type. Dr. S. was smart and quick at repartee, Dr. D. was profound with much depth of thought.[11]

The Austin School of Theology, which began with great hopes in 1884, was discontinued when Dr. Smoot and the instructor in languages, William J. Tidball, tendered their resignations to the Presbytery of Central Texas in April of 1895. Dr. Dabney, though almost blind, continued his efforts. Later that year when he had moved to be with his son in Victoria, he was still calling for candidates to study with him, offering to teach the whole range of theological studies except Hebrew. He couldn't see well enough to "point" the Hebrew consonants. Three men who studied with him in Victoria were Eugene Lowrance, Lawrence E. Selfridge, and John V. McCall.

Factors contributing to the closing of the Austin School of Theology were the advancing age and deteriorating vision of Dabney, the feeling on the part of some in the Synod of Texas that Austin College in Sherman, Synod's own college, should offer training in theology if any school in Texas did, rather than an institution in Austin with a board not elected by Synod nor established by Synod's initiative, and the small degree of financial support realized from the Presbytery of Central Texas (aggravated, no doubt, by the Panic of '94).

The Panic of '94 was especially hard on Texas. Conditions of drouth, ten-cent corn and ten per cent interest were driving many to despair. This was during the second term of Grover Cleveland, the era when Coxey's Army of 20,000 desperate unemployed marched on Washington and when their leader was arrested for walking on the grass at the capitol. Texas farmers' plea for the government to

11 D. A. Penick letter to T.W.C., Jr., April 22, 1956, and in the hands of the latter. Dr. Smoot came to his Austin pastorate in October 1876. The Church was chartered as "The Free Presbyterian Church" June 9, 1887. The Corporate Charter was amended June 23, 1919 to read "The First Southern Presbyterian Church." See William A. McLeod, *The Story of the First Southern Presbyterian Church Austin, Texas* (n.p., no publisher, ca. 1939), p. 62.

7

supply seed for new crop planting was refused on the grounds that to furnish seed at government expense would be socialistic and discourage private enterprise.

During its eleven years Austin School of Theology showed forty-six names on its roster of students. In addition to Smoot, Dabney, Bitzer, and Tidball, others who taught at one time or another included A. A. Little, W. S. Red, J. A. Lefevre, Thomas Cary Johnson, and J. M. Purcell.

In a letter to Dr. S. B. Campbell bearing the heading, "Austin, May 15, 1895," Dr. Dabney includes this closing paragraph:

> Our School has received scarcely anything from Texas; the little which it has came almost wholly from other Synods, mainly through my agency. At the approaching end of this term (possibly its last), it will have given to the Synods twenty-seven licentiates. Meantime, during the twelve years I have been in the state, only three of your own candidates, as far as I now remember, whom you allowed to go to Seminaries across the rim, have returned to labor for your Synod.
>
> Faithfully yours,
R. L. Dabney[12]

The above paragraph was in a letter addressed to Dr. S. B. Campbell because he was chairman of an ad interim committee of the Synod of Texas which had been formed for the purpose of gathering information concerning the need for a Theological Seminary and which was expected to report to the 1895 meeting of Synod at Palestine. In 1895 Synod appointed two men from each of the eight presbyteries "to receive and consider propositions for the location of a ("trans-Mississippi") seminary, and to take such measures for raising funds as they may deem advisable. . . ."[13]

The Synod of Arkansas of the Presbyterian Church, U. S., in 1897 was extended an invitation to join the Synod of Texas in founding a "Trans-Mississippi Theological Seminary." This invitation received an affirmative answer in 1905. The Synod of Oklahoma offered its support in 1908, shortly following its organization.

The Synod of Texas in 1898 voted to set May 1, 1899, as the time for the final decision as to the location of the Seminary. By 1899, when Synod was in session at Temple, the following report was heard and its recommendations adopted:

---

12 Thomas Cary Johnson, *op. cit.*, p. 503.
13 *Minutes of the Synod of Texas of the Presbyterian Church, U. S. Fortieth Session in Session at Palestine, Texas, October 25–29, 1895*, p. 37.

Your committee appointed at last meeting of Synod, to locate a Theological Seminary, held two meetings, the last at Fort Worth, on the 20th of June. All the members except Rev. C. J. Ralston were present at one or the other of these meetings, and by a unanimous vote accepted the offer of the buildings and grounds of Stuart Seminary, at Austin, Texas, for that purpose. This offer comes from the Trustees of the Austin School of Theology, who are enabled to make it, through the generous liberality of the heirs of Mrs. R. K. Red, in connection with the assets of the School of Theology.

This Seminary is beautifully located, on the highest grounds of East Austin, overlooking the whole city, and not very distant from either the State Capitol or The University of Texas. The buildings consist mainly of one large Seminary building, 54 x 108 feet, three stories, built in the most substantial manner of stone and brick, and well-finished throughout.

It has dormitories for some thirty-five students, class rooms, parlors, a library room, with 1100 choice volumes as the nucleus of a library; a large dining hall, an assembly room or chapel that seats 300 persons. It is well lighted with electric lights, and well supplied with good water, and an immense cistern cut out of solid rock, and also from a good well and the city waterworks. It has bathrooms, with both cold and hot water.

Everything is in perfect repair, and ready for immediate occupancy. The grounds are beautified with grass, and a grove of 84 nice shade trees, and are enclosed in front with a good iron fence. An electric car line passes in front of the buildings, with cars running every ten minutes, so as to afford easy access to any part of the city.

By accepting this timely and generous offer, our committee has reached a point in our work which we had not hoped to reach within less than two years of constant effort. With a Seminary building already finished, that will answer our purpose for years to come, we can now begin to raise funds for the endowment of professorships and for the erection of professors' houses and other purposes, with our people encouraged, and none of their resources exhausted in the erection of Seminary buildings.

The deed to the property of Stuart Seminary has been placed in the hands of Rev. S. B. Campbell, Treasurer of the Trustees; and also the library of some 1100 volumes, all of which is now at the disposal of the Synod.

In addition to this Rev. J. W. Sexton of Ennis has made within the last two or three days, a donation of about 140 or 150 volumes which he has not yet had time to select from his library, but which will in due time be turned over to the Seminary.

Your committee was also directed to employ a financial agent when the Seminary was located, but circumstances were unfavorable for doing so, and indeed all legal proceedings for the location of the Seminary have just now been completed.

Your committee would recommend:

1st. That Synod appoint a temporary Board of Directors with Rev. W. H. Leavell, D.D., as President of the Board and the representative of this Synod, to lay the whole matter of endowing the Seminary before the church, and to raise if possible, an endowment of not less than $200,000.

2nd. We recommend that the thanks of this Synod be tendered the heirs of Mrs. R. K. Red for their generous gift of the property of Stuart Seminary, and to the Trustees of the Austin School of Theology, through whose hands it was presented to the Synod, and that as a perpetual memorial of this gift the Seminary building be known as Stuart Hall.

We also recommend that the thanks of Synod be tendered the Trustees of the Austin School of Theology for their donation of the library of that institution, and to Rev. J. W. Sexton for his donation of books to the library of the Seminary.

3rd. We recommend that the legal title of the school be "The Austin Presbyterian Theological Seminary," and that it be regarded as the successor of the Austin School of Theology.

4th. We recommend that the Trustees be elected at the present meeting of the Synod, and that they be granted all powers necessary for the opening of the Seminary, when the Board of Directors shall have raised and deposited with the Treasurer of the Board of Directors a sum of not less than $100,000 in cash or good interest bearing notes, and that they prepare a constitution for the Seminary and report to the next meeting of the Synod.

5th. We recommend that the Seminary building and grounds be left in the care of Mr. A. L. Purcell, subject to the action of the Board of Trustees.

6th. In conclusion we would ask the Synod to call upon the Presbyterians of our State and of our land, to render the remaining year of our 19th century illustrious in the history of our church by thoroughly endowing and equipping this new Seminary, that it may be ready with the opening of the 20th century to enter on a grand career of usefulness in training young men for the Gospel Ministry, on down through all coming ages.

All of which is respectfully submitted.

S. B. Campbell, Chairman.

A committee consisting of Revs. A. H. P. McCurdy, A. G.

Stuart Seminary, Ninth & Navasota

Jones and W. L. Lowrance was appointed to nominate 7 Directors and 11 Trustees for the Theological Seminary.

The committee to nominate a Board of Directors and a Board of Trustees for the Austin Presbyterian Theological Seminary, made the following report which was adopted, and the parties therein named were elected Directors and Trustees:

Your Committee would nominate the following Board of Trustees for the Austin Presbyterian Theological Seminary:

From Presb'y of Brazos .... Rev. W. N. Scott, D. D.
   "   "   " Brownwood .... Rev. B. T. McClelland, D. D.
   "   "   " Central Texas .. Rev. R. K. Smoot, D. D.
   "   "   " Dallas .... Rev. S. B. Campbell, D. D.
   "   "   " Fort Worth .... Judge S. P. Greene
   "   "   " Eastern Texas .. Judge G. H. Gould
   "   "   " Indian .... Rev. C. J. Ralston
   "   "   " Paris .... Dr. T. J. Bell
   "   "   " Western Texas . Rev. A. G. Jones

From the Synod at Large—Rev. S. A. King, D. D., W. H. Leavell, D. D., and John S. Moore, D. D.[14]

The Stuart Seminary located in East Austin on the northwest cor-

---

[14] *Minutes of the Forty-fourth Session of the Synod of Texas of the Presbyterian Church in the United States,* October 19th to 24th, 1899, pp. 22–25, 38.

ner of Ninth and Navasota Streets had been erected by Dr. G. C. Red in 1875 for the use of the private school for girls to be operated by his wife. The school had officially opened its doors in January 1876. The last available catalogue is for the year 1895–1896. The last session ended in June of 1899.

The school building had been enlarged in 1893 in the course of which work the Rev. J. M. Purcell incurred a personal debt of $9,000. It is estimated that the Stuart Seminary grounds and improvements had actually cost in excess of $30,000.[15] However, some years later, in 1907, the sale price was $10,300.[16] The heirs of Mrs. R. K. Red, as a donation, deeded the property of the Stuart Seminary to the trustees of the Austin School of Theology. Then the funds[17] of the Austin School of Theology, approximately $4,600, were used to satisfy loans incurred in the improvement of the Stuart Seminary property and to compensate in part one of the heirs, and the Stuart Seminary property was conveyed to the trustees of Austin Presbyterian Theological Seminary. On May 11, 1905 authority was given for there to be placed on the wall of the building a tablet bearing the inscription, "Stuart Hall—in memory of Mrs. R. K. Red."[18]

Meanwhile Dr. Campbell was elected temporary chairman of the Board of Trustees. The Board of Directors, though appointed, had been dissolved December 19, 1899, and all its duties declared to repose in the Board of Trustees.

The period between the close of Austin School of Theology in 1895 and the opening of Austin Presbyterian Theological Seminary in 1902 was one in which the American Eagle was spreading its wings. On July 8, 1896 at the Democratic National Convention William Jennings Bryan delivered his "Cross of Gold" speech. The

---

[15] Mabelle Purcell, *Two Texas Female Seminaries* (Wichita Falls, Texas: The University Press, Midwestern University, 1951), pp. 106, 135, 190, 191.

[16] *Ibid.*, p. 196. This figure does not include the sale price of the additional property in the neighborhood. The total sale price was $14,000.

[17] Red, *op. cit.*, p. 308. The AST lecture room and library building at 23rd and Nueces Streets was sold to the Highland (now University) Presbyterian Church for $1,250.

[18] R. K. Smoot, *The Austin Presbyterian Theological Seminary, A Statement of Facts* (Austin, Texas: no publisher, October 10, 1904). In the safe in the office of the Seminary.

Minutes of The Board of Trustees of Austin Presbyterian Theological Seminary 1900–1908 Book "A," May 11, 1905, p. 150.

12

Samuel Blair Campbell, First Chairman of Board of Trustees
(1899–1905)

next August 16, gold was discovered near the Klondike River in
Canada, and more than 100,000 prospectors rushed into the Northwest Territories and Alaska. By April 21, 1898 the United States was
at war with Spain. Commodore George Dewey destroyed the Spanish
fleet in Manila Bay May 1. The Battleship Oregon was ordered from
there to Cuban waters. The fact that it had to go all the way around
Cape Horn, an extra 8,000 miles, dramatized as nothing else had for
the United States the need for a canal across the Isthmus of Panama.
By July 1 Theodore Roosevelt and his Rough Riders had taken San
Juan Hill in Cuba. Spain's sovereignty in Puerto Rico ended July
28. The Philippines became a United States possession by the Peace
signed December 10 in Paris. In this year six nations including the
United States sought to establish the "Open Door Policy" in China
and the Boxer Uprising occurred. The last year of the nineteenth

century saw Dr. Walter Reed and others mount a campaign to wipe out yellow fever in Cuba.

In Texas the century approached its close with the tragedy of September 8, 1900 when a hurricane hit Galveston Island and some 5,000 lives were lost. Another event was in the making hardly 75 miles to the northeast. Just south of the sleepy village of Beaumont in Jefferson County was a little smelly mound in an area ambitiously called Gladys City.

> One of the attractions there was the sour wells resort. It con-sisted of a half-dozen square boxes fashioned out of cypress boards, containing blue, green and yellow waters, with a range of palatability and odor from that of lemon phosphate to kerosene and the revolting flavor of rotten eggs. Some waters were to bathe in. Others were to drink. The range of its effects was equal to that of its colors and odors. The water would either bind its partakers tighter than the head of an Indian war drum, or send them scampering to the tall timbers with a case of what was quaintly referred to as the flying axe handles.[19]

Patillo Higgins had been sure since 1892 that beneath this mound there must be oil. But it was Captain Anthony F. Lucas' well drilled to a depth of 1,060 feet that blew in at 10:30 the morning of January 10, 1901. Oil had previously been found in Baku, Russia, at Oil City, Pennsylvania, at Corsicana, Texas, but here at Spindletop the gas pressure pushed up such a river of black gold, liquid energy, that it virtually catapulted the globe into the petrochemical age. It was in 1903 that the Ford Motor Company was organized. On December 17 of the same year at Kill Devil Hill near Kitty Hawk, North Carolina, Orville Wright flew a heavier than air mechanically propelled airplane 120 feet in twelve seconds.

America's youngest President, Theodore Roosevelt, in office since the death of William McKinley, September 14, 1901, was leading as the United States shouldered its way into the twentieth century.

---

[19] James Clark and Mike Halbouty, *Spindletop* (New York: Random House, 1952), pp. 5, 6.

Beginnings of the Infant Institution   2

In many different ways the churches had their attention called to the opportunities in distant places. For instance, of the meeting in Vadstena Castle in Sweden in 1895 to organize The World Student Christian Federation, Dr. John R. Mott could write, "Never since the Wartburg sheltered the great German reformer while he was translating the Bible for the common people has a medieval castle served a purpose fraught with larger blessing to all mankind."[1]

The vision espoused was that of Christian college students of every land across the world being challenged to unite for "the evangelization of the world in this generation."[2] The great Student Volunteer Movement quadrennial conventions which began with the one in Cleveland, Ohio in 1891 with 680 in attendance, continued until 1932 in Buffalo, the largest (6,890) being at Des Moines in 1920. These thousands of Christian young people in this and other lands were invited to consider whether to sign a pledge, "God willing, I will become a foreign missionary." Thus a virtually unparalleled stream of devoted, able, adventurous discipleship was offered each denomination. The Presbyterian Church, U.S. sent missionaries to Greece, Cuba, Brazil, China, Africa. The need for training for missionaries abroad as well as at home provided a stimulus for establishing the Seminary. The Southwest was calling, the Orient was calling, South and Central America were calling, Africa was calling.

In response the Board of Trustees appointed by the Synod of Texas of the Presbyterian Church in the United States met in Dallas May 3, 1900, at 11:00 a.m. Present were the Rev. S. B. Campbell, D.D., the Rev. J. S. Moore, D.D., the Rev. W. N. Scott, D.D., and Judge S. P. Greene. The following resolution was adopted:

[1] Basil Mathews, *John R. Mott World Citizen* (New York and London: Harper and Brothers Publishers, 1934), p. 108.

[2] This was the watchword of the Student Volunteer Movement of North America. It expressed the incandescent hope that inspired missions in many parts of Christendom. See John R. Mott, *Five Decades and a Forward View* (New York and London: Harper and Brothers Publishers, 1939), p. 22.

Thornton Rogers Sampson, President 1900–1905, Professor of Church History and Polity

On motion, it was resolved that, Rev. T. R. Sampson, D.D., be, and he is hereby elected President of the Austin Presbyterian Theological Seminary, his term to commence on June 10th, 1900, at a salary of $2500 per annum, payable monthly; provided however that the same is payable only out of funds raised by said President, he to pay his own expenses.

Said President shall, ex-officio, be financial agent of said Seminary and is hereby directed to proceed at once after commencement of his term to endeavor to raise funds for general expenses and endowment for said Seminary; and shall pay all cash raised and notes and other evidence of property received for said Seminary over to the Treasurer, who shall out of same pay the monthly salary of the President, taking his receipt for same. Said

16

President is hereby cordially and earnestly commended to the liberality of our people.[3]

To this Dr. Sampson agreed, first for twelve months from June 10, 1900, and later as a permanent assignment. Thus, Dr. Sampson had the Stuart Seminary property and a license to seek money for an operating budget and a $100,000 endowment, professors to teach, and as the goal of all, candidates anxious to be better prepared to pursue their calling to the ministry.

"Dr. Sampson," wrote Thomas Watt Gregory, "would have been a success in any business or profession because of his catholic love for humanity, his ability to appreciate the ordinary man, and his lack of cant."[4]

In 1901 the Synod of Texas heard that more than $53,000 was on hand. A constitution was adopted. Permission was given for the Seminary to be opened in 1902 if $100,000 in endowment funds had by then been received.[5]

Mrs. Sarah C. Ball of Galveston was the benefactor by whose gift of $75,000 the chairs of Systematic Theology and Old Testament Languages and Exegesis were endowed. Dr. Sampson was able to count $10,000 on hand and an additional $17,000 in a scholarship fund. A part of this latter fund was given on condition that it be lent to Daniel Baker College. However, it never proved to be of any financial benefit to the Seminary.[6]

In April of 1902 the announcement went out in the form of a leaflet:

Does the Southern Presbyterian Church need another Seminary now?

This is a question which nine-tenths of the members of the Church, and four-fifths of the ministers will possibly answer in the negative.

It cannot, indeed, be denied by any one that such necessity, if it exists at all, does not appear from the surface, as viewed from the East. Not only so, but many feel that there are already too many seminaries, and that two or more of those now in op-

---

[3] Minutes of the Board of Trustees of the Austin Presbyterian Theological Seminary, Book "A," 1900–1908, pp. 5–6.

[4] Arthur G. Jones, *Thornton Rogers Sampson* (Richmond, Va.: Richmond Press, Inc., Printers, 1917), p. 128.

[5] Thomas W. Currie, Jr., *A History of Austin Presbyterian Theological Seminary, Austin, Texas 1884–1943*, manuscript in Library of Austin Presbyterian Theological Seminary, pp. 251–253.

[6] *Ibid.*, p. 45.

Sarah C. (Mrs. George) Ball. *Courtesy of Ball High School, Galveston, Texas*

eration could be combined, with great economy of both men and money. Certainly this is a proposition which no one will deny, as viewed from the West.

Still, notwithstanding all this, the Synod of Texas has unanimously decided to establish another Seminary, and no one, who is at all familiar with the facts and conditions in this State, can doubt that it is a necessary step, not only for further progress, but even "to hold its own."

What are the facts and conditions which have led to this unanimous conclusion here, so different from what is thought elsewhere?

It may be well to attempt to set forth briefly some of these. Many of them are certainly not generally known, and others, not a few of them indeed, it may not be possible for those who have not lived under them fully to appreciate.

1. The Growth of the Church in Texas.   18

The ratio of increase of church membership in the State of Texas, in the Southern Church alone, since 1870, has been over *nine hundred per cent,* or *three* times as great as that in any other State! The increase in Florida has been only three hundred percent, and in no other State has it been much more than half that in Florida.

In 1870 there were only 2,000 members in Texas. In 1900 there were over 18,000. At this rate, in another ten years the Synod of Texas will be *second* in numbers in the General Assembly. It is now *fifth.*

It has been absolutely impossible to keep up with this increase in the churches by supplying ministers from the eastern States.

A pathetic letter recently received, one of a large class, from a loyal son of South Carolina, laboring in this State, contains this sentence:

"The whole Southwestern Church feels that this is the one great thing we now need, and by Southwestern I do not mean our little Presbytery down here, but our Synod. Our Presbytery feels that the one supreme matter now to be pressed, pressed, pressed, is the Austin Theological Seminary."

There are today more than three hundred and seventy churches, and less than one hundred and seventy ministers. Of these ministers, more than twenty are on the invalid list or engaged in educational and editorial work. There are about one hundred and ten pastors. So that there remain only about forty ministers to supply the remaining *two hundred* and *sixty churches.* This mighty cry, "Come over and help us," has gone, so far, unheeded.

The fact that many of these are weak churches only accentuates the necessity, because it will never be possible to secure pastors, with wives from the eastern States, who can live on the salaries or under the conditions which prevail in these churches now, although a few years' work, in some cases only a few months' work, will make many of them self-supporting and independent organizations.

Many of the most weighty considerations which make a seminary and a native ministry, trained on the ground, a necessity for Japan or South America, apply to this field.

2. The Number of Candidates for the Ministry.

It is not in ratio of increase in the church membership alone that this field is remarkable; but also in the proportion which its candidates for the ministry bear to those of the older States. The minutes of the assembly show that there were thirty-four candidates in the Synod of Texas, and thirty-six in the Synod of Virginia, in 1900. That is, Texas has only two less than the

Synod of Virginia, which has double its church membership! Texas, with one-twelfth of the membership of the whole assembly, had one-eighth of the candidates for the ministry! The year before the proportion was even still higher.

With the rapid increase in educational advantages through the Church and public schools, which has recently set in, it is only reasonable to expect that there will be an increase even in this number.

3. The Cost of the Present System.

To send these young men to the seminaries in the old States, costs a great deal, in money.

It takes more than the Assembly's Committee of Education for the Ministry allows a young man to carry him from Austin, Texas, to Richmond, Va., and back again. But the money is only a small part of what it costs.

The old States levy a "child-tax" upon Texas, keeping many of these candidates for all time.

They become weaned during their student life in various ways, from the State. Attracted by churches, young ladies or social conditions, many of them never come back, or if they come back do not remain, and, in not a few cases, they are among the most talented of the students.

Even when this is not the case, the weak churches of the State are deprived of such services as they could render and are rendering, while pursuing their studies in the States contiguous to the seminaries. It is impossible to say how much has been accomplished in Virginia, South Carolina, Kentucky and Tennessee, by the labors of the students in the vacation.

Of four students who went to Union in 1899 not one was able to come back the next year to Texas, although they all desired to do so. The distance from Austin to the nearest seminary, east of the Mississippi is twice as great as from Richmond, Va. to New York, and the distance from Austin to Richmond is more than four times as great as that from Richmond to New York.

When there is added to all this what the professors can do during the same period of vacation, as well as during the session, it is possible to appreciate, in some measure, what this great and needy and promising field is losing by being so distant from the existing seminaries.

This seminary in Austin is the great hope, and it would seem the only hope, of Home Missions in this State.

4. The Extent of the Field to be Reached.

But a seminary in Texas will not only meet the necessities of Texas. There are great fields, north, south and west of it, in Indian Territory, Mexico and New Mexico, to say nothing of

20

Arkansas, which must look to it for help.

The Church at large is not alive to the great opportunities it is losing in these sections. The stream of immigration is pouring into them, almost doubling the population in ten years, and the soil—as productive as can be found within the borders of the United States—insures a prosperous people.

In the Indian Territory, especially, the sentiment of the people is now most favorable to Presbyterianism, because of the work done in the past by this Church. Still there are many large towns in which there is no Presbyterian organization.

This stream of immigration must largely increase in the immediate future, for no State has received, in the last year, so much and such favorable notice from the press as Texas.

The discovery of the special adaptation of large sections of the State for rice culture, the opening of the great oil fields, the visits of influential committees of business men from New York, St. Louis and Kansas City, as well as the magnificent crops, and the consequent large accumulation of deposits in the banks, have all focussed the attention of the whole country and of Europe upon it, to a degree that has no parallel in any other State.

5. What it May Accomplish.

The great value of having an institution on the ground easily accessible, to increase the number of students, can readily be seen in the case of The University of Texas.

It was opened in 1883, and for several years had only a few hundred students. It has had over one thousand during the past session, and, at present, is making preparations to accommodate twelve or fifteen hundred next session.

The Austin School of Theology, during its brief existence of ten years, put more than forty men (only 37 of these can now be identified) into the ministry, and over half of these are now among the most useful and influential men in the Synod of Texas. While several are dead, others are filling positions of honor in their native States.

Whatever may be thought of the expediency or wisdom of the consolidation of Seminaries effected in Kentucky, it is confidently hoped and believed that there will never be any need for more than one in Texas to supply the necessities of this field.

The Austin Presbyterian Theological Seminary will be glad to help equip all young men, with proper qualifications, who may present themselves, and to help preserve them from the attractions and temptations of eastern institutions, churches and ladies.

Organic union is neither desired nor feared in Texas by the Southern Church, as the sentiment and tendency are almost solidly one way here. The opening of the Seminary will only further that tendency.

— — —

There is no antagonism in this movement to the existing institutions in the eastern States, of which the ministers here are nearly all alumni. On the contrary, any one of them, or any two of them combined, would be warmly welcomed to this free field.

Indeed, it is an open secret that one of the greatest difficulties with which the institutions of Texas have had to contend, has been at this point. The ministers and elders have, out of a natural loyalty to the theological and academic institutions from which they have come, so often sent their own sons, and encouraged their friends to send their sons, east of the Mississippi to be educated.

There are now three institutions in Texas—Daniel Baker College, Austin College, and The University of Texas—which are fully able to give necessary academic training for the young men of the Church, and a seminary in this field will be absolutely without competition, with a territory to draw from, and to supply, unequalled by any within the bounds of the General Assembly.[7]

So it was that on the evening of Wednesday, the first day of October 1902, the Seminary was formally opened with a service at the First Southern Presbyterian Church.

The president, Thornton Rogers Sampson, was a Virginian of exuberant vitality. He studied at Hampden-Sydney, The Universities of Virginia, Edinburgh, and Leipzig. He learned Arabic at the American University in Beirut, represented the American and British Bible Societies in Greece, and was a missionary of the Presbyterian Church, U.S., there. He had traveled in Europe, Palestine, and the Orient. He came to the presidency of Austin College in 1896 and became the president of the Seminary in 1900. In addition to his duties as president, Dr. Sampson taught Church History and Polity.

Dr. Sampson was a close observer of the situation of the church in the Southwest. He believed that the hope for the Presbyterian Church, U.S., was a native ministry, locally trained:

Doctor Sampson used to say that to be sure of a ministry in

---

[7] *The Austin Presbyterian Theological Seminary*, Austin, Texas, Catalogues, vol. 1, n.d. (issued approximately April 1902), pp. 5, 6, 7, 8.

this great Southwest, "you had to born 'em, and educate 'em, and marry 'em out here; then", he said, "you had 'em." One of the strong reasons which he gave for a Seminary in this section was that the boys from this section would go to Richmond, or Louisville, or Columbia, and in the midst of all that culture and refinement would marry a "guinea" wife. She would consent to come out here, but in just about a year she would begin to cackle, "Go back, go back, go back", and we would lose a fine man for these mission fields.[8]

Robert Ernest Vinson, who was the Seminary's professor of Old Testament Languages and Exegesis, was born November 4, 1876 at White Oak, Fairfield County, South Carolina. He was graduated from Austin College in 1896 and from Union Theological Seminary in Virginia in 1899. For the following three years he served as co-pastor of the First Presbyterian Church, Charleston, West Virginia. He was not only scholarly and personable, but, as the president of Union Theological Seminary, Virginia, said, "a superior man."[9] He also was to serve as librarian, with some twelve to fifteen hundred volumes under his care.

Samuel Alexander King, who had for some forty years served as pastor of First Presbyterian Church of Waco, became the professor of Systematic Theology. Dr. King was 68 years old the day the Seminary opened. He was from Woodford County, Kentucky, and he had been educated by his father. He studied theology under Dr. J. H. Zivley and was ordained in 1856 by the New School Texas Presbytery. Prior to coming to Waco he served in Crockett, Centerville, and Milford. He served as Moderator of the Synod of Texas in 1867 and of the General Assembly in 1892. On February 28, 1903 in the lobby of the First National Bank of Waco, Dr. King was presented a gold watch in which was engraved: "Samuel A. King, D.D. A token of love and esteem from citizens of Waco, 1863–1903."[10]

The entering class in the fall of 1902 was composed of: Leonard Gill from England; Charles Frederick Hancock from Arkansas; William Angus McLeod from North Carolina; John Leighton Read from Texas; William Henry Trainum from Virginia, but more recently from Manor, Texas; and James Robertson West from Missis-

---

8 J. F. Hardie, paper sent to T.W.C., Jr., August 23, 1957, and in the hands of the latter.

9 Catalogue, APTS, vol. 1, *op. cit.*, p. 3.

10 C. T. Caldwell, *Historical Sketch of the First Presbyterian Church, Waco, Texas* (Waco, Texas: Methodist Home Press, 1937), p. 34.

John Leighton Read and Charles Frederick Hancock, Class of 1905, at the entrance of the building first used by Austin Seminary

sippi. One year later John Black Hudson from Barboursville, Kentucky, who had taken the first part of his work at Danville joined this class.

Before two months had passed certain policies had been adopted and rules posted. Students were encouraged to take part in Sabbath schools and prayer meetings but were discouraged from undertaking regular preaching assignments. Students were earnestly requested not to deface furniture, walls, or woodwork, and admonished to direct any expectoration solely to cuspidors provided in the hall unless at their own expense they provided such necessities in their rooms.

As the senior professor Dr. King followed R. L. Dabney and Charles Hodge as a teacher of what he termed *Federal* theology. It was said, "When old Doctor King dies, the last man will have passed away who had a speaking acquaintance with Adam." Dr. King believed, "In Adam's fall, we sinned all." He had the highest hopes for his students when he would tell them, "Young men, your hands were made to hold a sceptre; your brows were made to wear a crown; and your frames were fashioned to wear royal robes."[11]

Dr. King viewed the church as one from Eden to eternity, as a stream is one from the tiniest trickle at its source all the way to the ocean. The visible church is composed of penitent believing sinners and their children under a special covenant, the "Great Charter" of which was the Covenant with Abraham. In the church, Christ alone legislates; the courts of the church may not. They only adjudicate and execute. As to the inspiration of the Bible, Dr. King believed

All books are inspired, and every part of each book is the inspired Word of God. . . . Inspiration extends not only to all the books, but also to the words. At the same time the Church does not hold what has been known as the "dictation" or "machine" theory. The inspiration was *dynamical.* Inspired men wrote in their own style in words which were their own, but were so "moved," borne along by the Spirit, that what they said God said.[12]

As to his view of education and religion and their relation, in a Thanksgiving address in 1894 Dr. King held that American Calvinism never

Dreads the skeptic's puny hands
While near the school the church spire stands;
Nor fears the blinded bigot's rule
While near her church spire stands a school.[13]

Concerning Dr. King, S. K. Dodson (Class of 1909) writes,

I believe that Dr. King left a more lasting impression on my life than any one of the other [of the faculty]. He might have been classed as an old man, seventy-five years of age, according to the calendar. But there was nothing old or feeble about his mind. For though he was a very ripe scholar, he was still a hard student, and brought to his classes a rich result of his studies.[14]

---

11 Currie. *op. cit.,* p. 69, and J. F. Hardie letter to T.W.C., Jr., September 20, 1955; in hands of the latter.

12 Samuel A. King, *The System of Doctrines of the Westminster Standards* (Richmond, Virginia: Presbyterian Committee of Publication, c. 1905) , p. 7.

13 Samuel A. King, *A Sermon On Thanksgiving,* November 29, 1894 (Columbia, Missouri: E. W. Stephens Printer, 1895) .

14 S. K. Dodson letter to Rev. Stuart Currie, dated Hamburg, Ark., October 15, 1975, and in the hands of T.W.C., Jr.

I do not remember how it came up, but it seemed that [in the fall of 1908] the matter of shouting was being discussed in one of Dr. King's classes, and he calmly remarked that he never had shouted, but that if [William Jennings] Bryan was elected President he was going to shout. So on the night of election day, almost the whole personnel of the Seminary went down town where the results of the election were being shown on a huge bulletin, many of them hoping that they would have the experience of hearing Dr. King shout. And for a while it seemed that they might have that privilege. But alas! You know, without my writing it here, that it did not come to pass.[15]

Dr. King retired to the status of Emeritus Professor of Systematic Theology at the age of 80 in 1914 and died September 21, 1918.

One of the early additions to the faculty was Dr. R. K. Smoot. He came in the fall of 1903 to assume duties in the area of Church History and Polity. This vacancy had come about because of Dr. Sampson's consent to lead a financial campaign. Dr. Smoot was given leave to continue as pastor of First Southern Presbyterian Church until his chair should be endowed, being also allowed a year to decide whether he would accept the Seminary work for an indefinite period. However, before this decision was made, Dr. Smoot died on January 10, 1905.

Dr. Sampson became the spearhead in Texas for the denominational effort known as the Twentieth Century Fund. At the Synod of Texas in 1903 Dr. Sampson agreed to be chiefly responsible for raising $50,000 each for Austin College, Daniel Baker College, and Austin Seminary. An anonymous donation of $5,000 assured his salary and relieved the Seminary of this expenditure for two years. Unfortunately, incessant travel and other burdens proved too much even for Dr. Sampson's robust constitution, and on the advice of his physician he gave up his responsibilities for the Twentieth Century Fund. On December 9, 1904 he tendered his resignation as president of Austin Presbyterian Theological Seminary.

Dr. Sampson took up again the courses in Church History and Polity for the spring of 1905. The Board not only noted the death of Dr. Smoot and the illness of Dr. Sampson but also the illness of Mrs. Sarah C. Ball (she died June 10, 1905) and the death of Judge S. P. Greene who had been a faithful member of the Board since its inception.

[15] S. K. Dodson letter to T.W.C., Jr. dated Hamburg, Ark., November 11, 1975, and in the hands of T.W.C., Jr.

26

In the spring of 1905, on May 10, the infant institution sent forth its first graduating class: Leonard Gill, Certificate (to Charlotte area of North Carolina) ; Charles Frederick Hancock, B.D. (to China as PCUS missionary) ; John Black Hudson, B.D. (served in Southwest) ; William Angus McLeod, B.D. (served in Southwest, taught Theology at APTS 1914–18) ; John Leighton Read, B.D. (served in Southwest) ; and James Robertson West, B.D. (served in Southwest) .[16]

[16] Minutes of the Board of Trustees of the Austin Presbyterian Theological Seminary, Book "A" (all written by hand) , Board meeting, May 11, 1905, p. 152.

A New Location and Some Teachers   3

Following the resignation of Dr. Sampson as President, the faculty as a whole assumed the duties of administration. Dr. King was Chairman of the Faculty until May, 1907. During this period, the Seminary acquired and began to develop a new site.

The Austin School of Theology had been located a scant two blocks from The University of Texas' original forty acres. Stuart Hall, on the other hand, at Ninth and Navasota Streets was two miles from the campus, or farther if one went by street car. Thus, in order for a student to attend classes in The University and in the Seminary the same morning, or for a teacher to teach in both, a decrease in the distance between the two schools was necessary.

On May 10, 1906, Dr. Sampson "read to the Board certain papers relating to the removal of the Seminary to a site nearer to the State University."[1] After receiving assurances that there was no legal barrier to the relocation of the Seminary within the city limits of Austin, the Board heard from Dr. Josephus Johnson, pastor of First Southern Presbyterian Church, and from Dr. Sampson that certain friends in Austin would help. An option had been obtained for a site north of 27th Street and west of Speedway. The cost would be $4,700 plus accrued interest. Friends in Austin previously at various times had given the Seminary $3,925. Now, the Board heard, The Business League of Austin would endeavor to help bring this to a total of $15,000 on condition that the Board would locate the Seminary permanently in Austin.

After a proper inspection of the site these five and one-fourth acres were bought for $5,029[2] by unanimous action of the Board, and the Seminary was declared to be definitely and permanently located in Austin. The property at Ninth and Navasota was sold for

[1] *Minutes of the Board*, Book "A", 1900–1908, p. 203.
[2] According to the *Audit Report Austin Presbyterian Theological Seminary*, Austin, Texas, April 30, 1946, by R. A. Moore Company, Certified Public Accountants, Fort Worth, Texas. On page 2 Mr. Moore reports that these 5¼ acres was bought at a cost of $5,029.

William Hayne Leavell, Board Chairman 1906–1907. *Courtesy of James L. Bayless*

$14,000.[3] Dr. Johnson secured plans for a brick and stone building to cost approximately $20,000. Dr. Sampson was given permission to use the last three weeks in April to travel outside the state in search of more funds. A contract for the building of a dormitory was let on the condition that no more would be erected than money was available to pay for. A bequest from Governor Frank R. Lubbock of $4,000 was used to erect a dining hall to bear the name of the testator. Temporary quarters for classes for the fall of 1907 were rented for $50 per month at 2408 Nueces.

The construction of the dormitory building stopped for lack of funds. Then Dr. Sampson and Dr. Vinson borrowed the money to complete the building with the prospect that rental of the rooms to university students would amortize the loans.

[3] See Chapter I, note 16.

30

Sampson Hall (left) and Lubbock Hall (right), 1908

In order to provide homes for the faculty, the Board agreed that "there seems to be no reason why a portion of the endowment funds should not be used therefore, and to that end recommend the erection of three or four residences to meet the necessities of the several members of the Faculty to range in cost from $4,000.00 to $6,000.00, and that such houses be rented to the said members of the Faculty at such yearly rental as will yield six per cent net upon their respective cost."[4] In March of 1908 the new premises were occupied. Soon four faculty homes were erected on the north side of 27th Street between Speedway and Lubbock Hall. The fifth residence at 2621 Speedway was erected a little later on land donated by Dr. and Mrs. Vinson. The cost of the five brick homes was $37,076.[5] Each professor vowed to pay rent and insurance on the residence he occupied.[6]

The character of the Seminary was largely wrought by its professors. Former students particularly remembered vivid stories about Dr. Sampson.

He was redheaded . . . He once remarked in chapel, "Enough

[4] *Minutes of the Board*, Book "A," *op. cit.*, p. 291.
[5] R. A. Moore, *Audit Report 1946, op. cit.*, p. 2.
[6] *Minutes of the Board, Book "A," op. cit.*, p. 293.

grace to last some of you all day would not last me fifteen minutes."[7]

He frequently used in chapel Psalm 27, especially the 4th verse, "One thing have I desired of the Lord, that will I seek after, that I may dwell in the house of the Lord all the days of my life, to behold the beauty of the Lord and to inquire in his temple." He desired, after the forms of worship were over, that the spirit of worship and the presence of the Lord might be with him continually, and that he might find a solution for his perplexities in the spirit of worship.[8]

His comments after student preaching sometimes were acrid. He helped us walk where the makers of history had walked. One of his sermon criticisms was, "The sermon was both good and original. But the good portion was not original, and the original portion was not good." . . .

He was asked by a prominent Catholic priest, "Where was the Presbyterian Church before the Reformation?" And he replied, "Where was your face before you washed the dirt off this morning?"[9]

Doctor Sampson was the linguist. He was asked by a member of my class one day what language he spoke when he was in Switzerland; his answer was, "It depended on what corner of it I was in." T. W. Currie, Sr., said he was the greatest teacher that ever touched his life. We will never forget what he said about *facts*: "A fact is like a louse: when you get it in your head it is hard to get out."

He said he was sitting in a beer garden in Germany with Philip Schaff, who said "Sampson, your America is crucified between two thieves, your poor beer and your Sunday newspaper!"

Doctor Sampson had what he said was the hardest class period, from twelve to one, and when any student would nod he would come up with an awakening story. He told about going with another scholar to an ancient monastery, high up on a "precipitous rock." He and his friend had to go in a small boat, pull a rope which sounded a bell at the monastery, and when the monastery was satisfied about them a basket was let down to bring them up. They anchored their boat and were lifted aloft. Their intentions were to read the ancient Greek manuscripts

[7] E. W. McLaurin letter to T.W.C., Jr., December 7, 1955, and in the hands of the latter.

[8] *Ibid.*

[9] T. C. Vinson letter to T.W.C., Jr., received November 5, 1955, and in the hands of the latter.

kept in the monastery. But a monk, with a long black robe and a small rope about his middle, was assigned to watch them.

In looking over the monastery they finally went below to the catacombs, where, Doctor Sampson said, bones were piled up in a large heap in one corner. But as they went down the stairs they noticed on the wall the painting of an angel climbing out of purgatory. One of them remarked to the other, "It would take a long-legged angel to climb that ladder with the rungs so far apart." They were leaning against one of the pillars down there, talking, when the old monk, to whom they were paying no attention, spoke in English, "Let's go up stairs past that long-legged angel." Doctor Sampson said in wondering amazement, "How is it that you are speaking English?" The old monk remarked, "I guess I am from Old Kentuck," and then explained that he had fled in the days of reconstruction, "and finally," he said, "I drifted down to this durn hole."[10]

Dr. Sampson never lost his love of the mountains. In the summer of 1915 he took his family to Colorado and, leaving them in Denver, he went on a fishing and tramping trip in the Grand Lake country. He writes a charming letter from Rand August 21st,

> . . . The air and weather and mountains are as fine as ever, but these abominable autos have invaded the place and the hunting will soon be all gone and the fishing sadly interfered with. There were three camping parties here last night and at least a dozen have passed through today. The government is working on the roads and soon there will be no place inaccessible to these miserable little Fords except the Peaks.
>
> Tomorrow I am going up to see some friends who live out of reach of anybody else, about half a mile from the top of one of the most difficult passes. They say I am the only visitor they have ever had. I shall take up the mail and some fresh meat and spend the night with them, possibly.[11]

He did not return from this trip. The following appeared in a Seminary *Bulletin* in 1932.

Thornton Rogers Sampson, D.D., LL.D.

He "deserved that the horses and chariot of fire should carry him aloft as they did Elijah . . ." So wrote his friend, Dr. J. P.

---

10 J. F. Hardie letter to T.W.C., Jr. September 20, 1955, and in the hands of the latter.

11 Arthur Gray Jones, *Thornton Rogers Sampson, D.D., LL.D.* (Richmond, Virginia: Richmond Press, Inc., Printers, 1917), p. 116.

Mahaffy, of Trinity College, Dublin, on receiving word of Dr. Sampson's death.

* * * * * * * * * *

Dr. T. R. Sampson, minister, missionary, first president of Austin Seminary, on summer vacation in Colorado, 1915, left Denver for a mountain tramp August 11th, and was last seen by fellow-climbers as they passed each other on the Continental Divide, September 2nd.

* * * * * * * * * *

Having been a leader of wide repute in religious and educational circles, with a host of friends the world over, in personal touch with President Woodrow Wilson, Attorney General Gregory, and Secretary Houston of the Department of Agriculture, his loss inspired the greatest search in the history of Colorado. The President of the United States ordered all available forest rangers into action, while Denver and other cities organized searching parties which scoured the trail leading over Flat-top Mountain.

* * * * * * * * * *

On July 13, 1932, seventeen years after the strange disappearance of his father, Mr. Frank Sampson of Atlanta hurried to Denver, having received news of discoveries which gave promise of solution of the mystery locked so long in the silence of the Rockies. Three miles beyond Flat-top summit, over the range from Grand Lake, and thirteen miles southwest of Estes Park, there lies what is known as Fern Valley. Here, in a kind of cove, Mr. Sampson was shown and was able to identify, by the side of the mortal remains, a diary still legible, a knapsack with toilet articles, a pipe, carved by himself, a can of tobacco, and unburned matches.

* * * * * * * * * *

All friends of Dr. Sampson and of his family and of the institution which he loved, will be reverently interested in the story as outlined by his son upon the basis of the data available:

Without doubt he failed to survive the first night out of Grand Lake. Having been slightly indisposed (as according to his diary), despite the usually unabated vigor of sixty-three years, his lowered vitality, on a hike of more than seventeen miles and a vertical climb of more than 4000 feet, failed to react to the exposure of a cold rainy day. It is very comforting to know that he was neither hurt nor lost. From the trail, the last three miles he traveled, the two lakes he was to pass, were in plain view. Had he had a minor injury he would have smoked his pipe and written in his diary. If he had had a fall

34

he could never have climbed up to the cove where his kit was found. He had got over the top. He was on the west side at 11,000 feet elevation at 2 p.m., having started that morning at 8500 feet. He passed over the Divide, at 12,000 feet, about 5 p.m., and was descending evidently when night caught him, at the timber line. He must have built a fire and have fallen asleep for the night—to awake with the Lord.

It seemed providential that the only minister of the only Church in Estes Park was Presbyterian, and that the pastor, Rev. Mr. Kuykendal, himself knew Dr. Sampson's record. The worship was beautifully appropriate, in the quiet valley decked by nature's hand with ferns, fifty feet above the trail, under a large overhanging rock. The preacher read the 61st and 121st Psalms and spoke fittingly of Dr. Sampson's life. Among other things he said: "No one need tell me of the influence of this man's life throughout the world, nor can one doubt that it will live forever; for I have visited Athens, where more than fifty years ago he laid the foundations during seven years of labor; and I visited Salonika, where his work is still going on for the Lord, and where the good man labored seven more years; and I have visited China and talked and prayed with missionaries who studied at his knee."

What Providence that God should bring such factors into focus at that mountain sepulchre! There was no music, and no flowers save a wreath of the rangers' making, of pine and spruce and other evergreens, fitting and beautiful. And when the minister, hand uplifted, said, "the trumpeter will sound 'taps' for this soldier of the King," the bugle's requiem rang out from high above, reverberating from height to height. So, his works to follow him.

> And hath he not high honor,
>   The hillside for a pall;
> To lie in state while angels wait,
>   With stars for tapers tall!
> The dark rock-pines, like tossing plumes,
>   Over his bier to wave;
> And God's own Hand in that lonely land
>   To lay him in his grave![12]

Eugene Craighead Caldwell came to the chair of Old Testament

---

[12] *Austin Seminary Bulletin* XLVII, 3 (October 1932). The poem quoted is "The Burial of Moses" by Cecil Frances Alexander. It appeared in *Golden Numbers*, Children's Crimson Series, by Kate Douglas Wiggin and Nora Archibald Smith (New York: Grosset and Dunlap Publishers; copyright by Doubleday, Page and Company, 1902) and is used here by courtesy of Doubleday and Co. Inc.

Languages and Exegesis in the fall of 1906. He had graduated from Hampden-Sydney and was a Hoge Fellow at Union Theological Seminary in Virginia to which he returned in 1914.

His careful outlines of the books of the Bible and his useful bibliographies together with his approach to the Scriptures that was at once full of faith and devotion and fearless to encompass the best critical scholarship gave his students a grasp of the Bible and the tools of Bible study that was to bless them throughout their ministry. Little if any of his writing was published while he was in Austin, but perhaps his Richmond books and papers were an indication of his earlier teaching.

He taught his students how to wrest from the words of the Bible a defensible position on a disputed point. For instance, in his lectures on Rev. 20 entitled, "The Millennium," after a cogent and closely knit study of the text, he brings the matter to a close with:

> Let us briefly sum up the results of our study and state the conclusion to which we have been led. The expression, "a thousand years," is a symbol of the whole Christian era and chapter 20 is a condensed panorama of the conflicts of the church from her first temporary victory over Satan on to the final and complete victory. Throughout this whole period the victims of Nero and Domitian, the first Christian martyrs, "the first fruits unto God" (14:4) reign with Christ in heaven. This signal honor is theirs, because they were the pioneers and pointed the way to victory for others to follow in their train. How far into this period we have already advanced we can learn only from the progress the church has made in the evangelization of the world; for the gospel must be preached in all the world, and then cometh the end. As the church approaches the completion of her task, the time draweth ever nearer for the appearance of the Saviour. In the meantime, the church, by reason of the presence and power of her Lord in the person of the Holy Spirit, is gradually extending her conquests over the earth, and on the eve of her final victory Christ will appear in person and will himself lead her in the final battle against sin, and with her share the honors and glories of the victory and establish the kingdom of God in its full perfection and abiding splendor.

> This view of the Millennium and the Second Coming, derived from a study of chapter 20 in the light of the whole book, possesses certain distinct advantages. For one thing, it banishes all notions of a period of a thousand years from our consideration of the Lord's return. Thank God for that riddance; for

where to put that long period, before or after Christ's appearance, has been the chief bone of contention and the prolific source of error, confusion and division. Another advantage is that it saves us from the distressing and absurd thought that after so long and so glorious a reign of God's people on earth the whole thing is to be spoiled by a fresh outbreak of Satan's power. This view removes all such dread. Furthermore, it accepts all the good points of both post-millennarianism and pre-millennarianism and rejects all that is bad in both. And last, but not least, it harmonizes some apparently contradictory New Testament teachings concerning Christ's coming and the establishment of his kingdom.[13]

The position stated here by Dr. Caldwell accurately represents the continuing point of view of the faculty of Austin Seminary as contrasted with the premillennial and dispensational views. A later reference will be found to the deliverance of the General Assembly with respect to the latter doctrine in a subsequent chapter. This deliverance was in part formulated by Dr. E. W. McLaurin who had by then been added to the Seminary faculty.

Dr. Chalmers Vinson had a further recollection of Dr. Caldwell. "Dr. Caldwell was a scholar and profound thinker. He spent far more time in study than any student. When he led the "Hebrew Children" through the fiery furnace with a particularly tough assignment he would always remind us that John Calvin never slept more than FOUR hours any night."[14]

Dr. Cecil H. Lang also remembered:

E. C. Caldwell was far and away the best teacher. He was thorough, even to the point of being meticulous. He had a wonderful gift of repeating the same truth over and over again but in different words and from a different angle. The students who sat under him had to work—they knew it, but they always knew that they were coming out of his classes well rewarded for the effort they had put forth in their studying.[15]

Wade H. Boggs wrote:

While lecturing on Hebrew one day he quoted Proverbs 22:6 (Bring up a child in the way he should go. . . .) and then paren-

---

[13] Eugene C. Caldwell, "The Millennium," *The Union Seminary Review* XXXI, 3 (April 1920) , pp. 232–34.
[14] T. C. Vinson, letter, *op. cit.*
[15] C. H. Lang letter to T.W.C., Jr., November 3, 1955, and in the hands of the latter.

thetically remarked, "Young gentlemen, if you ever decide to preach on this text, be sure to do it before you have any children of your own. . ."

Dr. Caldwell was a great teacher and expected every man in his classes to do his very best. I was a member of a small class in Hebrew, and it seemed to the members of our class that he had made unreasonably long assignments. The class asked me to register a respectful protest at the next meeting of the class and his reply to my protest ended the discussion. It was as follows: "Young gentlemen, the assignments in this class are made on the assumption that the members of the class have at least average ability."

Dr. Caldwell's criticism of my sermon before the faculty in my senior year was typical of his incisiveness: "Mr. Boggs, you had a good text tonight, and your outline was excellent, but the body of your sermon was starved to death. Feed it."

Dr. Caldwell was particularly hard on any student who spiritualized a text in his faculty sermons. On one occasion while I was at the Seminary we had a baccalaureate sermon preached by a prominent pastor, and the sermon was a high degree of spiritualizing from start to finish. We students decided among ourselves that it would be fine to hear Dr. Caldwell's criticism on this sermon. That afternoon we planned our strategy to corner him with it by asking him what he thought of the sermon that morning. His immediate reply was, "Let's not go into that!"

Both of these men (R. E. Vinson and C.) were indefatigable workers, and early in my associations with them convinced me that hard work would never kill anybody. They created in me an undying love for hard work which has been an inspiration all through my ministry. This they did by precept and example. . . .[16]

Dr. J. F. Hardie was also impressed by Dr. Caldwell.

Doctor Caldwell was all business. He had little or no small talk. But when he preached it was with fire, and tears would flow down his cheeks. He was noted for his capacity for work. In addition to his teaching load, he was superintendent of Home Missions for his presbytery. He was sent to McGregor, Texas, by his presbytery to dissolve the church, but before he was through a new church was built. He and Doctor Vinson ap-

---

[16] Wade H. Boggs letter to T.W.C., Jr., November 2, 1955, and in the hands of the latter.

peared to us to know all the best and latest books. Their approach to things was so new and fresh. When the time approached for us to leave the Seminary and go out on our own, we begged these men into meeting us in the afternoons and after supper. How gladly they contributed this supererogation! I will never forget a remark Doctor Caldwell made when we were leaving: "Young men, we can't make prophets out of you." And we had learned that a prophet was one who stood in the presence of God until a message was given.[17]

Robert Ernest Vinson was twenty-five when he came to the first class of the Seminary in 1902. He was Professor of Old Testament Languages and Exegesis and also taught New Testament Language and Exegesis. He was ardent in his labors, personable, an immediate favorite with all who made his acquaintance.

Dr. Vinson was in demand as a popular Bible teacher both in the churches and among the students on the campus of The University of Texas. "So forceful was his teaching and preaching that his very mannerisms were woven into the preaching style of a whole generation of young preachers."[18] He pleaded with the students to use imagination and originality in their preaching and give no one the chance to say, "The preacher spoke for twenty-five minutes and did not say anything that would not have occurred to anyone else to say on the same subject."[19]

Dr. Lang remarked, "Robert E. Vinson was certainly a master in his teaching of the Bible. I have never heard anyone in all of my life who could present the actual Word itself with the attractiveness, appeal, and accuracy with which he presented it. He could literally make the Bible in its scenes live again. He was clear in his outline and you were always able to take something definite away from the class with you. He was a marvelous, yet simple preacher, as well as teacher of The Word."[20]

An indication of Dr. Vinson's point of view with respect to Bible study and interpretation was to be found in his inaugural address delivered in 1903. After showing an appreciation for the archeological discoveries in the Bible lands and the bearing of these on the setting and record in the Old Testament, Dr. Vinson contended

---

17 J. F. Hardie letter, 1955, *op cit.*
18 Malcolm L. Purcell, "Reminiscences of Austin Seminary" (undated letter to T.W.C., Jr., and in the hands of the latter).
19 T. C. Vinson letter, *op. cit.*
20 C. H. Lang letter, *op. cit.*

Robert Ernest Vinson, President 1909–1916, Professor of Old Testament Languages and Exegesis, English Bible, Practical Theology

that the Old Testament was not primarily a book of general history.

. . . Instead of its being history, let us rather say that it is the history of redemption, the history of the progress of a great truth, and not the history of any nation or set of nations. It is the tracing of the revelation which God made of himself to man in its successive stages, and the gradual unfolding before man's uncomprehending mind of the glorious purposes of redemption. All that is related bears upon this theme. If we will look upon the Old Testament as the preparation for the New, upon the law as opening the way for the cross, upon Christ as revealed therein, it becomes in our hands a new book. Redemption is set forth in the beginning, and after this all that it relates, of history, prophecy, poetry, all bears upon the one grand purpose of the ages, God's love for man, and God's redemption of man

40

by the blood of the Crucified. The entire Old Testament falls into line with this great purpose.[21]

. . . this (was) the conception of the Old Testament which was held and taught by Jesus himself. He said to the Pharisees, "Ye search the Scriptures, because in them ye think ye have eternal life, and they are they that testify of me." The object and purpose of the Old Testament is to testify of the Christ.[22]

Dr. Vinson did not hold with the ideas of the record of the flood in Genesis having been derived from a combination of sources, J, E, P, etc. He felt that the Old Testament in all its particulars would be vindicated, or better, illustrated, when the fruits of archeological research had been fully gathered.

With the coming of Dr. Caldwell in 1906, Dr. Vinson, at his own request, was transferred to the Chair of Homiletics and English Bible, yet to be financed. By 1908 the chair had been endowed by gifts from friends of Dr. Josephus Johnson and by a donation of more than $30,000 from J. W. Allen of Edna, Texas.[23] Not only did Dr. Vinson refuse calls for his service elsewhere, but he raised money for his own salary and for the endowment of it. In 1909 the Board called him to be President[24] and he accepted.

Dr. James Lewis Bell came to the Chair of New Testament Language and Exegesis in January of 1910. To the duties of this work, he added those of instruction in music.[25]

The report of the Faculty in May of 1910 was, in part, as follows:

It is with great gratitude to God that we report what has been in many ways the most successful year in the history of the work under our care. The number of students who have availed themselves of the privileges of the Seminary in whole or in part has been the largest since the establishment of this institution in 1902, and we believe larger than at any time in the history of the Austin School of Theology. There have been enrolled in all departments for the session 36 students, 16 of whom have taken the full course . . . .

In accordance with the instructions of the Board at the last

21 R. E. Vinson, "The Old Testament in the Light of Its Own Times," *The Presbyterian Quarterly* XVII, 64 (October 1903), 173.

22 *Ibid.*, p. 174.

23 William A. McLeod, *Story of the First Southern Presbyterian Church, Austin, Texas* (no publisher, 1939), p. 69; Minutes of the Board, Book "A," 1900–1908, pp. 276, 277.

24 Minutes of the Board, 1900 to 1919, p. 165.

25 *Ibid.*, pp. 176, 236.

annual meeting, the Faculty had admitted to the privileges of the Seminary thirteen women students, who have taken the English Bible course with the Middle Class, for either the whole or a part of the session.[26]

One of the five on whom the Board conferred the B.D. degree in 1911 was Thomas White Currie. At the same time he was elected Assistant Professor in Dr. Vinson's Department of English Bible.[27]

During the academic year 1913–1914 the Rev. Samuel McPheeters Glasgow was instructor in Greek and Homiletics. The spirit displayed by Sam Glasgow and others like him must have influenced the increase in the number of congregations in the Synod of Texas of the Presbyterian Church, U.S., between 1880 and 1910 from 155 to 451. During this period the number of communicants was multiplied by five, while the population at large a little more than doubled.

Dr. Glasgow reports of a colleague, Rev. M. W. Doggett, D.D., that "For a stretch of eighteen months at one time, so untiring and efficient were his efforts, that he organized an average of one church a month. . . ."[28] And of his own work in the town of Mission, Dr. Glasgow writes:

An experience that is rarely given to men in this day and land was mine in the infant town of Mission in the summer of 1909. I visited that town unheralded and found a little city teeming with life in which there had never been a Protestant service of any kind held. I did not know a single living soul among them all, and finally, at a loss where to begin, I stopped in a store and spoke to the woman behind the counter and asked whether they had ever had a service there; she replied, "No." "Would you like to have one?" "Yes, I would." "Would you like it bad enough to prepare a place for me to preach next Sunday afternoon?" She promised, and I left. That Sunday afternoon, having driven from a nearby appointment, I had the exquisite pleasure of preaching the first sermon ever preached in that town, and with the Sunday-school missionary, Mr. R. Waller Blain, of organizing a Sunday School, the services being held in an unoccupied pool hall. This little infant was nursed about from home to vacant store until now it is housed in three splendid church

[26] Minutes of the Board 1900–1919, May 1910, *ibid.*, p. 176.
[27] Minutes of the Board 1900–1919, May 1911, *ibid.*, p. 199.
[28] Samuel McPheeters Glasgow, *Border Trails* (no date, no place, no publisher), p. 15. In library of Union Theological Seminary, Richmond, Virginia.

buildings, each with its own Sunday-school and with its own pastor and preaching services.[29]

Dr. Cecil H. Lang says,

Samuel M. Glasgow was one of the most helpful teachers I had in my Seminary years. I particularly remember his courses in pastoral theology. He was young but he had come for a season right out of a very busy and challenging pastorate in the new territory of the Rio Grande Valley of Texas. His continual emphasis upon giving a spiritual emphasis to every pastoral visit, always having a prayer in the home if it were at all possible, has stayed with me all of my ministry and has been helpful and determining in the carrying on of my pastoral activities.

Two expressions of Glasgow's were repeated frequently but in such a way as that they have stayed in my mind through the years. One was, "Give them the meat, young brethren, give them the meat." He would then lay strong emphasis upon the value of expository preaching and ever sticking close to The Word itself.

The other favorite of his was, "Give them the emancipated eye." This, of course, was his starting point for giving us some very strong and practical exhortations on the value of preaching without note or manuscript.[30]

When Dr. S. A. King, at the age of eighty, retired in 1914, he was succeeded by Rev. William Angus McLeod (Class of 1905) in the Chair of Systematic Theology.[31] Rev. Robert Francis Gribble (Class of 1914) was engaged to teach Old Testament Language and Exegesis. The next year Robert Lawson Jetton (Class of 1911) became professor of New Testament Language and Exegesis.

Thomas Chalmers Vinson (Class of 1912), brother of Dr. R. E. Vinson and from 1912–1928 a missionary in the Belgian Congo, reminisced of his years at the Seminary:

We had a great faculty and comparisons are difficult. Ed Tolliver, Janitor, cook, and General Factotum aptly expressed it, "There was giants in the land in them days." The Bible was central. They had all walked with the Master and they made our hearts burn within us as they opened unto us the Scriptures. . . .

Unforgettable in those days was the board bill; never over $14 a month—and we lived high on the hog. And the evenings,

29 S. M. Glasgow, *Border Trails, ibid.*, p. 19.
30 C. H. Lang letter, November 3, 1955, *op. cit.*
31 Minutes of the Board 1900–1919, *op. cit.*, p. 257.

after supper, on the dormitory steps when Jim Hardie and Sam Joekel (in the University) would relate their inexhaustible supply of jokes to hear John Kidd and Cecil (Runt) Smith "die laughing."

And about the first weekend preaching trip we took as Middlers (Prohibited to Juniors then). Six or seven of us on the I.&G.N. with Clergy Permits. The Agent had sold us children's tickets, *green* with ½ fare in sign board figures. When the Conductor had collected the lot he remarked to the Auditor, "That Seminary Kindergarten must be having a holiday." . . .

To sum up. We did not have very much in the way of physical equipment in "Our day." Not much beyond the proverbial Mark Hopkins and his log. A rather short log, but it served the unforgettable purpose of bringing the students and professors very close together in the most intimate, personal contact. I consider this the outstanding feature of our Seminary life.[32]

Rev. Henry M. Bailey who entered as a junior in the fall of 1915 writes of another member of the class,

Herbert Wager, who gathered up laundry and delivered it to help make his expenses. Wager worked in a mission in South Austin, died young, and is the only member of our class of four who has a church named for him, the Wager Memorial Church of Austin, Texas.

Our class had Homiletics under Dr. R. E. Vinson, a master of the subject. . . . He urged that every sermon have a definite aim and all that went into the sermon should contribute to the accomplishment of that aim.

Our professor of Hebrew was Dr. Robert F. Gribble, who also knew his subject-matter and whose bow still abides in strength at Austin Seminary. He urged his pupils to look for the pictures behind the Hebrew words. Dr. Gribble's Christian influence has been very fruitful.

Our professor of New Testament Languages was Dr. R. L. Jetton, . . . One who took work under Dr. Jetton had to work. Our professor of Church History was Dr. Sam L. Joekel, who was a Senior when we four were Juniors. The summer before . . . Dr. Sampson had lost his life. . . . Dr. Joekel was a fine teacher who made Church History interesting. Despite his profound intellect, he could preach the Gospel in a fine way in revival services as he did at the country church in Maysfield, Texas.

Our professor of Systematic Theology was Dr. Angus McLeod, a noble saint as well as a teacher of theology, an example to young ministers of what a Christian minister ought to be. Dr. S. A. King was still living on the campus (and Dr. Mc) would take us over to Dr. King's house occasionally to get instruction from a stalwart Christian soldier of large experience. In Dr. King's presence one felt a little closer to heaven.

The Seminary had no chapel in those days, so we preached our sermons before the faculty and students in the University Presbyterian Church for their prayer meeting services. This writer preached on "Pressing Toward the Mark" for his first sermon and remembers that Miss Edleen Begg, now a fine Bible teacher, played the piano.[33]

---

[33] Henry M. Bailey letter to T.W.C., Jr., November 3, 1955, and in the hands of the latter.

Financial Troubles 4

While Dr. R. E. Vinson was President, 1909–1916, The Synod of Texas was seeking to remedy the financial difficulties of Austin College, Sherman, Daniel Baker College, Brownwood, Texas Presbyterian College, Milford, and Austin Presbyterian Theological Seminary, Austin. Dr. Sampson's view that the schools should be considered as a pyramid, closely integrated, with the Seminary at the summit seems to have continued. Dr. Vinson became chairman of first one committee of Synod and then of another, whose purposes were to liquidate the debts of each institution and to raise more funds for the growing needs of all four.

In 1902 Dr. Sampson had received a gift of $12,000 for the endowment of scholarships at Austin Seminary on the condition that it be used to liquidate pressing indebtedness to Daniel Baker. Daniel Baker would then be obliged to repay principal and interest to the Seminary endowment.[1] Such payments were never made. In 1912 Synod "authorized and directed" the Board of Daniel Baker to negotiate a $40,000, 7 percent, ten-year loan (to include the prior loan and accrued interest). No more was paid on the second loan than had been on the first. Dr. Vinson evinced optimism at the prospect of consolidating the debts of Synod's committee and of the four schools (by 1915, some $275,000) and launching a campaign for $1,000,000. But neither was done. The crescendo of war hysteria was one distraction.

On May 11, 1916 the Board congratulated "the President and the Faculty on the successful management" of the school, found endowment funds totalling $168,496.60 which, with other anticipated income, warranted a budget for the coming year of $37,322.05.[2]

It was to this meeting of the Board that Dr. Vinson tendered his

[1] Thomas W. Currie, Jr., *A History of Austin Presbyterian Theological Seminary, Austin, Texas 1884–1943, op. cit.*, p. 47, footnote 16.
[2] Minutes of the Board, May 1912–Oct. 1922, May 1916, p. 287.

resignation in order that he might become President of The University of Texas.

Dr. Daniel A. Penick remembered Dr. Vinson as being

. . . showy, bright, eloquent, and a good executive. . . . Dr. Vinson was a very able man. I may be prejudiced because it was under his administration that I became a full professor. I have a very high regard for him. I think he made a good president for the Seminary and for the University. . . . He was a far sighted man. He had the vision. He suggested that the University be moved to 500 acres on the lake. The citizens of Austin rose up and said, "No!" I haven't kept up with Dr. Vinson since he left for Cleveland, but I have always believed he was a straight and clean man.[3]

Dr. Cecil H. Lang expressed it as his conviction that, "To my thinking the greatest spiritual and ecclesiastical tragedy of this generation lies in the fact Robert Ernest Vinson saw fit to turn aside from a spiritual ministry to give himself first to educational and then to more purely secular pursuits."[4]

The choice of the Board for the successor to Dr. Vinson fell on the Rev. Neal Larkin Anderson, D.D., pastor of the First Presbyterian Church of Winston Salem, North Carolina. A letter from Dr. Vinson dated July 6, 1916 assured Dr. Anderson that the Seminary had ". . . nearly $200,000.00 of invested funds and have had an annual income for some years past of from $15,000 to $16,000. . . . We shall endeavor immediately to secure $40,000 of additional endowment for the chair of New Testament Greek, and also about $50,000 for the general endowment. . . ."[5]

Arriving about mid-September, Dr. Anderson found a faculty consisting of T. W. Currie, R. F. Gribble, R. L. Jetton, and W. A. McLeod, and a student body of six juniors, three middlers, four seniors, and six special students. However, his examination of the financial position of the Seminary prompted him on the eve of the meeting of the Synod of Texas, October 10, in Bryan to wire the Chairman of

---

[3] D. A. Penick conversation, July 1957, recorded by T.W.C., Jr. and in the hands of the latter.

[4] C. H. Lang letter to T.W.C., Jr., received November 3, 1955, and in the hands of the latter. Dr. Vinson went from the presidency of The University of Texas to a like office in Western Reserve in Cleveland, Ohio and then entered some ill-fated business ventures.

[5] Faculty Minutes, Austin Presbyterian Theological Seminary, 1914–1927. The pages in this book are for the most part not numbered at all and certainly not in sequence. This letter bears the designation "G."

Arthur Gray Jones, Board Chairman 1907–1920, Professor of
Systematic Theology 1921–1927

the Board, Dr. Arthur G. Jones, pastor of the First Presbyterian
Church of San Antonio. The following letter sets forth something of
what had come to light:

> Reverend Arthur G. Jones, D.D.
>   Austin, Texas
> My dear Dr. Jones,
>   In conference with Dr. Vinson and Mr. Boone of the Ameri-
> can National Bank last night I learn that the liquid assets of the
> Seminary, what would be doubtless known everywhere as "pro-
> ductive endowment", amounts to something over $50,000.00,
> more or less—the exact amount would be disclosed by a detailed
> statement of the Treasurer of the Board.
>   This is clearly indicated in the report last (May 1916) year,
> which shows that receipts available from the "endowment
> funds" amounted to about $3,000.00, the rest of the expenses of

the institution not paid out of this amount coming from "overdrafts" or rentals of rooms in the West Dormitory ($306.00), and from a donation of $3,046.47.

This creates, or discloses a situation so difficult and surprising that I wired you at 2:00 a.m. today, "Cannot go to Synod until conference with you here. Stop on way Tuesday. Urgent. Answer." and am just in receipt of your wire stating that you would reach here on the "Sunshine Special" today at 11:20.

My wire to you in August last, accepting the offer of the Presidency of the Seminary was based upon three representations made as to the financial status of the Seminary:

(1) Dr. Vinson's letter of July 6th, in which he wrote as follows:

"The present financial condition of the Seminary is, of course, not up to the mark which it ought to reach for its best development. We have, however, nearly $200,000.00 of invested funds, and have had an income for some years past of from $15,000.00 to $16,000.00."

(2) Report of the Board of Trustees to the General Assembly in Session at Orlando:

"The total endowment of the Seminary is $186,000.00 and the estimated value of the grounds and buildings is $125,000 and the addition to the endowment and equipment during the past year is $5,000.00."

As grounds and buildings are not termed "endowment" in the general language of educational institutions, I naturally understood that the $125,000.00 was in addition to the endowment, particularly in view of Dr. Vinson's statement above quoted.

(3) In reply to my letter dated July 21st, whether the necessary expenses of the Seminary are met from the productive funds, or if it is required of the President to hustle for funds for running expenses, you replied under date of July 29th:

"I am not able, the records not being at hand, to give you the detailed information as to our invested funds. I do know, however, that in our annual meeting of the Board last May it was brought out that our anticipated income for the next year was expected to meet our budget. Other funds will be needed to equip and endow the Seminary as we purpose it to be, but there is no element of urgency which would make it imperative for the new President immediately to make such effort."

I find now that our anticipated income from invested funds is in the neighborhood of $3,000.00, and at least $1,000.00 of the expenses approved by the Board not included in the present budget.

The facts brought out in my conference last night are so contrary to what I have been led to expect when I wired you in August last in response to the call of the Board, that I can only say if the Board, after receiving this letter still desire to have my election confirmed by the controlling Synods, I am willing to continue at the head of the Seminary for the present, and will do all in my power to further its interests in every way, provided the Board itself will arrange to finance the work for the current year, and will also set clearly out on its records a plain, clear statement of the exact status of the finances of this institution at the time of my entering on this work.

I am sincerely desirous that the Seminary should not suffer through any act of mine, and for that reason, am willing to continue, at least so far as the public is concerned as the official head of the institution for the present, but I must consider de novo my attitude toward a position so entirely different from what was set before me when I acted on this call.

This letter is written only after an entire night spent in prayerful consideration, and from a sincere conviction of duty I owe the Church as well as myself.[6]

The Board requested Dr. Anderson to remain with the Seminary for the present[7] and proceeded to go into its financial position in detail. It became apparent that the operating and the endowment accounts had not been kept separate and that after provision was made for the current year's budget, the unencumbered liquid assets capable of being used to produce interest or dividends was no more than $15,000.[8]

Synod's Executive Committee on Schools and Colleges had been granted sole permission to canvass the churches for funds for the colleges and for the Seminary. On December 18, 1916, Dr. Jones, Dr. Anderson, and, at their request, T. W. Currie presented the appeal of the Seminary to the Executive Committee.

1. It (the $100,000 debt) is not, as we might say, an obligation on the side of the institution's life, or even upon its back as a heavy load; and which, however burdensome, would permit

6 Minutes of the Board 1912–1922, *op. cit.*, meeting Oct. 11, 1916, p. 292.

7 Minutes of the Board 1912–1922, *ibid.*, p. 294.

8 Minutes of the Board 1912–1922, November 9, 1916, *ibid.*, pp. 305, 306. David L. Stitt letter to T.W.C., Jr., August 30, 1957, and in the hands of the latter states that all funds ever placed in the endowment of the Seminary were then intact and income-producing investments. Much, if not all, of the restoration of the endowments to their original totals was accomplished during the administration of Dr. Stitt.

the institution to go on with the hope that by some means it might be liquidated. This debt is of a nature which has cut the very ground from under the institution's life by destroying the corpus of its trust funds, so that we have left no resources with which to continue the Seminary.

2. But this debt has even a more serious aspect than the possible closing of the Seminary. Until now this condition has not been known to us. Grievous as it indeed is, yet it has come upon us unawares. But now that it is known, unless it is very wisely and promptly handled, it contains the possibility of destroying the confidence of the people in our administration of trust funds. . . .[9]

The called meeting of Synod the next day agreed for the Executive Committee to consider payment of interest on the $100,000 indebtedness of the Seminary to its endowment if and when it had funds available,[10] but there were no "available" funds. Dr. Anderson felt that it was difficult if not impossible to elicit further donations to the endowment unless what had been given had been restored, and no progress could be seen in such a direction. Consequently, on March 20, 1917, Dr. Anderson notified the Board that as soon as his duties of the spring semester had been discharged he would depart to become pastor of the Independent Presbyterian Church, Savannah, Georgia.[11]

The state of finances of the Seminary had been reviewed in a seven and one-half page report by one of the Board, the Honorable Thomas Watt Gregory, prior to his becoming Attorney General under Woodrow Wilson. His unheeded alarm, sounded in one sentence, was, "We are unable to state what the original amount of this fund was, but on page 149 of your Minute Book, it, as indicated at that time, amounts to $5,266.75; there was included in this last mentioned amount, however, a $1,000 bequest in the will of a lady at Victoria; she is still living. . . ."[12]

Another feature of the financial picture which eliminated the income-producing characteristic of the endowment funds was the

[9] Minutes of the Board 1912–1922, March 20, 1917, p. 309.
[10] Minutes of the Board 1912–1922, *ibid.*, p. 310; see also Minutes of the Synod of Texas, Called Meeting December 19, 1916, p. 357 included in Minutes of the Sixty-second Session of the Synod of Texas of the Presbyterian Church in the United States, 1917, pp. 339–412.
[11] Minutes of the Board 1912–1922, *ibid.*, p. 313.
[12] Minutes of the Board of Trustees of Austin Presbyterian Seminary from February 6, 1900 to May 1914, p. 195.

action of the Board in 1914 cancelling the obligation of the occupants of the professors' houses to remit rental payments. This feature was highlighted in a special audit in 1946.[13]

By May 10, 1917 the current debt at the bank had risen to $20,000.[14] The financial picture was bleak for the future of the Seminary.

By May of 1916 T. W. Currie was chairman of the faculty.[15] By May of 1917 the Board had agreed on at least one step: to support the chairman of the Auditing Committee, T. H. Williams, and the Treasurer, H. A. Wroe, in the policy, "that no loans will be made to ourselves, or to schools, colleges or churches."[16]

Although the first American Expeditionary Force landed in France June 26, 1917, and most Americans in the Southwest as well as elsewhere were preoccupied with events relating to war, at the Seminary the struggle continued over funds. Through unabated appeals to the Synod's Executive Committee on Schools and Colleges, the Seminary was able to deposit $8,000 in its account in September of 1917. The faculty, who knew how precarious its support was, called for freedom from the Executive Committee to appeal to the churches in Texas as they could in Arkansas and Oklahoma.[17]

September of 1917 saw an enrollment of four seniors, two middlers, four juniors, plus twenty-two special students, but the whole university community was being engulfed in the war effort. By April, 1918 the finances available could no longer support the Seminary, and many of the faculty and students were leaving for war services. T. W. Currie who had been secretary of The University of Texas YMCA since 1911 in addition to his duties at the Seminary was called to "remain with the Seminary."[18] Dr. Gribble became student secretary of the Texas State YMCA, and the other two professors went overseas as YMCA secretaries.

With four faculty homes, Sampson, and Lubbock Halls available, the premises were leased and rented. The only teaching offered was

13 R. A. Moore Company, Certified Public Accountants, Fort Worth, Texas. *Audit Report Austin Presbyterian Theological Seminary*, Austin, Texas, April 30, 1946, section 1, p. 3.

14 Minutes of the Board 1912–1922, May 10, 1917, p. 323.

15 Minutes of the Board, May 1912–October 1922, May 10, 1916, p. 281; May 10, 1917, p. 328.

16 Minutes of the Board 1912–1922, *ibid.*, p. 324.

17 Faculty Minutes, Austin Presbyterian Theological Seminary, 1914–1927, paper "Z."

18 Minutes of the Board 1912–1922, *op. cit.*, April 4, 1918, pp. 337, 338.

the courses offered for credit to university students by T. W. Currie in a classroom at the YMCA at 22nd and Guadalupe.

Less than a month after the Armistice was signed, on December 3, 1918, Dr. Jones convened the Board and urged the following action which was adopted:

1. On motion it was ordered that inasmuch as the attention of the Board had been called to an action which was taken by Board of October 9, 1902, and record of which is found on page 35 of the Minute Book, and which record is as follows:
"In view of the present peculiar conditions and exigencies of the Seminary:
Resolved: That until otherwise ordered by this Board, the treasurer is authorized and instructed to pay from any money in the treasury (of either the general or endowment fund) all expense authorized by this Board, and the money so used be charged to the fund to which it is taken, when the funds are in hand:"
and the Board having been further advised of the possibility that the above action which was taken to meet an exigency of that time and which does not appear in the records ever to have been repealed might be interpreted as indicating the settled policy of the Board in handling the funds of the Seminary, the Board does now definitely rescind the above action.
2. On motion it was ordered that the Board instruct the treasurer of the Seminary, Mr. H. A. Wroe, Austin, Texas, to transfer to the permanent endowment funds of the Seminary any surplus which may remain from the income of the Seminary after the expenses of the present year are paid.[19]

This same meeting of the Board agreed to amend the corporate charter so as to read: "No debts shall ever be created that shall ever be or become a liability against the corpus of the endowment funds of the Seminary: Provided that this article shall not apply to any debts or obligations now outstanding or any renewal of the same or any part thereof."[20]

The matter of increasing the Seminary's assets absorbed much of the time and prayers of the Chairman of the Faculty. By May 1919, $40,000 in pledges to the permanent endowment was reported.[21] As a part of the Synod-wide campaign, some churches designated gifts

[19] Minutes of the Board 1912–1922, *ibid.*, December 3, 1918, pp. 346, 347.
[20] Minutes of the Board 1912–1922, *ibid.*
[21] Minutes of the Board 1912–1922, *ibid.*, May 7, 1919, p. 349.

to particular institutions. The First Presbyterian Churches in Taylor, Waco, and San Antonio and the First Southern and University Presbyterian Churches in Austin earmarked gifts for the Seminary. More than $32,000 in the permanent endowment funds plus another $6,500 in endowment for the library was reported in the spring of 1920.[22] The church in Waco pledged more than $42,000, and the church in San Antonio more than $52,000 to the Seminary.[23]

Many were anxious to reopen the Seminary because of needs and possibilities, but it was still barely hanging on. The Rev. R. D. Campbell and the Rev. C. R. Womeldorf asked the Board to offer training for Spanish-speaking candidates. The Board obtained the first of a number of annual grants for this purpose from Assembly's Executive Committee of Home Missions in the amount of $3,000.[24]

Dr. W. J. Battle of the Classical Languages Department of The University of Texas offered help from another direction.

> Dr. Penick tells me that you are planning to reopen the Seminary next fall. Can the University be of help in offering the Greek that you will need? Dr. Penick has made a special study of New Testament Greek, and of course we offer each year the usual college and University work in Attic and Homeric Greek. We shall be glad to help you, if we can.
>
> Cordially yours,
> (signed) W. J. Battle[25]

So for many years Seminary students studied Greek at The University of Texas under Dr. Daniel Allen Penick, who was Synod's Moderator at the time this arrangement began.

A Brazilian, The Rev. Antonio Horatio Perpetuo, taught Hebrew Language and Exegesis.[26] The chair of Systematic Theology was held by Dr. Arthur G. Jones.[27] T. W. Currie, chairman of the Faculty, was professor of English Bible.

Since the Seminary property was mostly under lease, classroom space was rented at the YMCA for the 1921–22 school year. The an-

[22] Minutes of the Board 1912–1922, *ibid.*, May 12, 1920, p. 353.
[23] *Ibid.*
[24] Minutes of the Board 1912–1922, *ibid.*, February 23, 1921, p. 378.
[25] *Ibid.*, p. 383.
[26] *Ibid.*, May 10, 1922. He was actually employed by the Executive Committee of the Board May 6, 1921 which action was approved May 10, 1922. The page is unnumbered.
[27] *Ibid.*, May 12, 1920, p. 376.

Charles Henry Hardin Branch, Board Chairman 1921–1922.
*Courtesy of Presbyterian Historical Foundation, Montreat,
North Carolina*

nouncement went out: WEDNESDAY, SEPTEMBER 29, 1921, 9:00 A.M.
Seminary Opens. Enrollment of Students.[28]

---

[28] *Announcement of The Austin Presbyterian Theological Seminary for the Session of 1921–1922* (Austin, Texas: Von Boeckmann-Jones Co., Printers, 1921), pp. 3, 24. In the Seminary Library.

The Faculty: 1921-1930   5

As the faculty for Austin Seminary took up its work anew in the fall of 1921, the members displayed a variety of backgrounds.

Dr. Arthur Gray Jones, Professor of Systematic Theology, was a native of Memphis, Tennessee, and was graduated from Arkansas College with honors in 1888. He finished his theological studies at Union Seminary, Hampden-Sydney, in two years, then returned to be pastor of the church at Batesville, Arkansas, for five years. Dr. Jones came to First Church, San Antonio, the first Sunday of March 1895. During his service there, that congregation grew to be the largest of the denomination.

The untimely death of a son in 1912 seemed to make even keener his outgoing pastoral affection. The loss of hearing made him the more attentive, and he became an expert at reading lips. When T. W. Currie once asked him how he could be pastor of such a large church, he replied, "Well, Tom, it works like this. I will go to my study and read, and write, and preach, until one day it will sift up through the good wife: 'the pastor is neglecting his visiting,' and then I will visit, and visit, until one day the wife will say, 'Arthur, if you don't get into that study again pretty soon, you are going to pound that Bible to pieces!'"[1]

As a theologian he was a Calvinist.[2] His dominant concern was less in tracing the trends of ancient and modern doctrines than in a vital faith. He once remarked: "We are not called to build our hope upon any creed, however rich or elaborate its doctrines may be. But we are called to put our trust absolutely, utterly and forever in

---

[1] Some of the above is from the recollections of T.W.C., Jr., who had a vivid memory of the Joneses and some from the information contained in Dwight A. Sharpe, "Arthur Gray Jones, Nobleman of God" (unpublished minor paper, Austin Presbyterian Theological Seminary, Austin, 1952).

[2] Arthur Gray Jones, *Calvin: The Times: The Man: The Historic Significance* (Fort Worth, Texas: Keystone Printing Company, n.d.), in the Seminary Library. Also, address delivered at Synod Nov. 18, 1909.

Christ Himself, the divine Saviour."[3] His was a jovial dignity, an infectious friendliness, a boundless faith.

Dr. Daniel Allen Penick, though born in Cabarrus County, North Carolina, moved to Austin at an early age. He grew up in the First Southern Presbyterian Church where he served in many capacities including janitor, usher, pumper of the pipe organ, member of the choir. For a time Dr. Smoot was his Sunday school teacher. Many of the students at Austin School of Theology boarded at his home. His father, Dixon Brown Penick, was one of the organizers of the University Presbyterian Church. Dr. Penick graduated from The University of Texas in 1892 and received his Ph.D. from Johns Hopkins in 1898. He came to teach at The University in Austin in 1899 and became a full professor in 1917 in what came to be known as the Department of Classical Languages. He became the widely honored unpaid coach of The University tennis teams. For many years he taught a class of students at the University Presbyterian Church. Seminary students registered in The University of Texas to take Greek under Dr. Penick, and the Seminary refunded the cost to the students.

The Rev. Antonio Horatio Perpetuo had been born in the state of Sao Paulo, Brazil, in 1883. He was graduated from the College of Wooster, Ohio, in 1909 and from Princeton Theological Seminary in 1912. In 1920 he was in the work of the Presbyterian Church of the U.S.A. in El Paso and from there he came to the Seminary to teach Hebrew and to be responsible for preparation offered for the Spanish-speaking candidates. Mr. Perpetuo left the Seminary after two years.

The Rev. Robert Francis Gribble was called as Professor of Old Testament Language and Exegesis and head of the Spanish-speaking work, from a pastorate in Mercedes, Texas. He began teaching in the fall of 1923. A native of Waco, Texas, Dr. Gribble was a graduate of Austin College and Austin Seminary. He had taught Hebrew at the Seminary 1914–1918 and had taken post graduate work at The University of Texas and at The University of Chicago as well as having served as Texas State Student Secretary of the YMCA during the war. Dr. Gribble's father served on the Seminary Board 1914–1916.

In addition to his teaching, Dr. Gribble was more or less in charge

[3] Arthur Gray Jones, *Temple Builders and Other Sermons* (New York: Fleming H. Revell Company, 1929), pp. 101, 102.

of things mechanical around the Seminary. He was in charge of the dormitory part of Sampson Hall. He was a stone mason who built many a flower bed, retaining wall, and some stone garages. He would "h'ist the tune" at the chapel services which were held in the northeast first floor classroom of Sampson Hall.

He was sometime owner of a Franklin car which he serviced. He and his charming wife, Joyce, and their children, Nancy, Bippy (Elizabeth), and Robin, were active in the First Southern Presbyterian Church. Dr. Gribble supplied the congregation, first at Bartlett and later at Leander.

Although to Dr. Gribble the idea of Moses not being the author of the Pentateuch was as offensive as the Auburn Affirmation,[4] his cheerful wit, his unbroken courtesy, and his ceaseless and disciplined energy assured him the admiration and gratitude of a host of students and many others.

In 1926 the Rev. Samuel Levinson Joekel came to the Chair of English Bible and Religious Education. Dr. Joekel was born in Giddings, Texas, in 1893 and was graduated from The University of Texas in 1913 and from Austin Seminary in 1916. He served the church in Clarendon, Texas, before entering the Army YMCA and then the Army Chaplaincy. For seven years, until 1926, he was pastor of the First Presbyterian Church in Waxahachie, and he taught Bible during most of that time at Trinity University, then located in Waxahachie. Dr. Joekel was in demand as a preacher and as a speaker at a variety of civic affairs. While he taught at the Seminary he supplied the church at Lockhart. For a number of years he was the Presbyterian preacher at the Blois Camp Meeting. His kindly spirit and his reservoir of humorous stories and retorts made him a great favorite.

Dr. George Summey came in 1927 to meet an emergency vacancy caused by the poor health of Dr. Jones. Upon his resignation, Dr. Jones was made Emeritus Professor of Systematic Theology and Dr. Summey succeeded to that task and title. Dr. Summey, born in Asheville, North Carolina, in 1853, received an A.B. from Davidson College with a Phi Beta Kappa in 1870 and an M.A. from Davidson as well as a B.D. from Union Theological Seminary of Virginia in 1873. After several pastorates he became Chancellor of Southwestern Presbyterian University, Clarksville, Tennessee, in 1892. From 1903

---

[4] R. F. Gribble, "When is a Christian Not a Christian?," *The Southern Presbyterian Journal* I, 5 (September 1942) , 16.

until he came to the Seminary, he was pastor of Third Presbyterian Church, New Orleans, Louisiana. He was Moderator of the General Assembly in 1925. He had written extensively, having served in an editorial capacity for no fewer than five Presbyterian periodicals.

Dr. Summey's contribution most valued by the students was his generosity and the personal interest he took with each one. Nell (Mrs. J. Martin) Singleton recalls, "I remember Dr. Summey for his Tuesday night coffees after [student] preaching. We all wondered how his pot plants lived on so much Louisiana coffee. His car was called 'Honeymoon Special,' and he was always as interested in the girl as the boy. He wrote to me all through Assembly's Training School and I met him in Washington when he went for committee meetings. His eccentricities were legion."[5]

During the illness of Dr. Jones in 1925, the Rev. T. Chalmers Vinson, Litt. D., who was on furlough from his mission work in Africa filled in for a time. Dr. E. R. Sims of The University assisted in the Spanish-speaking department. Rev. Lawrence Hay Wharton, D.D., pastor of the University Presbyterian Church, taught homiletics. In 1928 Rev. Orin Conway Williamson, returning from mission work in Mexico, took up work in the Spanish-speaking department.

The man who had begun teaching in the Seminary in 1911, had become Chairman of the Faculty in 1916, had been made custodian of the Seminary's affairs when it was closed in 1918, had reopened it in 1921, was elected president in May of 1922: Thomas White Currie.

Dr. Currie had been born in 1879 near Carolina Cemetery between Durango and Lott in Falls County, Texas. When he was fourteen he went to work at Sam McCall's Grocery Store in Lott. Not long afterward he began also teaching a Sunday school class in the Lott Presbyterian Church. Sam's brother, John V. McCall, was a minister. In 1902 Sam moved to Norman, Oklahoma, and opened a haberdashery. Tom also moved and went to work in the new store. On his visits to his brother, John talked to Tom about becoming a minister. Tom Currie matriculated at Austin College in Sherman in 1903. It was during a meeting conducted by Dr. Nathan Bachman in Grand Avenue Church in January 1906 that Dr. Currie decided to heed a call to the ministry and notified John McCall he was ready to apply to be taken under care of Presbytery.

At Austin College, Tom Currie played guard on the football team and became the manager for it. He was graduated with honors and

[5] From a letter, August 2, 1975, to T.W.C., Jr. and in the hands of the latter.

60

Thomas White Currie, President 1922–1943, Professor of English Bible, Church History

agreed to fill in the year after graduation, teaching for a chemistry professor who was on sabbatical. Coming to Austin Seminary in 1908, he entered The University, graduating in 1911 with a B.D. from the Seminary and an M.A. from The University.

His Master's thesis was written under Dr. L. M. Keasby, a professor in the History Department who was infected with the virus of race prejudice. The thesis was an inquiry into the state of culture of people in the Kasai area of Zaire in the Congo basin. When Dr. Keasby insisted that the source of his data be identified, Currie said, "a Black." Keasby immediately pronounced this thoroughly unsatisfactory. Currie responded that this gentleman was the Rev. Mr. William H. Sheppard, a member of the Royal Geographical Society of

London and a pioneer missionary of the Presbyterian Church, U.S. in the Congo. Dr. Keasby approved the thesis. Later concerning Currie he remarked, "I could have made him my successor if I had gotten hold of him before he went to the Seminary."[6]

During his days in the Seminary and The University, Dr. Currie took a great interest in developing the YMCA whose building was located at the northwest corner of Guadalupe and 22nd Streets across from the campus. In 1911 he was called to be the full-time secretary of that YMCA and continued that work along with his duties which began the same year at the Seminary. He was frequently called on to preach and supplied the University Church on a regular basis from the time the Rev. R. W. Joplin left in 1920 until the Rev. L. H. Wharton came as pastor in 1922.

Dr. McCall knew the T. H. Roe family in Colorado City, Texas. One of the five Roe girls had an appointment with Dr. McCall August 26, 1913. He solemnized the wedding of Miss Jeannette E. Roe and Thomas W. Currie.

So it was, first, as a teacher of English Bible and later as Professor of Church History and as president, that Dr. Currie found his life's work at the Seminary.

One of Dr. Currie's concerns was the library, no small part of the resources of a theological seminary. To the books donated by Rev. R. E. Sherrill to the Austin School of Theology, others were added. Clara Caswell Dismukes Vanderlass in 1914 began the Library Endowment with a gift of a house in Phoenix, Arizona, which netted the fund $6,500.[7] However, more than books and money were needed as the Rev. Wendell Crofoot notes.

> I had to have some means of support while I was in the Seminary and went to Dr. Currie for help. He wanted to know what I could do and since I had been working in the University of Texas Library for several years, I asked him if I could be of help in the Seminary Library. He said, "Sure, go to it." The books had been over in the house located at 102 W. 27th Street and in the other houses occupied by the Seminary professors; but during the summer preceding, the Seminary had bought a Model-T Ford dump truck and during that summer the books had been removed from the houses, piled in the dump truck, and taken

---

[6] Katherine Gray letter to Dr. Samuel L. Joekel, October 14, 1943, and in the Seminary archives.
[7] Minutes of the Board, February 23, 1921, p. 384.

over to the basement of Sampson Hall. Apparently the dump truck had backed up to the back door and simply dumped the books out, because I have never seen such a conglomeration in all my life. The first thing that had to be done, was to build some shelves. The Reverend Jose de la Luz Guerrero, who was a student at the Seminary, was a carpenter. He and several of the other students took upon themselves the responsibility of building the shelves. They were built and we stacked the books on them. One day I came down to the basement where the library was located. The shelves had pulled away from the walls and the books were down on the floor again. All of this work had to be done over. Some type of order had to be brought out of the chaos. The shelves were rebuilt and I talked with my friends at the University of Texas Library about a system for cataloging the books. The Library of Congress method was suggested, and it was started at that time. Dr. Currie was interested in the growth of the library and encouraged me in every way possible. The library of today is a far cry from what it was in 1925, but what it is today can be attributed in no small way to the vision he had then of what it ought to be.[8]

In 1928, Dr. S. M. Tenney, Curator of the Presbyterian Historical Foundation, was requested to buy "research materials."[9] In the spring of 1929 the report of Crofoot, the Librarian, read in part as follows:

Since the last meeting of the Board of Trustees, the Library has been entirely rearranged and quite a number of shelves and book cases have been added. All books have been placed on the shelves and arranged by subject and author. Until this year we have been embarrassed by having to keep some of our books stored because of lack of shelf room. A satisfactory beginning has been made on the repairing of books. Proper materials and tools have been purchased and it is our purpose as rapidly as money is available to continue this work until each book in the Library is in as good condition as it can be made. . . .

During the past year 440 volumes have been added. . . . We have almost a complete file of the Minutes of the General Assembly of the Presbyterian Church U. S. and U. S. A., and an increasingly complete record is being gathered of the minutes of the several presbyteries and synods. . . .

. . . [G. W. Crofoot] has not only served the students and fac-

---

8 G. W. Crofoot paper in the hands of T.W.C., Jr.
9 Minutes of the Board 1923–1931, May 16, 1928.

ulty but he has put in a great deal of time in repairing books and in cataloguing and in arranging the Library. . . .[10]

In 1930 authority was given to improve the lighting and heating in the Library and for at least eight chairs to be provided for the students to use when studying in the Library.[11]

Effort was made to bring in other leaders of the church for the benefit of the students.[12] In 1925 lecturers included J. E. Purcell, M. E. Melvin, Brooks I. Dickey, J. W. Skinner, and T. A. Wharton. Outside speakers in 1928 and 1929 included:[13]

Year ending May 1928
Rev. Wade C. Smith
Rev. H. W. McLaughlin, D.D.
Rev. Neal L. Anderson, D.D.
Rev. S. H. Chester, D.D.
Rev. B. K. Tenney
Rev. Motte Martin
Rev. C. R. Hemphill, D.D.
Rev. W. M. Anderson, D.D.
Year ending May 1929
Mr. Arthur Rugh
Mr. L. A. Coulter
Rev. Darby Fulton, D.D.
Rev. J. D. Leslie, D.D.
Rev. A. A. Little, D.D.
Miss Julia Lake Skinner

Continuing education was a Seminary concern. Following the close of the spring semester in 1927, ministers of Central Texas and Western Texas Presbyteries were invited to be the guests of the Seminary, and the next year the Presbyteries of Brazos, Brownwood, and Eastern Texas were invited. On occasion a lecture by a University professor was added to the program. Each member of the faculty delivered two or three lectures. Dallas, El Paso, Fort Worth, and Paris Presbyteries were invited in 1929.[14] The ministers from Arkansas, Oklahoma, and Louisiana as well as Texas were invited in 1930, but the site was moved to Westminster Encampment, Kerrville. Board and room were offered to the out-of-state ministers to help

[10] Minutes of the Faculty 1928–1939, May 15, 1929.
[11] Minutes of the Board 1923–1931, May 14, 1930.
[12] Minutes of the Board 1923–1931, March 20, 1923.
[13] Minutes of the Faculty 1928–1939, May 16, 1928, May 15, 1929.
[14] Minutes of the Faculty 1928–1939, May 15, 1929.

compensate for their added travel expense. Two of the speakers came from a distance: John Wesley Field, M.D., Ph.D., of the General Hospital, Kansas City, Missouri, and John Timothy Stone of McCormick Presbyterian Seminary, Chicago.[15]

The Spanish-speaking program had as one of its earliest features the first of a number of annual conferences in November of 1921. In connection with the conference an evangelistic meeting was held each evening in El Buen Pastor Presbyterian Church in Austin. Lecturers at this first conference included W. S. Red, T. W. Currie, R. D. Campbell, Elias Trevino, W. S. Scott, and G. A. Walls.[16]

The Synod of Louisiana became one of the supporting and controlling Synods of the Seminary in 1929.

Although the campaign for $1,350,000 ordered by the Synod of Texas in 1923 was of great help to the Seminary, it now appears that hardly more than $750,000 was realized by all the colleges and the Seminary combined, and gathering this sum took ten years. By then it became virtually impossible to identify funds to be credited solely to the campaign.[17] The funds lent by order of Synod from Seminary endowment to Daniel Baker were never returned in interest or principal.[18]

The auditor's report for the year ending April 30, 1929, counting the Seminary Building and Grounds in at $125,000, listed the Seminary's assets at $463,232.37 and showed during the course of that fiscal year $22,287.02 to have been derived from investments.[19]

Sampson Hall had a basement housing the furnace and the library and the custodian's quarters. The first floor offered space for three classrooms, each on one corner, a small faculty office just to the north of the east entrance, and the Seminary office just to the south, with the office of the President adjoining and occupying the southeast corner. The second and third stories were dormitory floors. The single men were housed there and as many University students as could be accommodated. In 1924 Sampson Hall and Lubbock Hall were again occupied by the Seminary.

The experience of one of the students, Charles M. Campbell, in

15 Minutes of the Faculty 1928–1939, May 14, 1930.

16 Minutes of the Faculty 1914–1927, November 8, 1921.

17 Minutes of the Seventy-Eighth Session of the Synod of Texas of the Presbyterian Church in the United States 1933, p. 240.

18 R. A. Moore Company, Certified Public Accountants, Fort Worth, Texas, *Audit Report Austin Presbyterian Theological Seminary*, Austin, Texas, April 30, 1946, p. 9.

19 Minutes of the Board 1923–1931, May 15, 1929.

talking to students in Arkansas about coming to the Seminary prompted his suggestion to Dr. Currie that it would be helpful to have a piece of publicity that would depict something of the Seminary campus and student life. Dr. Currie suggested that he compile such a publication.[20] Consequently, the Student Edition of the bulletin was issued, the initial issue bearing the date May 1, 1926. The opening article recounts a student-faculty seminar on evangelism that had been held in the late spring of 1925 and of its sequel:

What was the outcome of this evangelistic "council of war"? The result was 127 additions by professions of faith and 31 by statement and letter. Unusual experiences of grace were the fruits of the personal work and preaching of faculty and students. In a week's meeting in a small country school house Dr. Robert F. Gribble, assisted by four of the seminary boys, was blessed with 45 professions of faith in less than a week. The student preachers in charge of regular work reported professions all through the summer, some students having professions every Sunday for a month, and almost all having decisions for Christ all through the summer. . . .

In the fall, after the harvest season, all students and faculty having assembled, a testimony meeting was held in which each man reported on the experiences of the summer. Great joy and almost astonishment were experienced when one after another of the men told what God had done for them and their work.[21]

The Seminary was glad to be able to be represented again in the councils of the church at large. In 1925 the Board agreed "That the amount of $1250.00 be appropriated for the expenses of President Currie's trip to Europe as a delegate to the Pan Presbyterian Council at Cardiff, Wales, and the World Conference on Life and Work at Stockholm, Sweden."[22]

Where Dr. Currie taught, his students felt the ebb and flow of the tides of Christendom. Wherever he was, the welfare and growth of the men at the Seminary toward a fruitful ministry was not far from his heart.

Dr. Currie was, more than any other individual, the Seminary to me. His great heart and vigorous mind, his love for the Seminary and the church, his personal interest in the students, his

[20] C. M. Campbell conversation, August 7, 1957 with T.W.C., Jr.
[21] *The Austin Presbyterian Theological Seminary Bulletin, Student Edition* II, 1 (May 1, 1926), 1.
[22] Minutes of the Board 1923–1931, May 13, 1925.

expectations of them, confidence in them, his "down-to-earth" relationship he was willing to have with them—all these things and many more endeared him to me, and I think practically to all. He was a rare combination of dignity and homely humor.

He had a way of incidentally dropping bits of advice during class sessions with these future preachers. Warning us not to resign in a huff before having a call to other work, he advised us to take a lesson from the "old parrot who never turns loose with her feet, till she's got a new hold with her beak." Again, urging the desirability of finding ways of getting along with cantankerous elders, he used to observe, "You'll move on— They'll stay!"

Two conditions almost certain to result in a minister's having to move were, according to Dr. Currie: "1) Marry a girl in the congregation. 2) Build a church building."

Believing in a minister's duty to provide for his family, he encouraged plenty of insurance. His formula was: "Decide how much you can carry—then take out twice that much, and you'll never regret it."

Dr. Currie's beautiful diction, particularly in the reading of the Scripture made a lasting impression and served as a model for many of us. I believe I remember him best for his unique method of teaching the Bible, making its characters and writers live in a thrilling way.[23]

The vigor and interest of his devotional life was shared by the students. "From time to time he used to invite us into his office for prayer. We would talk about things that ought to be done, the needs of people, and our own needs, and then we would get down on our knees and pray."[24]

He loved the students. ". . . He never became impatient at some of the crazy things we students did. He was blessed with a grand sense of humor and an optimistic spirit. We seemed to catch that wonderful spirit, and Dr· Currie led us on to the completion of our Seminary work."[25]

Some of the students drove him to his appointments. The Rev. Ellis Mosley was one of these.

I travelled with Dr. Currie many times as he preached in the

23 Dwight A. Sharpe letter, December 23, 1955, to T.W.C., Jr. and in the hands of the latter.
24 G. W. Crofoot letter, n.d., in hands of T.W.C., Jr.
25 M. M. Miller letter to T.W.C., Jr., November 25, 1955, and in the hands of the latter.

churches in Central Texas 1923–26. He loved life and good country ham. I cannot eat ham but enjoyed watching him and the Rev. J. P. Kidd eat ham and "red eye" gravy at Mr. Hubert Atkinson's in Maysfield. I recall telling Dr. C. that I was like Moses and did not eat ham. Dr. C. replied, "Moses would have eaten it if he had ever tasted a Swift Premium ham."[26]

Another was impressed by the many-sidedness of Dr. Currie's work.

I was impressed with the magnitude of his heart and spirit; and with the prodigious amount of work he did, not only in preparation for his teaching of History and Church Polity in the Seminary and Bible at the University, but [by] the vast amount of reading he did in many areas; and the scope and interest of his devotional life.

On one occasion he told some of us that he prayed daily for each of his students by name, and this fact has been an inspiration and I believe has supported me throughout my ministry.

We have a great Seminary in the Southwest today chiefly because of the toil, sweat, tears and prayers of Thomas W. Currie. He had faith and a great dream and a devotion to his dream which made it come true.[27]

In discussing the evangelistic work of the Seminary students and faculty, the *Bulletin* for the fall of 1929 records an attitude supremely characteristic of the President: "Austin Seminary has the conviction that scholarship and spiritual life are cooperant and not antagonistic."[28]

As the decade came to a close, the Seminary was offering instruction to thirty-five to forty candidates and to some ninety to one hundred University students.

Late in the spring of 1930 there was a trip out west of Austin:

On April 29, 1930, the students and faculty members [wound] their way to the top of Mount Bonnell, about five miles out of Austin, for an hour of prayer and meditation. Dr. Currie, President of the Seminary, led their devotion. There, away from the noise of automobiles and of the city, with the beautiful Colorado lying beneath and the sun sinking noiselessly behind the western hills, Dr. Currie spoke earnestly on the subject of "Making God Real in One's Life." At times our president showed

---

26 Ellis G. Mosley letter, n.d., in hands of T.W.C., Jr.
27 Maurice C. Yeargan letter to T.W.C., Jr. November 4, 1955, and in the hands of the latter.
28 *The Austin Seminary Bulletin* XLV, 3 (October 1929), 1, 2.

emotions as he mentioned the absolute dependence upon God of the minister as he undertakes to solve problems in which the hopes of making the work grow seems as impossible as to make alive the "dry bones" that Ezekiel saw in his vision.

When Dr. Currie had finished talking and during the silence the students began one by one to pray, some praying in English and some speaking in Spanish, but all talking in the same language to God. At the end of the prayers of the students, Dr. Summey, whose knees are much accustomed to being bowed in prayer, closed the period of communion with the prayer that God would go with each one as he goes to the work which had been given to him.[29]

Less than a month later another honor came to the Seminary, for when the General Assembly convened at the Charlottesville Presbyterian Church, Charlottesville, Virginia, May 22, 1930 at 11:00 A.M., a commissioner from the Presbytery of Central Texas was elected Moderator, "Rev. Thos. W. Currie."[30]

[29] *The Austin Presbyterian Theological Seminary Bulletin, 1930 Student Edition* XLV, 2 (July 1930), 24.

[30] Minutes of the Seventieth General Assembly of the Presbyterian Church in the United States, A.D. 1930, p. 19.

The Period of the Thirties   6

As the Depression of the 1930's settled upon the country, the Seminary could not escape the staggering weight of its burden. The bedrock principle of financial policy adopted in 1918[1] was tried on the occasion of each annual budget but had never been tested more severely than at the beginning of the decade of the Thirties. Income from investments which in 1930 was $25,971.37 by 1935 had slipped to $11,177.69. Total income from investments and other sources decreased from $39,276.65 in 1929 to a low of $20,282.77 in 1935.

If the Seminary were not to go into debt, something had to be done. Should one or two of the teachers be terminated? On September 9, 1931, the faculty by unanimous vote cut its salaries by ten percent.[2] Soon another ten percent cut was necessary.[3] The salary of the President was cut by an additional $1,000 when he was called as stated supply of the Highland Park Presbyterian Church in Dallas. On the second Sunday of December 1932, Dr. Currie began a schedule that included preaching morning and evening at Highland Park Church and at the Sunday school hour teaching a men's Bible class that grew to average more than one hundred in attendance. Monday he cared for the administrative work of the congregation. The official boards met on Monday evenings. That night he boarded the pullman on the MK&T for Austin. Tuesday morning he was met at 7:00 A.M. Dr. Currie spent from nine to twelve hours with lectures on Church History at the Seminary and three hours Bible teaching for credit for students in The University of Texas classes which met at the YMCA. In addition to the matters in the President's office, there were the matters devolving upon Dr. Currie as Chairman of Home Missions for the Presbytery of Central Texas. On Saturday afternoon he would board the Katy going north and arrive in

---

[1] Minutes of the Board 1912–1922, December 3, 1918, pp. 346, 347.
[2] Minutes of the Faculty 1928–1939, September 9, 1931.
[3] Minutes of the Board 1932–1940, May 11, 1932. This represented an additional salary cut for the faculty, the second in 12 months.

Dallas that evening. He used to say that a minister ought to feel as embarrassed to be without a book as he would be to be without clothes. Thus, some of his studying was done on the train. Indeed, few of his waking moments were idle.

John E. Owens, an officer of one of the Dallas banks, wrote of Dr. Currie:

He was a very great minister in my opinion. . . . I [went] into his class and [came] under his wonderful charm once a week. Seldom indeed did I miss a meeting of this character. I really believe his Sunday School work was superior to his church work, as he seemed to have left the printed page and talked from the heart. I think he was one of the greatest ministers the South has ever produced. His combination of knowledge, of humor, of history and of faith is the greatest thing I have ever seen in any living man. In my opinion his teaching and preaching here has never been equalled. His knowledge was universal. He had read and studied so much religion, so much of history, so much of philosophy and, added to this was his wit and eloquence that made him one of the most powerful figures I have ever seen in any pulpit. His friendships were all loyal—they were true and sincere and heartfelt. I have never met a man who represented the ideal minister as did Thos. Currie.[4]

Rev. Girard Lowe, sometime pastor of First Presbyterian Church, Memphis, Tennessee, wrote:

It was my privilege several times to have him in my pulpit while in Memphis and the people there came to admire him and look forward with eagerness whenever he was to occupy the pulpit. I have always felt that the Synod of Texas was the most evangelistic portion of our church, and I believe this was due in large measure to Dr. Currie's love for the souls of men and his evangelistic spirit which through his great personality permeated the whole Synod. He was indeed a great soul and gave unstintedly of himself to the cause of Christ. In fact, probably, if he had not tried to do two men's work after the death of his brother Morgan, who was killed in the last war, his life would have been prolonged. I remember that after Morgan's death he felt he must not only do his own work but try to do what he felt Morgan would have done too.[5]

[4] John E. Owens letter to Sam L. Joekel, October 13, 1943, and in the Seminary Library Archives.
[5] Girard Lowe letter to Samuel L. Joekel, October 5, 1943, and now in the archives of the Seminary library.

Something of Dr. Currie's approach to Church History was illustrated in his article on "Theological Education Today," published in *The Union Seminary Review*.[6] There his emphasis was that the church was always at its authentic best when it was most seriously involved in evangelism and missions. His approach to Bible study was illustrated by the courses offered through the Extension Department of The University of Texas and by his studies in the Psalms printed in 1941 by The Tex-Mex Printery.

Dr. H. Y. Benedict, President of The University of Texas in the thirties, was not a professing Christian, but he and Dr. Currie were dear friends. On one occasion Dr. Benedict, whose field was physics and astronomy, was brought by Dr. Currie to address a church conference at Westminster Encampment in Kerrville. He brought a telescope so the heavenly bodies might be examined more closely by the conferees. In May of 1937 Dr. Benedict died. On May 12 Dr. Currie conducted the funeral service. O. E. Sanden recalls,

Perhaps the time Dr. Currie rose highest in my estimation was on the occasion of his being called to conduct the funeral service of the late Dr. H. Y. Benedict, President of The University of Texas. It is said that this man once called Dr. Currie to the death bed of his son, and said that he would wish that he could have the kind of religion Dr. Currie had. We filed into the great Gregory Gymnasium, and there before one of the most select audiences, this master preacher delivered a eulogy, eloquent, thoughtful, truthful, alarming. He referred to the ceaseless activity of nature, the throbbing of all things. Central in the Universe is the heart of the Creator, who incites all action, and whom Christ teaches us "is most wonderfully kind." Without compromising any of his theology and his insistence of a need for a regenerating faith, he yet managed to arouse the admiration of the faculty and student body by his wonderful grasp of the mighty challenge to one's best, that it seemed almost less than a funeral and more of a searching sermon. After the service, I said, "Doctor, you were at your best today." "And I was up until two this morning before the Lord gave me that," was his rejoinder.[7]

The arrangement with the Highland Park Church was continued through the summer of 1937. During this period the church grew

6 T. W. Currie, "Theological Education Today," *The Union Seminary Review* XL, 1 (October 1928), 58–73.

7 O. E. Sanden letter to Samuel L. Joekel, October 25, 1943, and in the Seminary Library Archives.

in membership from seven hundred fifty to more than one thousand. The church, as a token of esteem, gave Dr. and Mrs. Currie money for them both to go to Britain where in August Dr. Currie was a delegate to the Edinburgh "Faith and Order" conference. Beginning in September of 1937 the financial picture was improving enough for Dr. Currie to return and give full time to the Seminary.

Even during the troubled times of the Depression, Austin Seminary found a distinctive reason for its existence both in its relation to the needs and opportunities of the Presbyterian Church, U.S. in Arkansas, Louisiana, Oklahoma, and Texas, and in its obligations elsewhere. By the end of the thirties, twenty-six who had studied at the Seminary had become foreign missionaries.[8] The rationale of this abiding concern of generation after generation of students may be seen in a statement published in the 1932 Student *Bulletin*:

> . . .We believe in a Christ-like world. We know nothing better; we can be content with nothing less. We do not go to the nations called non-Christian, because they are the worst in the world and they alone are in need; we go because they are a part of the world and share with us in the same human need—the need of redemption from ourselves and from sin, the need to have life complete and abundant and to be remade after this pattern of Christ-likeness. We desire a world in which the Christ will not be crucified but where His spirit shall reign.
>
> We believe that men are made for Christ and cannot really live apart from Him. Our fathers were impressed with the horror that men should die without Christ—we share that horror; we are impressed also with the horror that men should live without Christ.
>
> Herein lies the Christian motive; it is simple. We cannot live without Christ and we cannot bear to think of men living without Him. . . . Christ is our motive and Christ is our end. We must give nothing less, and we can give nothing more.[9]

One of the earliest alumni to go as a missionary abroad was John Walker Vinson. His brother, Thomas Chalmers Vinson of the Class of 1912, became a missionary to the Congo. Their brother, Robert Ernest Vinson, was President of the Seminary.

The story of John Vinson appeared in the *Seminary Bulletin*:

> On Monday, November 2, 1931, the press in the United States reported the capture of the Rev. John W. Vinson, D.D., of the

8 Currie, *A History of Austin Presbyterian Seminary, op. cit.*, pp. 251–53.
9 *The Austin Seminary Bulletin*, Student Edition, XLVII, 2 (July 1932), 6, 7.

John Walker Vinson, Class of 1906

United States Presbyterian Church Mission in China, by bandits ravaging the country around Haichow, where Dr. Vinson had been stationed. On Wednesday, November 4, reports indicated that our missionary had been executed by these bandits. The following telegram was received by Austin friends the next day:

November 5, 1931

"Not much information available. Cable received Tuesday from Shanghai: 'Robbers captured J. W. Vinson November 1, fifty kilometers southeast of Haichow.' Immediately this office cabled Shanghai full power to act and wired State Department at Washington for official action through the consul in Nanking. Cable received this a.m., Shanghai: 'J. W. Vinson killed. Particulars not yet in hand.' All other news we have comes from press dispatches. Please express to relatives and friends the Executive Committee's deep sympathy."

(Signed) EDWARD D. GRANT

Upon receipt of this confirmation, the Faculty at Austin Seminary, in a meeting on November 6th, ordered the framing of the following Memorial, to be spread on the minutes, printed in the October Bulletin, and sent to the family and the brothers and sisters of the martyred missionary:

The Austin Presbyterian Theological Seminary Faculty, alumni, and students, together with our friends who knew and delighted to honor the Rev. John W. Vinson, D.D., of China, mourn the loss of a friend, the first martyr of this institution.

In sympathy and love our hearts go out to the members of the family of this alumnus. We rejoice in his loyalty, integrity, and devotion to his Lord. Faithful unto death, receiving the crown of life, we know his departure will be regarded by all as a triumph of the gospel which he faithfully preached even more than as a loss, severe and shocking though the sense of that loss is.

Sherman was his home, Austin College his Alma Mater, Austin Seminary his theological training school, the everlasting gospel his life work, China his field of labor, God his exceeding great reward.

The anachronism of a martyr's death in the twentieth century of our Lord's era, vindicates the more certainly the cause of the Christ whom this distinguished alumnus represented.

If his death shall be instrumental in stirring our whole church to a more diligent devotion and sacrifice in executing the Great Commission, as his life has counted in the dispensation of the gospel by whose terms he proclaimed salvation even to such depraved humanity as cause his death, all who grieve at his loss shall yet thank God and take courage in the consolation that he has not died in vain. He being dead, yet speaketh.

"Awake! Awake! Put on thy strength, O Zion!"

"Servant of God, well done!
Rest from thy lov'd employ;
The battle fought, the victory won,
Enter thy Master's joy!" [10]

Beneath his picture in the Seminary *Bulletin* the following appeared:

JOHN WALKER VINSON   MISSIONARY – MARTYR

John Walker Vinson was born in White Oak, Fairfield County, South Carolina, December 29, 1880. He was one of eight children. In 1887 the family moved to Shermán, Texas. John

[10] *Austin Seminary Bulletin* XLVI, 3 (October 1931).

was trained in the public schools of the city and was graduated from Austin College in 1903. He completed his work and was awarded the B.D. degree from Austin Presbyterian Theological Seminary in 1906.[11]

The official magazine of the church, *The Presbyterian Survey*, featured J. W. Vinson on its cover in February 1932 and reported the circumstances surrounding his death. More yet is to be found in a letter from E. H. Hamilton in possession of T. Watson Street.

Jack and Jeanie de Forest Junkin Vinson had six children, only three of whom attained adulthood. Jeanie died March 25, 1923. By 1929, with three children studying in the United States, Jack continued his efforts in China, writing,

June 5, 1929. In addition to looking after the hospital accounts, I have been privileged to take over Mr. Grafton's evangelistic work during his absence on furlough. I have just returned from a two weeks visit to six of the out-stations in his field. . . .

The cordial, hearty welcome, the friendliness, kindness, hospitality shown me by the Christians and inquirers at Yang-Djia-Gee will always be filed away among the sweet memories of my life. . . . I spent six days there in the closest, most intimate fellowship with our evangelist, Mr. Liu I-sheng. . . .

As the fruits of his loving labor there, seventy-one persons came up for examination, eight of whom were received on profession of faith in Jesus Christ. These came from all conditions of society in the community—merchants, well-to-do farmers, students and teachers—from the most ignorant to the most noted scholar in town, Mr. Chow Shih-chin.[12]

"Food, faith, and fellowship" were part of the story, but cold and fleas were also to be reckoned with. The fleas migrated in May from the water-buffaloes, cats, dogs, and pigs to the missionary's inviting frame. In the winter the damp cold was penetrating and merciless.

In December of 1929 Mr. Vinson reported that during a four-week tour he had baptized 46, 18 of whom were a part of the church at Yang-Djia-Gee. From there he wrote,

What a wonderful day this has been: sixty-seven examined

---

11 *Austin Seminary Bulletin* XLVII, 2 (July 1932), 5.

12 E. H. Hamilton, "I Am Not Afraid!" The Story of John W. Vinson, Christian Martyr of North Kiangsu, China. Unpublished paper received from Ethel (Mrs. Conway T.) Wharton by T. Watson Street with covering letter dated September 19, 1957 and in the hands of the latter.

during the past three days; baptism administered to eighteen. What a joy to break to them the bread, and to share with them the cup of their first Lord's Supper!

I have been witnessing here. . . .

I baptized Old Man Wang today. His face is full of a radiant joy since the love of Jesus came into his heart. . . . He came to his baptism, not only bringing his soul as an offering of first fruits to the Saviour who bought him, but bearing other sheaves of his own ingathering. His brother, his wife, and six of his neighbors whom he has been teaching, were brought to Christ by him, and received baptism at the same time.[13]

Mr. Vinson, not fully recovered from an operation in the summer of 1931, was back at work that fall. At the end of October he was again in Yang-Djia-Gee in a room at the Christian chapel with an evangelist, Mr. Liu. Bandits were a constant risk, and that night under the cover of darkness, the town was surprised and ravished. One hundred fifty prisoners, including Liu and Vinson, were taken. Vinson was led away in pajamas and deposited in a dirty inn. The innkeeper gave the shivering missionary his own spare clothes. Soon soldiers were approaching, and the bandit chief, hoping to go unpunished, spoke to Vinson:

"Do you want to go free?"

"Certainly," came the reply.

"All right. If you will write a letter to the general of that army, and get him to withdraw his troops, I will let you go free," said the bandit chief.

"Will you also release all these Chinese captives you are holding?" the missionary asked.

"Certainly not," answered the bandit chief.

"Then neither will I go free," said Mr. Vinson.[14]

When the bandits tried to escape they suffered heavy losses. Though some of the prisoners found their way to safety, Vinson remained captive. A little girl whose name is beyond recovery reported a conversation that shortly preceded the martyrdom. She told how she had seen and heard a bandit trying to intimidate Mr. Vinson. She said the bandit pointed a gun at Mr. Vinson's head, and said, "Are you afraid?"

"No, I am not afraid," came the answer.

And again, "I'm going to kill you. Aren't you afraid?"

13 *Ibid.*
14 *Ibid.*

Once more he replied, "No, I am not afraid. You kill me, and I will go right to heaven."[15]

A fellow missionary found in these words the inspiration for the following poem:

Afraid? Of What?

Afraid? Of What?
To feel the spirit's glad release?
To pass from pain to perfect peace,
The strife and strain of life to cease?
Afraid—of that?

Afraid? Of What?
Afraid to see the Saviour's face,
To hear His welcome, and to trace
The glory gleam from wounds of grace?
Afraid—of that?

Afraid? Of What?
A flash—a crash—a pierced heart;
Darkness—light—O heaven's art!
A wound of His a counterpart!
Afraid—of that?

Afraid? Of What?
To enter into Heaven's rest,
And yet to serve the Master blest,
From service good to service best?
Afraid—of that?

Afraid? Of What?
To do by death what life could not—
Baptize with blood a stony plot,
Till souls shall blossom from the spot?
Afraid—of that?
　　　　　　　　　　　—E. H. Hamilton

Suchowfu, Kiangsu, China,
November 7, 1931[16]

---

15 *Ibid.*
16 *Ibid.* The poem is by E. H. Hamilton, *Afraid? Of What?* (Bristol, Tennessee: Mallicote Printing, Inc., copyright 1968 by E. H. Hamilton), p. 7.

Through the Eyes of a Student 7

Oscar Gardner of the class of 1935 was a Choctaw Indian born in Bennington, Oklahoma. After finishing his work at the Seminary, he served for a number of years as Superintendent of the Goodland Indian Home near Hugo, Oklahoma. His memories of days at the Seminary bring the reader into the Austin of the 1930's and illustrate the fashion in which The University community and especially the students and faculty of the Seminary touched the life of a young man in preparation for the ministry.

"The first organized effort to bring Christ to the Choctaw Indians began in Mississippi in 1819 under the American Board of Commissioners of Foreign Missions. This being a joint agency of the Congregational and Presbyterian Churches. Eventually, the Congregationalist disappeared and my family knew nothing but the Presbyterians. My father was the third ruling elder in our rural church from my family and he believed the Presbyterian Church was a special stairway from earth to glory. 'I can pick out Presbyterian preachers from a picture of all sort of preachers,' he said. 'There is something about Presbyterian Doctrine that gives a man security,' he felt, 'and if a man really believes in the sovereignty of God it is reflected in his face.' He also told me from infancy to observe Presbyterian Preachers because they are well educated and know how to act. He stressed that they should be watched at the table, but in this capacity I neglected the clergy while looking after my own interests.

"It must have been in September, 1932 that Dr. R. M. Firebaugh took Grady James and me to the Seminary. I fain would have gone via The Katy Railroad but went with these brethren in a reliable Ford touring car. The Depression was a reality then and not a shadow in a history book.

"What to expect of a seminary was beyond my knowledge. Sampson Hall was standing there with the third story just a little higher than some few pecan trees. The dining room was a thing of delight.

Never have I seen such an abundance of good food. Real fattening, too. And elegance hithertofore seen only in an occasional movie. Silverware in abundance with two forks and two spoons and napkins big enough for baby diapers. Within a month I fain would have renounced Presbyterianism but tradition is deep-rooted and in a dream my Grandfather Gardner seemed to be with me and when leaving admonished me to not leave. Hikes to Mount Bonnell and hours down at the depot when the Katy trains rolled in from Oklahoma helped me soon to like The Seminary in spite of unlimited silverware, Greek and Hebrew. In due time I knew beyond any doubt that I was immune to all this and began to enjoy life.

"It was customary in Dr. Summey's Theology to have students offer a prayer at the beginning of class. When my turn came I asked 'that we may understand these things.' As soon as I said 'Amen,' Dr. Summey cleared his throat with a roar that any lion would have appreciated and said: 'You are not supposed to understand everything. God be true though every man a liar!'

"Sometime that first year a petition was handed me asking that Dr. Summey be relieved from his work. I did not sign and explained that since it was my first year I had no idea of whether he was an able instructor or not, and suggested that since he was then 80 that the petition be dropped and let God remove him in due season. 'Never do anything to wound an old man. . . .' This set the brother with the petition into an eloquent rebuttal: 'No, he isn't about to die. He can out walk you right now. Every so often he sends to New Orleans and gets a bunch of young people and then a gang from around the Seminary and walks all of us down climbing to the top of the capitol and all over Mt. Bonnell. No telling when that old man will die. . . .'

"And so I settled back to enjoy good, old Dr. George Summey. In a short time I was at his house for 'hemlock' as the boys called this Louisiana Coffee. That night I took on a demitasse of this potent beverage which Dr. Summey said had been thoroughly purified as far as any stimulant was concerned. That night The Katy Flyer whistled Northward around 2:00 a.m. and I had not been to sleep. Grady James sighed on the lower bunk and said he could not sleep. I asked, 'What is wrong with us?' And Grady said, 'It's Dr. Summey's old coffee.' Again and again, I took hemlock at Dr. Summey's socials. His home was a place I dared touch nothing but the door knob and that with apprehension. He collected gadgets everywhere. To a studious person he would hand a small volume with some comment on the author's erudition. The moment the book was opened it fired like a shotgun. You lifted the lid of a box and a monkey leaped in your face. A rose by any other name doubtless is still a rose but some of Dr. Summey's flowers squirted water in your face. . . . And he set two to debating the merits of certain contemporary theologians and then passed the sugar. One debater put three tiny spoons of sugar in his hemlock except the spoon had no bottom.

"Dr. Summey had a wealth of stories. He feared being absent minded and told of a certain minister, sitting in his study reading Dr. Bull on Infant Baptism. A couple came to be married and the minister's wife rushed the parson into his coat and on down the stairs. He stood before the young couple with Dr. Bull's works much in his thoughts and asked: 'And what will you name the child?' . . .

"Dr. Summey confessed that he had driven a Model T but these gear shift cars were too much for him. So sundry boys chauffeured him around. It was hardly a stone's throw from his backdoor to his garage, but he let the boys take their dates on little drives and confessed that it was often 15 miles from his backdoor to his garage according to the speedometer on the faithful Buick. He also confessed that when in New Orleans a distinguished person died and he was conducting the funeral. Enroute to the cemetery the funeral procession went through an intersection. . . . Fancy cars and then Dr. Summey's Model T, and when the Model T came abreast of the policeman he commanded, 'You get out of that funeral procession.'

"H. Grady James, also came from the Indian Presbytery, and was as much Choctaw as I could muster. He was not given to foolishness and it grieved him when I nicknamed Dr. Summey: 'No. 10.' It was not possible for me to advance in Greek and Hebrew but I did get to be a waiter and manipulate that silverware. The minute the bell rang for a meal here would come Dr. Summey to the dining hall. Having always appreciated trains it was a compliment I wished to pay him, but some of the boys did not understand calling the beloved Old Gentleman, 'No. 10.'

"And at the close of my last year I hung around the Southern Pacific Depot just to see No. 10 swing aboard that pullman for Houston and thence to New Orleans. 'He is old in many moons and I will not see him again.' About 11:00 Dr. Summey caught sight of me and asked, 'What are you hanging around here for at this time of night?' I did not tell him that he was the attraction and it was some years before I learned that occasionally some of the folks around a station that late at night aren't going anywhere. . . . But I was mistaken. Again and again, I was to meet Dr. Summey. The last time at the General Assembly at Massenetta Springs in 1950. He was then something akin to feeble. The second day of this Assembly mumps took charge of me and I spent ten days in the Memorial Hospital in Harrisonburg, Virginia. On Sunday, Dr. Summey led the Assembly in prayer and I heard him through radio earphones. At first his voice was unsteady and I thought, 'His years are too many,' and then he gained strength and once again his voice was strong and resonant with the old familiar words, 'Grant and Fill' and spoken with something that sounded to me like an echo from Mount Sinai. A few years later No. 10, being old and full of years was gathered to his fathers.

"Dr. Joekel interested me from the beginning. 'Half German and half Hebrew,' they said. He could tell yarns on both nationalities. And he had a wealth of stories, but I remember few of these tales. . . . His presence to me was like music, delightful music, music gay as a Strauss waltz, a curtain that camouflaged sorrow. . . . In time I called him affectionately and always to his back: 'The Rabbi.' Soon after entering the Seminary, Dr. Joekel picked me up down near the University Presbyterian Church one afternoon, and asked how I was liking the institution, I told him that Dr. Currie told some of the funniest things I ever heard and that I laughed and sniggered so much in his classes that I feared lest Dr. Currie believe I had come to the wrong institution in Austin. He said, 'No, just go ahead and enjoy every yarn Tom tells. He likes for a fellow to appreciate his stories and wisecracks. . . .' I hoped this were true for I never stopped enjoying Dr. Currie's remarks. And one time Dr. Joekel told me, 'Dr. Summey is the only man I ever knew that regardless of where he went, he always clicked.' Dr. Summey's teeth did no end of clicking.

"Dr. Joekel was a wonderful man and I liked to see him glance down at his Bible to be sure of a reference. Two additional chins appeared while he scanned the page. Mother always said that if you mocked others the same thing would come to you. Now with my dim eyes undoubtedly TIME will supply another extra chin.

"The children of the Professors astonished me by being so normal. Dr. Joekel had two boys, Robert and Sam, and they were artist's models in my sight. The Curries numbered four: a girl and three boys. In front of Sampson Hall there was quite a hedge and beyond this a circle of tall grass. Many are the times when these small children were animals in the jungle and the sound effects were quite convincing. Dr. Joekel claimed these children were evidence enough

84

of Total Depravity. Said he happened to look into a rendezvous down the hill and they had his Sam tied to a tree and the wood already stacked around him.

"Following Seminary I met beloved Dr. Joekel here and there and his interest in me was something I treasured. . . . It is strange how we take people for granted. Never occurred to me that Dr. Joekel would soon be going home, and then one day he was not for God took him. . . .

"The Old Testament has always been the most fascinating reading to me but the first time I saw it in Hebrew, my appreciation of the English language skyrocketed. Dr. Gribble was trying hard to innoculate me with Hebrew and before I was immune many rash statements left my tongue. It took something more than an immunity to Hebrew to disturb Dr. Bobbie. . . . During my first year I went to Sunday School and church at Hyde Park as that seemed more like the places I would know than the larger congregations. Times were very hard and I discovered a friend in Hyde Park Church whose family was having a hard time. It was decided to move back to Fort Worth as the family would be eligible for some assistance there. My young friend was well established in the public school and the family did not wish to leave Austin. I took this matter up with Bill Hazel, a fellow student, living in the Leper Colony and sometimes secretly referred to as Major Hoople. Hazel was the kind of a man who found adventure in every nook of the woods. Enroute to a preaching point he would pick up a hitch hiker and more than likely have a dramatic conversion. Hazel and I took this matter to Dr. Gribble. He heard us gladly and thanked us for our interest in people. Some days later, following a conference with Dr. Currie, Dr. Gribble brought me the verdict I expected. The Seminary could ill afford to let anyone live in one of the houses of the Leper Colony rent free lest every Depression-pressed Presbyterian in the four supporting synods apply for free living quarters until economic changes brought relief.

"Dr. Gribble had a story about Napoleon which I fain would catch but his speech moved at a speed which I could never catch. He did tell of an American enjoying a bowl of soup in a Chinese restaurant. He felt that he should tell the Oriental that he appreciated the soup. Thinking it was Duck Soup, he looked at the Chinese and down at the soup and said, 'Quack, quack?' Instantly, the Chinese said, 'Bow wow!'

"Then there was a day when Bill Pruitt kept asking Dr. Gribble

85

questions and delaying a Hebrew lesson. Finally, Bill asked, 'Dr. Gribble is there much foundation for the idea that the New Testament was originally written in Aramaic?' Dr. Gribble turned and said, 'And now Mr. Pruitt I will ask you a question: Have you studied this lesson?'—The class continued.

"They sent us to The University of Texas to pick up a little Greek. The class met on the top floor of the Old Main Building and one had to pass through a collection of mutilated Greek statues. Copies of the famous originals and like anything in Texas these far exceeded the originals in that vulgar artists had taken crayons and left bloody smears on most mangled limbs and necks. Behind all this was a certain Dr. W. J. Battle who was long on Greek and culture but had failed in that he had no wife. Dr. Battle had all the wisdom of the ages boiled down into 'What is the color of Job's old, blue, turkey hen? Humbug and Humbug the second time.' I came out of Greek knowing forever the color of Job's old turkey hen and with a profound admiration for 'Dr. Humbug.' Years later I visited Dr. Battle a number of times with Grady James. He was always a model of courtesy and would chat contentedly with us for long periods. Once, I dared ask him about France when he mentioned having been abroad. I felt he would know that what I knew of France would be precious little, but the Old Gentleman gave quite a lecture · on the French.

"Church History was alive. There was never a dull moment. Dr. Thomas W. Currie was decades ahead of Hollywood in being able to present any subject in a fascinating style. They told me he had come from around Lott, Texas, and that his father had handled oxen along with mules. This was good news for here was a man as native to the land as John The Baptist. He walked with the great but kept the common touch. He could speak my language and any uneducated man could understand every word of this Lincoln of Texas. I hung onto his words and delighted in his going off on something aside from the lesson. He called these verbal extras 'Chasing jack rabbits.' Always, to me these Jack rabbit chases were like one going around switching floodlights upon the subject under study.

"I expected Church History to be somewhat like being on a mental tour of a dusty museum. Instead, Dr. Currie had the saints of all ages saluting us and marching around in spite of centuries, dungeons, fire and sword. Ancient difficulties took on new and modern dress. Once the Mohammedans of Spain granted the Christians the privilege of existing but they could do no mission work nor maintain schools to perpetuate their religion. Dr. Currie summed this up with: It was a matter of 'scratch them on the back and live; kick them in the pants and die!' He said, 'David told The Lord to get Himself an alarm clock' and I snorted and Dr. Currie then turned to the Psalm and put this in modern language. The last verses being somewhat after this order: 'Lord, we used to be some pumpkins. Once, we told the neighbors where to get off the boat. Now Lord, all the neighbors are kicking us around. Awake, Lord. Get on the job. Get yourself a Big Ben and get busy.'

"Faculty preaching was a time that was sometimes difficult to forget. . . . Dr. Gribble sat alert and sometimes took notes. Dr. Joekel sat with hands sometimes folded across his bay window. In this position he seemed to me a picture of being at ease in Zion. Dr. Summey was a beehive of activity until we sat down after the long prayer. In a few minutes Dr. Summey would clear his throat with a roar anything but muffled and in seconds he would be asleep. A time or two he snored but on the first note of the last hymn Dr. Summey was awake and abreast of the occasion. Dr. Currie seemed to me to like to sing at these services and he sat with dignity throughout the sermon. It was rumored that MAJESTIC SWEETNESS was one of his favorite hymns.

"Following the student preaching the Faculty began their remarks. I remember Dr. Currie would sometimes close his eyes and occasionally have a hand on the lapel of his coat. When most men close their eyes it is like the light going out but not so with Dr. Currie and these brief poses.

"The night came when I was to have the altar by the horns and as we were leaving for the service a number of boys wished me well. Grady James ran by and caught me from the back and surviving this bear hug, it seemed to me that the boys did not want to be disappointed. The Sufficient Christ—John 6:46–49. After a few minutes all seemed calm and I had woven a number of Indian tales into my message and people feel kindly toward the American Aborigine.— They got me for splitting infinitives, mishandling the King's English, and Dr. Summey caught me saying 'WUZ' for 'WAS.' To my surprise the Faculty were very kind in their remarks. Even favorable. . . . Dr. Currie pronounced my name with what I took to be an affectionate French touch, he called me 'Gairdner,' and I supposed that he had some knowledge of the Gare du Nord Railroad station in Paris and my habit of resorting along side the Katy trains. . . . That night he said, 'Gairdner, I didn't know you could talk until tonight.' And for several days the boys were kind enough to bring me reports of favorable words from Monsieur le President.

"During this first year Dr. Currie had suggested that I try to get by on what little I had at hand as The Seminary was hard-pressed. I had a $100.00 and was sharing this with a most considerate roommate. Later, I was to discover that certain boys had churches and other jobs which paid something and that they came from homes which I felt were able to do somewhat. About this time The Moderator of the General Assembly came to Austin and I went to hear him. He spoke at length about Presbyterians having been the backbone of the nation since the beginning. Sitting there in my one, old, shiny suit it occurred to me that perhaps I was attempting to be in a class above my financial status quo. It also struck me that during the depth of the Depression it hardly behooved any group to lay claim to being the backbone of the nation, for conditions in general reminded me that the country might be suffering from something like tuberculosis of the bones. These things were debated a few days and remembering Marshall Ferdinand Foch of France had said, 'Always take the offensive when possible,' I approached Dr. Currie and asked for a suit of clothes. In all kindness he asked me: 'Gairdner, you know that money doesn't grow on trees?' The interview ended with negotiations still open but no decision made. I was little enough to remark that 'Down at the Katy Freight Depot they save all their railroad magazines for me and when I come in the door they are glad to see me and introduce me around muchly. When I go in the Seminary office I am reminded that Indians sold Manhattan Island for some Dutch beads. . . .' Then a tailor shop burned on Guadalupe and one pair of trousers to my suit went up in the flames. Bill Hazel got word of this and by the time he caught his breath Dr. Currie doubtless expected me to appear as a Blanket Indian. He called me to his office and gave me $40.00 and I went forth to Scarbrough's with Lawrence Malloy and Grady James as style and financial experts. Came out of there with a suit with two pairs of pants and enough money to take in the next Will Rogers movie.

"About this time I was selected as a waiter. This was a lot of fun. Certain boys spoke Spanish fluently and others had a smattering of sundry languages. All this confusion of tongues amused and interested me and I enjoyed the work. Paul was ever aware of a more excellent way of accomplishing things and as a waiter it fell my lot to wake the boys each morning. Most of the waiters rang the bell down at the dining room and occasionally they would enter Sampson Hall and ring the bell. This was just a hand bell with considerable volume, but the young divines stayed up late and were slow to get up. I would enter the dormitory, parade each floor, and while ringing the bell call aloud like a train announcer in a large station: 'Board Katy, Texas Special North, Track 1, Georgetown, Temple, Waco, Waxahachie, Dallas, Greenville, Denison, McAlester, Muskogee, Springfield, and St. Louis. Board.' The first morning every man hit the floor feeling that disaster was pending for nothing of this kind had been done in those sacred walls.

"About this time Grady James heard that a lemon a day would prevent baldness. So each morning sans permission I carried to him a hot lemonade and then called the trains and disturbed the divines. This had gone on for a month when good Mrs. S. C. Leake happened to appear early in the kitchen and asked, 'Who is sick?' 'No one,' I answered. She continued, 'I saw you carrying something in the dormitory and supposed someone is sick.' 'No, the water is dingy up there and I always take Grady James a glass of hot water each morning.' This satisfied her, but the Negro cooks then took up the matter. 'Mr. Oscar, we likes you and likes to work with you and we don't want you to lose this job for the next boy might not be any fun. Now you spilled a little of that lemonade and Mrs. Leake done stepped on that place and she could feel the grains of sugar on that concrete and she knows dat ain't just water. You go tell the truth and get straightened up. Them boys what hangs around will tell her that there ain't nothing the matter with the hot water in that building.' I agreed and after breakfast, went to Mrs. Leake's room. She and Mrs. Green and perhaps David Stitt, Glenn Murray, Harvard Anderson, et al, whom we called 'The Double Breasted Gang,' were enjoying the homelike atmosphere as was their custom. Mrs. Leake wanted to know what I wanted as she doubtless supposed I had come with a message from the cooks. 'I want to make a confession,' I said. She asked me to continue. 'You know I come from Oklahoma and if a man cannot tell a first class lie up there he doesn't have much rating. So I just have to do a little practicing down here lest I lose the art. So this morning and every morning for a month or longer I have taken Grady James a hot lemonade. He believes it might help him to hold his hair and he wants to get married ere his hair is no more. So let me pay for the lemons and try to forgive me for lying. I am sorry.' At this the gracious lady replied: 'You are forgiven. Keep on carrying Grady lemonade as long as it seems to help him. I am glad to have that much invested in his appearance. And never apologize to me for lying. Remember I come from Arkansas.' I believe the pious Dr. Robert F. Jones, then sometimes frequently called 'Tail Feathers' was in on this confession.

"William F. Pruitt was given to considerable wrestling and was a mighty man of valor. He also had certain capacity as a dancer. During my waiter days I was pouring Dr. Summey's half glass of sweet milk at breakfast. I saw Pruitt come in the door and glide toward me. He extended an arm and a finger touched me under the arm. Lo, Dr. Summey's glass ran over and milk flowed freely over his vest. He exploded: 'Why don't you go somewhere and learn how to wait tables?' Instantly, Pruitt took a napkin and began to mop up the milk with such gusto that I feared Dr. Summey might be injured. 'It was my fault, Dr. Summey, my fault,' he explained, 'I accidently bumped into him.' After Dr. Summey had time to cool off I went and asked him to let me take the suit to the cleaners. 'No, my boy, no. It isn't even hurt. AND YOU ARE A GOOD WAITER!'

"The Negro cooks were good to me. When a Will Rogers' movie came to Austin I went and stayed in the theater until I had seen the show at least twice. And the cooks always saved me a good supper, too. At that time there were two Negro women of considerable avoirdupois. Sally and Corene. I believe it was Sally who had a sort of barbaric look and sometimes mentioned such delicate operations as 'knife in the heart.' Such talk was new to me, but I did not consider myself a target and felt that 'Mr. Monroe,' the Negro janitor with the wheelbarrow moustache, was a veteran and knew how to take care of himself. Sally told me through tears that Corene had made Mrs. Leake afraid of her and that she was being let out and would not come back. She confessed that she did a lot of rough talk but did not mean a word of it. The dining room was closed that noon and Sally and I were alone and she had dinner enough for me. At my suggestion we sat at the same table and ate.

"Monroe was a character. He swept floors and kept a fire and wore a cloth over his nose and whiskers when sweeping. He received telephone calls galore and always from a cousin. It was mean but I listened to several of these calls and Monroe's voice made me think he should have been an actor on a stage. Believe it was Shakespeare who wrote: 'All the world is a stage,' and Monroe was acting, too. Some phone calls were all soft and mushy as if the mere sound of Monroe's whiskers crackling was sufficient, a message needing no words. Other calls brought forth expressions of alarms: 'O my God. No!' And then at twilight Monroe would come forth from his quarters all spic and span. Or the Seminary would have a function and Monroe would appear as a waiter dressed in white and every whisker bristling. Monroe was a philosopher and he never mixed in the boys' affairs although he knew much about each of us. His special word was 'Graft.' Rodney Sunday and Bill Pruitt worked at SRD and so when these gentlemen were to preach before the faculty, we had to move many extra chairs into the place to take care of the girls who would venture forth from Scottish Rite Dormitory. Monroe said, 'Yeah, Mr. Sunday and Mr. Pruitt, they really got a graft.'

"Lawrence Wharton, Minister of the University Presbyterian Church, was also our Homiletics teacher. I liked him a lot and went to hear him on Sunday nights if possible. It seemed to me that his life could have been summed up in two words he used often: 'Tremendously Concerned.' Following his death I happened to be in Austin and went alone and sat in the University Church remembering him and how much I owed to him. He was along with all the Faculty 'Tremendously Concerned,' about each of us.

"Dr. Currie was my inspiration . . . my ideal. He never knew this and I did not hang around him. Several times I watched him down at the railroad station when he was about ready to leave for the Highland Park Church in Dallas. He never knew that I watched him with interest and delight. A time or so I was at Synod and saw and heard him with pleasure but did not feel it necessary to push in through the rank of admirers who were with him. Once, at Longview, he called, 'Gairdner, aren't you going to speak to me?'

"It was my last year in the Seminary and we all went to the top of Mt. Bonnell. Dr. Currie said: 'One of the things that haunts a seminary is Jealousy. Jesus had it in his seminary, and James and John went and got their mammy, and she came to Jesus and said, 'Lord, when you set up your kingdom I want John to be Secretary of State and James to be Secretary of The Treasury, and Simon Peter and the rest can take the other offices! . . . So on His last night Jesus decided to end all this jealousy and so he told John Mark, 'Go tell your Ma that I want the biggest Turkish towel and the largest wash basin she has in the house.' That night he took the towel and started in to wash their feet. They all knew that someone should wash their feet but each fellow thought: 'I'm too significant to do that task. So-and-so should do that job for us.' So Jesus began with the most self-righteous who stood thinking: Peter, James and John and others have all been mad and raising cain but not me. Jesus washed his feet first and then to the next most self-righteous. . . . They all took this in silence until He came to Peter, and Peter said, 'You are not going to wash my feet!' Jesus said, 'I am if you are going to get out of the Seminary.' Then Peter wanted to take a shower bath.

"One noon Alfred Seddon asked me to drop in the Library at The University of Texas while he checked out a book. I sat down at a table and read these words in a poetry magazine. They touched me and I copied them and until this good day have never learned another thing about the poet. Neither do I believe that all returns to clay. Nevertheless, these lines might be a good tribute to The Faculty who meant so much to me.

Madison Lane

Part V.

Man does not say good-bye. Somehow the soul
Keeps all that has been loved with it always.
The bodies break, friends go, the seasons roll
But of each cherished thing the spirit stays.
They are like summer shining on the air—
These forms, this breathing earth, these radiant friends.
From their remembered splendor I shall wear
Some light around me till my moment ends.
I cannot carve your lovely shape in stone,
Staying awhile its excellence from decay,
Nor fix your beauty into paint. Alone
A look upon my face will sometimes say
How beautiful are the things which I have known
That came from earth, that turn again to clay.

—By Lawrence Lee.[1]"

[1] Oscar Gardner letter to T.W.C., Jr., undated and in the latter's hands. The verse is a part of the poem "Madison Lane" by Lawrence Lee. It appeared in *American Mercury*, vol. 30, no. 119 (November 1933), 337, and is reprinted here by permission of *American Mercury, Inc.*, P. O. Box 1306, Torrance, California 90505.

Other Impressions

8

Dr. Daniel Allen Penick, a professor in the Classical Languages Department of The University of Texas, taught Greek to Seminary students who were registered for his courses from 1921 until Dr. Eugene McLaurin came to the Seminary faculty in 1938 and gradually assumed the duties of instruction in New Testament Languages and Exegesis.

Dr. Penick's mother had served meals to some of the students in the Austin School of Theology. Even after Dr. Penick retired he still did some tutoring of theologs, so for his entire life he was in touch with the Seminary.

James I. McCord, who was such a determinative influence on the Seminary in the 1940's and 1950's, recalled:

> Dr. Penick was an institution by the time I arrived in Austin. Of Scotch-Irish stock from the Piedmont in North Carolina, he had grown up in Austin, studied at The University of Texas, and taken his doctorate at Johns Hopkins under the great Basil Gildersleeve. He has told me that he had two great teachers: Robert L. Dabney in moral philosophy in The University and Gildersleeve in classics at Johns Hopkins. Returning to The University he became professor of Latin and Greek, tennis coach, president of the Southwest Conference, assistant dean of the College of Arts and Sciences, choir director of the University Presbyterian Church, teacher of a Bible class for students on Sunday, and founder of student work in the Presbyterian Church, U. S. He turned 70 about the time I came to Austin but continued to teach a full load in Greek. Most of his students were seminarians, although his courses were given in the University. He amazed me then by his liberal spirit and each year since my amazement has increased. On every issue (church union, social progress, economic justice, etc.) he has always been on the side of the angels. The fact that he was a ruling elder

and not a minister made his witness to us all the more profound.[1]

The Seminary had from 1921 onward shown a concern for witness to those of Spanish-speaking heritage. Tex-Mex at Kingsville and Pres-Mex at Taft had pioneered in education at the high school level. The Board of Home Missions had made to the Seminary an annual appropriation to underwrite, at least in part, a Spanish-speaking department. Pastoral leadership for the congregations where Spanish was a primary language was then provided. Dr. Gribble was the professor in charge. Dr. O. C. Williamson and Dr. R. D. Campbell also taught in this department during the thirties and forties.

E. A. J. Seddon, Jr. was a student whose experience in the Seminary turned his attention to the opportunity in the Spanish-speaking communities. "My decision to go into the Latin-American work was due in large part to O. C. Williamson. He talked to me a number of times about how he thought some non-Latin-Americans were needed in the work. When I asked him how could one tell whether God wanted him in a certain part of His work or not, Williamson gave me this bit of helpful advice: 'You can't turn a boat around unless it is sailing. You can't do anything with it if it is in port, but if it is moving, then you cause it to go in any direction you want. So it is with God and us. God himself cannot do much with us if we are not headed somewhere definite. We may start out in the wrong direction, but if we are moving, God can turn us around and guide us where He wants us to go.' The time came when I took his advice and headed for the Latin-American work with this prayer, 'If it is not thy will, O Lord, turn me around where you want me to go.' But He didn't turn me.

"It was about the beginning of the school year 1933–34 that Dr. Campbell assumed the teaching responsibility in the Spanish Language Department of the Seminary. He was at that time and for many years also chairman of the Home Mission Committee of Texas-Mexican Presbytery and treasurer of that Presbytery. This meant that in addition to teaching . . . the Mexican students . . . , he did much travelling throughout the extremely large presbytery and practically carried the full financial responsibility for the Presbytery. Yet

[1] J. I. McCord paper received by T.W.C., Jr., February 17, 1956, and in the hands of the latter. Dr. Penick died November 8, 1964, at the age of 95. See *Texas Presbyterian* (December 1964), p. 1.

he was a very patient man and carried in his heart the problems of the students as well as those of the ministers of the field and even of many individual members in churches throughout the field, for they all esteemed him most highly and still do.

"That was when the country had not fully recovered from the 1929 economic depression and the Mexican families in Texas were in particularly difficult status. Principally for that reason, but for others also, the Mexican students did not live in Sampson Hall. They rented a house in a Mexican quarter of Austin and pooled their resources and a pittance of Home Mission Funds, and with the culinary talents of one of the women of the Mexican Presbyterian Church in Austin, those students made their three-year Seminary course. Dr. Campbell also had to see that the students were well provided for.

"Typical of his spirit of self-sacrifice was his experience of telling one of the ministers that he was reasonably certain that he could secure him a $5 a month increase in salary through one of the women's groups in one of the Anglo-American churches. The minister had been in a special need and asked for an increase, but the women did not help as Campbell had anticipated. So for many months, unknown to the minister, Dr. Campbell contributed $5 a month to the Home Mission account and increased that minister's salary thereby. I think it was for more than a year, and Dr. Campbell's income was nothing to brag about, I am sure!

"One of the things for which I remember Dr. Currie most was the time when my year as a Senior [1934] was drawing to a close and I told him that I wanted to go into the Mexican work. He was trying to get all graduates located and was considering all the possibilities. Dr. Campbell had indicated a place available in Texas-Mexican Presbytery and there was also a vacancy in El Paso Presbytery, the Presbytery under which I had gone to Seminary as a candidate. Dr. Currie confronted me with the two possibilities:

" 'Here they are, Alf,' he said, 'Colorado City is a nice place, has a manse and pays $70 a month. If you go to Gulf (a town in Matagorda County no longer in existence) to the Mexican Church, they promise you a small place to stay in, no definite amount of salary though they hope to get some together, and meals that you may take with the church families, one week at a time. Which do you want? 'I'll go to Gulf,' I replied. 'All right,' Dr. Currie said, 'but if you don't get enough to eat down there, don't come back crying to me and saying that you would like to go to Colorado City instead!'

95

"I appreciated his frankness in making it clear to me that that kind of Home Mission work would offer many privations and that I ought to know what I was getting into before I made my decision. But at the same time it served as a challenge of faith to me."[2]

Dr. Robert Francis Gribble returned to the Seminary in 1923 and taught there until his retirement in 1960. He received a D.D. from Austin College in 1924. He served as Moderator of the Synod of Texas in 1935. He and his wife, Joyce, had two daughters, Nancy Joy (Mrs. C. Ellis Nelson) and Elizabeth Fonda (Mrs. Stephen L. Cook), and a son, Robert Fonda. Dr. Gribble was to some students a life-long inspiration.

Dr. Bobby, a title which few dared to bestow in the presence of the man, is revered by many beside myself because of his intense loyalty to duty. "Duties never conflict." With so much of life sliding any way it wants to, it is impelling to find one who seeks to do what he feels is right to the last point even if it kills him. He might be heartily disagreed with by the majority but it seemed not to matter—he tried to live up to his lights. Holding himself rigid, he expected the same from others. Herein lay the test. Most of the colts in Seminary pretended to claim he was wrong in his premise—but I feel they often knew he was right but they didn't want to discipline themselves. I felt that Dr. Bobby was not as strict as he seemed—there was the smile, the jokes he liked to tell in his jerky fashion, so fast that many found the punch line spit out at them before they had gotten the setting in mind. He would do anything in his power to help if you were even half sincere about it. I felt he assumed the burden of being the disciplinarian for the school for someone has to hold the line always and he was the logical one. If he tried to hold it tight, he was Hegelian enough to hope for a happy median sometime. His working with his hands around the buildings also betrayed him. He was by no means the cloistered ascetic who found the world about him strange. He knew how to lay a plumbed wall, bind a book, fix a leak, or trim up a tree. He enjoyed life.[3]

Doubtless, many a student had the seemingly incongruous experience with respect to Dr. Gribble that is confessed by Rev. J. Martin Singleton.

[2] E. A. J. Seddon, letter and paper, November 26, 1955, to T.W.C., Jr. and in the hands of the latter.

[3] Fred Tyler letter to T.W.C., Jr., November 30, 1955, and in the hands of the latter.

I suppose that I was closer to Dr. Gribble than to any other Professor. At the same time, we disagreed on more things. I respected him very much, but felt him to be wrong many times. His feeling on posture in prayer—*always standing*—is an eccentricity that stands out in my mind. His opposition to students getting married while still in the Seminary is well known, and since I was guilty of doing it, I ran head on into the opposition. I have heard him say that he doubted a man's call to the ministry if he married while still a student.[4]

I remember Dr. Gribble for his economy. . . . Our apartment had a cookstove he had abandoned, which I was glad to abandon also. He did plumbing chores to save money. He memorized the Bible while he shaved.[5]

Dr. Samuel Levinson Joekel had come to the Seminary as professor of Bible and Religious Education in 1926. He and his wife, Dorothy, had two boys, Samuel, Jr. and Robert Charles. The Doctor of Divinity degree came to him in 1926 from Austin College and from Trinity University. He was Moderator of the Synod of Texas in 1941.

Dr. Joekel was in great demand as a public speaker, book reviewer, toastmaster, and Bible teacher as well as a preacher. He represented the Presbyterians for years at the Blois Camp Meeting in the Davis Mountains of West Texas where his week of sermons was annually welcomed by the ranchers and their friends. He was no less in demand in the conference grounds in the church. One of his sermons, "The Eternalness of Christ," was widely circulated through The American Pulpit Series.[6] To many Seminary students he was the one who drew back the curtain and revealed the Bible for what it is.

Rabbi was an experience all his own. . . . Life to him had a sarcastically humorous tinge. His teaching of the Bible was life-centered, not at all studious or of higher criticism type. The characters were modern and lifelike as they shuffled off this mortal coil. The lectures were really sermons in running style. Perhaps this left much to be desired in the matter of research but it gave a running start to homiletic art and many preached Joekelistic sermons for years. At least this tended to warm

[4] J. Martin Singleton letter to T.W.C., Jr. received December 1, 1955, and in the hands of the latter.
[5] Nell (Mrs. J. Martin) Singleton letter to T.W.C., Jr., August 2, 1975, and in the hands of the latter.
[6] *The American Pulpit Series, Book One* (New York: Abingdon-Cokesbury Press, 1945), pp. 78–91.

people up by preaching instead of leaving them cold in facts and figures.[7]

Most famous of the stories about Dr. Joekel stemmed from his labors in the front yard of the house at 104 E. 27th Street when he was exerting himself fixing his flower beds or perhaps the big fishpond, and wringing wet with sweat. He straightened up and remarked to the small gathering of students who had stopped to observe his toil, "What this world needs is fewer Christian Observers and more Earnest Workers!"[8]

Dr. Eugene William McLaurin was a native of Mississippi (Near Mt. Olive), born there in 1888. He received degrees from Southwestern Presbyterian University at Clarksville, Tennessee (B.A. 1912) and from The University of Texas (M.A. 1916, Ph.D. 1952). He was pastor in Edna, then became a chaplain in the First World War. Before coming to the seminary in 1938 he served as pastor in Sweetwater and Ballinger, Texas, and as superintendent of home missions in Brazos Presbytery. The Doctor of Divinity degree was awarded him by Daniel Baker College in 1932, and he was Moderator of the Synod of Texas in 1949. He and his wife, Myrtle, had one son, Lauchlin Arthur.

Shortly after his severance from the service, Dr. McLaurin was deeply moved by two sermons preached by James F. Hardie: the first entitled "In Christ" and the second, "For Christ." He decided that each year thereafter he would read through the Greek New Testament. Thus, although he came to the Seminary as teacher of Theology, he worked toward the day when he would become the Seminary's professor of New Testament Languages and Exegesis.

Dr. McLaurin joined the faculty the year before James I. McCord came to Austin as a student. Dr. McCord said:

> His field was Greek but he taught systematic theology as well, since advanced age had caused Dr. Summey to give up some of his work. Dr. Mac's spirit won everyone immediately. He was, and is, "an Israelite, in whom (there) is no guile." But he won our respect also through his prodigious labor. He might be unfamiliar with a problem in one class but when the class met again he could cite all the authorities on the problem involved.
> Although all these men were in middle age and loaded with

---

[7] Fred Tyler letter to T.W.C., Jr., November 30, 1955, and in the hands of the latter.

[8] Larry M. Correu letter to T.W.C., Jr., December 29, 1975, and in the hands of the latter.

work over and above teaching (McLaurin served as librarian, Gribble as dean, and Joekel as registrar), they continued to study and grow, enrolling in graduate seminars in the University in 1940 and 1941. I took Spinoza with Drs. Gribble and McLaurin (they led the class) and Plato with Gribble, McLaurin and Joekel. Joekel's paper on Ezekiel and Plato's *Timaeus* should have been published. I recall that, at the end of the course, Dr. Gribble tried to change the professor (A. P. Brogan) from a Platonist to a Calvinist![9]

Dr. Thomas W. Currie made an impression on the lives of many students. One, Homer C. Akers, admits that "The professor who most profoundly affected my life was Dr. Thomas W. Currie, . . . I learned to love and admire all of the giants who made up the faculty while I was there, but he was my greatest inspiration.

"He was my sole reason for entering Austin Seminary . . . Dr. Currie came to Austin College at Sherman for the Week of Religious Emphasis sponsored by the College Y.M.C.A. I was active in the Y.M.C.A. so not only had the privilege of hearing him speak, but also of sharing in the counselling periods. I was immediately attracted to him as I am sure Timothy must have been to Paul. In his presence I was deeply moved, feeling that I was talking to a man who knew God intimately, who had a great warmth of spirit, and a vision as broad as the world. Later fellowship with him only deepened this conviction about him. I also learned that a part of his warmth of spirit was a deep affection for people. This affection cut across all race and color lines. There was added to it a jovial spirit with the quick and illuminating humor for which he became famous. Although their approach was different, he and Will Rogers had a great deal in common. His humor often brought to light his amazing ability to combine the visionary, the commonsense and the every day in perfect union.

"In my middle and senior years in the Seminary I was profoundly impressed by his power in prayer and his faith in its efficacy, not only to help the individual, but through it to join hands with God in the carrying out of His program. During these two years, I was privileged to organize and pastor a Community Church at Natalia, Texas, made up of ten denominations. This project was very close to his heart since he was a great believer in Church unity. He dreamed

---

[9] J. I. McCord paper to T.W.C., Jr. received February 17, 1956, and in the hands of the latter.

of the day not only when all Presbyterian bodies would be united, but firmly believed that some day the body of Christ would be one in the sense of the union of all denominations. Each Monday morning, unless he was out of town, I would go down the stairs of the dorm into his study for a period of prayer and fellowship which often lasted for an hour. He would be keenly interested in the happenings of the week-end and we would talk about it. Very often also we would then talk about the things of kindred interest at the Seminary. We would then agree upon definite things for which we would be in prayer. He believed in praying definitely and concretely. We would then enter into our period of prayer which was never hurried and during which we would both pray. In these prayer sessions I would discover his great desire to be completely a part of the will of God and his yearning desire to help to bring the Kingdom of God a little closer to fulfillment. I was also very aware in these prayer sessions of his great love for the Seminary. He was deeply concerned about the need of larger endowment to undergird it and make possible the larger future he envisioned. He would often have specific amounts in his mind for which we would pray specifically. Often he had specific people on his heart who he felt might be led to give the large sums for which we prayed. My remembrance of these prayer sessions will always be a holy of holies in my life.

"In the class room he literally made Church History come to life. However he was not as concerned with our gaining a knowledge of Church History as our feeling ourselves to be a part of the history of God's Kingdom in the making. He would often say things with the express purpose of shocking us into some realistic thinking. Although he definitely played down sensationalism, he was concerned with the rut into which ministers often get, and the way they are taken as a matter of course in a community. More than once he made this rather unusual statement: 'People should be aware that the man of God is in the community. If you cannot get to them any other way, try Isaiah's plan—go down the street in your shirt tails.'

"He believed firmly in the minister taking his stand regardless of consequences of jails. However, he was embarrassed by those who either for sensational purposes or for trivial reasons were self-made martyrs. I have never forgotten one of his statements on this matter. It came after a minister had literally forced himself upon the attention of the Presbytery in such a way that he was defrocked. Dr. Currie was a member of the commission. In the class room the next day he spoke of the line of distinction between real martyrs to a great cause and forcing martyrdom upon one's self for personal, even though misdirected gratification, or even for sensational publicity. He said, 'When the time comes for you to be a real martyr, walk right into the jail and take it like a man, but whoever heard of a *dog backing up to a fence to get a can tied to his tail?'*

"He was also concerned with the fact that so many fine sermons were preached without giving the listeners specific direction for life and decision. He would say, 'Be sure and put on some *rousements* in the conclusion of your sermon. Tell them what you want them to *do* about it.' "[10]

In commenting on student preaching, Dr. Currie once told the preacher that if that was the best he could do, he might as well go sell peanuts for a living, and to another he averred, "That sermon reminds me of the boy that drew a picture on the blackboard and wrote under it: 'This is a horse.' "[11]

. . . while he was generous and tolerant he was very emphatic about what a Presbyterian minister should be. I recall his criticism of a student's sermon when he had used the term "borned again." [Dr. Currie] said that, "No man had a right to stand in a Presbyterian pulpit who used such English."[12]

Dr. Currie's purpose was to make the students relive the Bible incidents. One student remembers his lying prone on the floor to illustrate Paul in prison at Philippi.[13]

Dr. Currie knew we needed sermon outlines, and whenever he discovered one, he would give it to the class. He might present it this way: "I got this sermon outline in my devotion this morning. I thought you would be interested." . . .
Here are a few of them:
Here is Paul's prescription to a preacher from I Timothy 1:5
1. Love out of a pure heart
2. A good conscience
3. Faith unfeigned.

10 Homer C. Akers letter, December 1, 1955, to T.W.C, Jr. and in the hands of the latter.

11 R. Gage Lloyd, paper, n.d., in the hands of T.W.C., Jr.; John C. Solomon letter received November 30, 1955, and in the hands of T.W.C., Jr.

12 S. P. Riccobene letter to T.W.C., Jr., November 29, 1955, and in the hands of the latter.

13 Harry H. Burch, letter to T.W.C., Jr., November 29, 1955, and in the hands of the latter.

If you are to win souls for Jesus, you must be:
1. Unselfish
2. Willing to die
3. Non-resentful (or non-resistant)

The following are five things the Gospel did for Paul:

I Thessalonians 2,3
1. Made him bold
2. Unselfish
3. Sincere
4. Sanely optimistic
5. Missionary minded.

Here are five things the Gospel will do for you:

I Thessalonians 1:9
1. Enable you to walk pleasing to God.
2. Subtract open sin from your life.
3. Make you have a spirit of unselfish interest in men.
4. Give you a new view of death.
5. Make you the best citizens in the community.[14]

. . . Dr. T. W. Currie, in his inimitable way, often chose to dramatize a particular teaching by any act that came to his mind at the moment. One morning in his class in New Testament, teaching from the fourth chapter of Mark, he came to the 26th and 27th verses in which the Lord was teaching of the Kingdom "as if a man should cast seed into the ground, and should sleep, and rise night and day—" To Dr. Currie and through him to the class this immediately became the worried farmer who set his alarm for midnight so he could waken and go out to his field and sit on the fence and watch the grain sprout. That, of course was ridiculous enough to be impressive to all of us in the class, but what impressed us most was Dr. Currie as he imitated the farmer climbing up on the fence. There being no fence in the class-room Dr. Currie seized one of the straight wooden chairs and stepped up on the seat of it. The chair was not equal to the task. The seat split, the rungs were torn from their sockets and Dr. Currie dropped the eighteen inches to the floor. Remarking, "That chair is just like a farmer's fence," he continued his lecture.[15]

I remember Dr. Currie as the best read man I have ever known. He knew more about more things than any other, and seemed to have never forgotten *anything* he had ever read.[16]

14 *Ibid.*
15 John C. Johnson letter to T.W.C., Jr., November 29, 1955, and in the hands of the latter.
16 J. Martin Singleton, *op. cit.*

Dr. McCord recalled that "Early in the summer of 1939 I made a trip to Austin to meet President Currie and discuss my program of study with him. He was in his office in Sampson Hall, the door was open (it was always open to students), and he was soon plying me with questions about John Baillie's *Interpretation of Religion* and Eugene William Lyman's *The Meaning and Truth of Religion.* . . . This was the beginning of an intellectual stimulation to me that continued in and out of the classroom until I left Austin. Dr. Currie encouraged me to buy for the Seminary library any book in philosophy or theology that I would read and then drop by and discuss the contents with him. He was especially interested in Dewey and had a far deeper insight into Dewey's real philosophy than many professional philosophers. For example, he understood that the key to Dewey was his *Logic*, and not his educational philosophy that had become so much the vogue. He was deeply interested in the problem of 'subject' and 'object' in philosophy and theology, one of the crucial issues in the thirties as now.

"My class in Reformation history met at 9:00 a.m., immediately after chapel. We worshipped in the senior class room, the space that now houses the offices of the Dean and secretaries. Dr. Currie was always eager to begin his teaching day—even before the bell gave the signal to go! He would say, 'Come on, saints, let's go to work,' and he would begin a schedule that involved four straight hours of teaching. Mrs. Currie was waiting at 9:50 at the door of Sampson Hall to drive him to the YMCA to meet his University of Texas Bible class, and she would return him to the Seminary campus at 11:00 for two additional classes, one with the juniors in Bible and the other with the seniors in history and polity.

"Dr. Currie's method of lecturing was unique. He would begin with the text (in middler history it was Fisher's *History of the Christian Church*) but this often furnished a point of departure for excursions into philosophy of religion, apologetics, contemporary issues, and a host of other fascinating by-ways. Not that the Reformation was neglected! We read all of Schaff's multi-volumed history and Calvin's *Institutes*. But the Reformation became contemporaneous and relevant. Dr. Currie would speak of Calvin with great respect but he could never subscribe to his double-predestinarianism. He saw that life had suffered at the hand of logic. He would say: 'Calvin wrote his theology around the sovereignty of God. You cannot beat it. But today's theology must be written around the love of God.' He would cite Gandhi and Kagawa as examples of such

103

love in action. One of his deepest concerns was the relation of theology and devotion, a concern expressed in an article he contributed to the *Earnest Worker* about this time.

"He had a knack of being able to reduce a book he read to a single sentence. 'The thesis of Latourette,' he would say, 'is thus and so.' And so it was with any volume he read. Whitehead's *Process and Reality* intrigued him. He was always eager that philosophy should be sensitive to the prevailing thought-forms; hence, his interest in the Gifford Lectures. He is the only man that I have known that had read all the lectures on this great series. . . .

"I believe it can be proved that he did more for the advancement of the Negro in Texas than any other person. . . .

"His intimate knowledge of even the smallest church in the Synod was amazing. Early in September, 1939, he sent me to Llano, a small town in the hill country northwest of Austin. He told me how many different views I would have of Lake Buchanan en route, who would meet me, who would be my host, who the deacons and elders were, and concluded: 'When you get through preaching, tell them you'll be back next Sunday.' I did, and continued in Llano for three years. Llano was no exception. He knew them all.

"The chapel was built toward the end of my Seminary career. Architecturally it is a jewel. I am sure that it was built before the library or other needed buildings because of Dr. Currie's primary concern for worship and his concern that the Seminary be a worshipping community. It was built, too, with the worship needs of the University in mind. When ground was broken for the chapel, Mayor Miller, President Homer P. Rainey, and Dr. Currie spoke, and both Drs. Rainey and Currie referred to the common faith binding the sister institutions and the need for a place of worship for faculty and students."[17]

How did Austin Seminary of the early 1940's strike a student who had spent his first year of theological study at Yale Divinity School? Such a one was David M. Currie who had graduated Phi Beta Kappa from The University of Texas in 1940.

"At the Choate School (in Wallingford, Connecticut)," he wrote, "I [had] heard about the theory that Moses did not write the first five books of the Bible, but that they were some sort of compilation. . . . But I simply thought that was another crazy idea of the 'Yankees.'

"At Yale Divinity School I audited a class where I saw and heard Richard Niebuhr 'doing' theology: visibly, audibly, struggling with Biblical concepts and contemporary situations. I sat under Dahl instructing us in the study of Hebrew and within the first year helping us interpret what was written in the Word. . . . I studied under Latourette who recounted the history of the church as living history, influencing persons in whatever culture they were—and being influenced by them. I knew Bainton as a scholar with a keen interest in the 'full life': home and family, art, municipal affairs, church affairs (and I heard him preach more than once at First Presbyterian Church, Stamford, where I did my field work). The student body was diverse as to denominational affiliation, as to native states, as to goals for studying in a 'divinity' school: pastoral work, scholarly pursuits, ministry at college campuses, Bible translation, etc.

"From there I came to Austin Seminary: small classes—with the same 'middler' students in each class I attended, small faculty, contrasting homogeneous student body (we had even had women students at Yale!), and a small library.

"In later years I drew comparisons with other seminary professors and those I had known at Austin: John Bright, Balmer Kelley, E. T. Thompson at Union, J. B. Green, Manford Gutzke at Columbia, Rhodes and others at Louisville 'published' while, to my recollection, only Joekel's Bible study for the Women (Fitly Framed Together) and Currie's Psalms (for the same purpose, I believe) were the only 'publishing' by Seminary faculty. In a way, the Mid-winter lectures later came to fill that void, vicariously, for the Seminary through them did 'cause to be published' scholarly works.

"Currie died, Stitt came, Nelson matured, McCord was added, McLaurin taught Greek rather than theology—and within two years I know change took place. My 'presbytery exam' was done by Chas. King in strict 'Westminster' categories. When Jan Owen was examined two years later by Marshall Munroe, Munroe made the mistake of asking: 'Mr. Owen, what, in your study of theology particularly caught your attention?' To which Jan responded: 'The teleological suspension of the ethical' . . . a concept to which he had been exposed by McCord's 'taking students to the original sources' of theological thinking. (I came through Austin Seminary without reading a word of Barth, Brunner, Niebuhr, Dodd, etc.) Nelson began to develop 'practicums' in the education field. Street came to lead students into the rich heritage (and diversity) of the Church's history (giving an elective in Personal Devotional Classics, etc.), and Street began the Easter vacation trips of interested students to the Mexico missions. Quinius arrived to offer 'techniques' for organizing a parish and its work—and to give some supervision to summer field work. Stitt . . . with [the enabling generosity of] Toddie Lee Wynne [made] available to seniors the famous spring trips to the headquarters of the agencies of the General Assembly.

"Currie 'held together' a diverse collection of persons at Austin Seminary and helped produce 'servants' of the Church.

". . . with the coming of McCord and Stitt 'scholarship' became a central point in the life of the school, Street 'gave it heart,' Nelson gave it strategy, Stitt gave it financial stability.

"I am glad I attended Austin Presbyterian Theological Seminary because it was assumed that the Bible was the text book for the church, the vehicle of God's continuing revelation for His people." [18]

There was that about the Seminary that tended to discourage cant and to foster concern for getting the Gospel where it was needed as attested by Dr. E. B. Paisley (Class of 1916) who had kept in touch with the Seminary from his posts of service in pastorates in Texas, with the Executive Committee of Home Missions in Atlanta, as professor and then President of Assembly's Training School in Richmond, Virginia, and as member of the staff of the Board of Christian Education of the Presbyterian Church, U. S. A., in Philadelphia. Over three decades a number of trends and observations had come to him.

"To me Austin Seminary has many unique characteristics giving great promise for future usefulness and these promises are the more assuring because of what it has already done and is doing now.

"I suppose the most outstanding characteristic from the very beginning has been an attempt to prepare men to make God known in a grand, new and growing frontier of American life. There is something sublime in the vast expanse of unoccupied territory of the West, rich, unconquered and untamed giving promise of almost limitless resources; and of a people ever increasing, with small fear of insufficient natural resources to match their highest aspirations— especially when this somewhat raw, rude, adolescent life is confronted with an older civilization such as is to be found among both primitive Indians and cultured Spanish grandees.

"This breadth of view, this happy confidence of youth, this faith

---

[18] David M. Currie letter to T.W.C., Jr., November 4, 1975, and in the hands of the latter.

that each day and year will certainly bring greater rewards than the present, whatever the struggles of the day may be, has been an element that has pervaded and shaped Austin Seminary from the beginning; and it is not alien to 'the hope that is set before you,' the anticipation of 'the Promised Land' of Faith.

"Emerson said: 'An institution is the lengthened shadow of one man.' It may be so, but Austin Seminary has within it the shadow of many men, some longer and larger than others. Smoot and Dabney, Sampson, Vinson, Caldwell, Currie—their shadows seem to me to dominate. All were daring men, devoted and gifted. All were 'men sound in the faith,' but none of them thought that 'soundness in the faith' was confined to a faultless creedal statement of what we hold, but rather an active commitment to the Lord of Life and the business of living accordingly. This has always meant not only the knowledge of God as obtained through His personal revelation of Himself in and through Jesus Christ as recorded in the Scriptures, but the knowledge of men in their daily lives and the ability to communicate with them in a language which they can understand and to which they can respond.

"No one could rightly accuse Austin Seminary of neglect of sound theological background—Smoot, Dabney, King, McLeod, Arthur Gray Jones, Summey . . . all speak of the Seminary's concern for the faith once delivered to the saints. But Austin Seminary has put its chief emphasis on Biblical rather than Systematic Theology. Hence the development of the grand tradition of the study of the English Bible, and the insistence upon a study of the progress of Christian thought and action through Church History. This fact, in my judgment, has given to the Seminary a great tradition of true Christian freedom; a liberality that is genuinely liberal in that freedom which is in Christ—not a freedom to think wanderingly and futilely, but a freedom to know God in Jesus Christ and to do His will which is none other than the salvation of mankind. The true Christian liberal is one who loving God as He is, loves man for what God has destined him to be in Christ, and devotes his life to glorifying God through his service to fellow-man. For this spirit Austin Seminary has been and is to be counted great.

"This has been achieved in Austin Seminary it seems to me in many ways, some of which can be listed. First, its professors have been strong men, informed, devoted men who were living out their profession. For them, 'I believe' meant 'I live by.' They have been men who, living as men, had little regard for pretense and sophistication. They, at a cost, had devoted their lives to making God known in a new territory offering little promise of selfish gain for them. They were scholars, yes, but not overly concerned with the recognitions of scholarship. They were thinkers, but never over-exalted the value of brilliant reasoning and that peculiar pride that comes to intellectuals who glory in their ability to think in terms beyond the appreciation of the common man. So they have kept a balance between 'rational' theology and Biblical theology: they have found in the life of the church the commentary on Scripture; and they have chosen to speak a language that can be understood and appreciated, and responded to by man as man.

"The evidences of these are the high regard for the study of the English Bible; the emphasis upon preaching relieved of all the mannerisms of the boor or the scholastic, or the over-pious and conceited ecclesiastic. The hearty acceptance of the value of association with the best that science can offer in university study; the necessity for close association with all Christian enterprises such as the Y.M.C.A., the Christian Student Movement, and the present ecumenical associations; the welcoming of students from all evangelical churches (or any other if they want to come) ; and the emphasis that before a man can effectively minister to men, he himself must be a man. I suppose one of the best proofs of all of this is the number of graduates who have gone out to serve fields having little to offer but people in need of the Gospel.

"For the future I can see great possibilities. They seem to me to lie along the line of (1) the opportunity to lead American Protestantism out in the development of better theological education in that a better place shall be given to the knowledge of how persons grow and develop and how this process is related to the communication of the Gospel, (2) Closer ties with the best knowledge that we have through study—as represented by a great secular university, and (3) the assuming of a place of leadership in all matters dealing with the Protestant Church in the Latin world."[19]

19 E. B. Paisley, letter to T.W.C., Jr., December 3, 1957, and in the hands of the latter.

Outside the Regular Curriculum   9

Beyond the stipulated curriculum, a number of features have characterized the life of the Seminary.

For instance, the Student Edition of the *Bulletin*, issued in the summer of 1933, mentions speakers who lectured the prior school year. Omitting pastors and missionaries from the list, others included: Rabbi Samuel Halevi Baron on some phases of the Old Testament; Sr. Von Son, an ex-Roman Catholic priest from Mexico on why he was converted; Dr. J. B. Wharey of The University of Texas on Robert Browning; Dr. Daniel Poling, President of International Christian Endeavor on Prohibition; Dr. W. A. Visser 't Hooft of the World Student Christian Federation on the Theology of Karl Barth; Dr. E. Stanley Jones on Evangelism; Mr. Robert Frost on poetry.

In April 1938 the students at the Seminary had a part in beginning the Southwestern Regional Interseminary Organization at the initiative of the National Interseminary Movement.[1]

Through the concern of Dr. Currie the Seminary made a contribution in the area of racial understanding. He taught in a school at Prairie View College sponsored by the women of the Synod of Texas[2] and also in a school at Samuel Huston College, Austin, led by Mr. Edgar Love, Superintendent of Negro Work of the Board of Missions of the Methodist Church.[3] He helped persuade the Texas Legislature to supply scholarship funds for graduate and professional training for black students.[4]

[1] *The Austin Seminary Bulletin* LV, 3 (July 1939), 21.

[2] Minna (Mrs. Geo. A.) Sprague, letter (and accompanying tribute) to Samuel L. Joekel, October 9, 1943, and in the Seminary Library Archives. Mrs. Sprague was a former president of the Women of the Synod of Texas, U.S.

[3] Edgar Love, letter to Samuel L. Joekel, October 28, 1943, and in Seminary Library Archives. Mr. Love was at the time Superintendent of Negro Work of the Board of Missions and Church Extension of the Methodist Church.

[4] Mrs. Jessie Daniel Ames letter to Samuel L. Joekel, October 26, 1943, and in the Seminary Library Archives. Mrs. Ames was Director of Field Work, Commission on Inter-racial Cooperation, Inc., Atlanta, Georgia.

Tillotson College was another black institution of higher learning in Austin. The president, Miss Mary Branch, said of the leader of the Seminary:

It takes a good deal of tact, courage, and genuine Christianity to champion the causes of minority groups anywhere. And to stand four-square for justice, and Christian brotherhood where the Negro is concerned is one of the greatest tests to which a member of the majority group can be subjected. Dr. Thomas W. Currie in every respect met this test. Though he was a very busy man, he could always find time to listen to a story of anyone who felt oppressed and, with the wisdom of Solomon and the deep sympathy of Christ himself, he would give a word of comfort and the assurance that he would do his best to help right any wrong which he felt existed.

Dr. Currie believed and practiced brotherhood. A man was a man with him. He believed in equality of opportunity for the Negro in education, in opportunities of work, in the exercise of the ballot, and in the comforts and conveniences of travel. The last conversation we had was about an injustice which had been meted out to a Negro by a railroad official here in Austin. This person had been refused pullman accommodation when an assured vacancy existed. All this evidence was reported to Dr. Currie. He immediately stopped his work, drove to the station and within fifteen minutes called and said, "I've straightened out the matter. Have the person go and get the accommodation and I hope she will have a pleasant trip to New York." His Christian courage, love of justice and tactful handling of a prejudice of long standing changed the view point of that official.

Tillotson College, one of the projects in Negro education supported by the American Missionary Association of the Congregational-Christian Church, and located in Austin, needed the sustaining influence and the wise counsel of an understanding Southern white man on the Board of Trustees, a person who could appreciate the efforts being made by Negroes in their attempt to secure an education. Dr. Currie readily accepted this added responsibility to his already heavy load and was always ready to help. I went to his office on several occasions to talk with him on difficult problems in connection with the work of the college, and I always came away with assurance.

Dr. Currie was President of the Inter-racial group in Austin for many years, and was genuinely interested in helping to make the relationships between the races good for each group. When a problem was especially knotty and many other members feared to touch it with a ten-foot pole, Dr. Currie volunteered to accept

110

the task, and in every contact of this kind he changed conditions for the better.

In Dr. Currie's death the Negro race lost a true and devoted friend, the white race lost a great leader who lived his democracy as laid down [in] the Constitution of the United States and the Declaration of Independence, and a Christian who practiced what he professed.[5]

The Seminary took an interest in preserving the place of the study of Hebrew in the curriculum of theological education. The General Assembly of 1935 appointed a committee to study seminary curricula. This committee proposed a revision of the Book of Church Order that would make the study of either Greek or Hebrew requisite for ordination. Dr. Gribble, a minority of one, but with the support of the faculty and Board of Austin Seminary,[6] presented and won his case at the 1936 Assembly.[7]

General Assembly's Committee on the Revision of the Confession of Faith included Dr. Summey and then later, in his place, Dr. Eugene W. McLaurin. In 1941 the committee was asked to consider the question of Bible interpretation known as Dispensationalism, a system embraced in the Scofield Bible.[8] Dr. McLaurin became secretary of this committee.[9]

The report of the committee which was adopted by the 1944 Assembly[10] observed that Dispensationalism rejects the Unity of God's people, rejects the One Way of salvation, rejects the One Destiny for all God's people, rejects the Bible as God's one Revelation to His One People, "rejects or minimizes the present kingly office of Christ, and deviates from the conception of the Resurrection and Judgment, as set forth in our Standards." The Assembly adopted as its own the unanimous opinion of the committee that "Dispensationalism as defined and set forth above is out of accord with the system of the

5 Mary E. Branch letter to Samuel L. Joekel, October 27, 1943, and in the Seminary Library Archives. Miss Branch was at the time president of Tillotson College in Austin.

6 Minutes of the Board 1932–1940, May 13, 1936.

7 Minutes of the Seventy-Sixth General Assembly of the Presbyterian Church in the United States, A.D. 1936, p. 117.

8 Minutes of the Eighty-first General Assembly of the Presbyterian Church in the United States, A.D. 1941, p. 60. See also Minutes 1943, p. 46.

9 E. W. McLaurin (secretary), Records of General Assembly's Committee on the Revision of the Confession of Faith and Catechisms 1941–1944. Seminary Library.

10 Minutes of the Eighty-fourth General Assembly of the Presbyterian Church in the United States, 1944, p. 123.

doctrine set forth in the Confession of Faith, not primarily or simply in the field of eschatology, but because it attacks the very heart of the Theology of our Church, which is unquestionably a Theology of one Covenant of Grace."[11]

Union between the Presbyterian Church, U.S. and the Presbyterian Church in the United States of America seems rarely to have been a matter of indifference to the faculty of the Seminary. Although R. L. Dabney and R. K. Smoot who had so much to do with the beginnings of the Seminary were uncompromising in their opposition to union, most of their successors viewed the possibility with open minds. Not many months after the death of Dr. Smoot, while Dr. S. A. King was chairman of the faculty in 1907, two paragraphs appeared in the faculty minutes:

> The following communication was received from Rev. H. F. Olmstead, Stated Clerk of the Presbytery of Austin, U. S. A., "The Presbytery of Austin, Synod of Texas, Presbyterian Church, U. S. A., does hereby declare its full confidence in the management and instruction of the Austin Theological Seminary of the Presbyterian Church, U. S., and we do hereby recommend to our ministers and churches this Seminary as an appropriate and convenient institution for the education of our young men for the Gospel ministry."
>
> The Secretary was instructed to answer this communication, expressing the high appreciation with which this faculty heard the action of Austin Presbytery.[12]

The division that occurred in 1861 has not been healed, but the Seminary was to be found more often than not to be placing the preponderance of its weight, though it might not be enough to tip the scales, on the side of reunion. And, cooperation between the denominations has been evident. Candidates from the Presbyterian Church, U.S.A., occasionally took their seminary work or a portion of it at Austin Seminary. The result of years of friendly relations is reflected in minutes of meetings in 1942.

The Minutes of the Synod of Texas, U.S. record the action of a committee made up jointly of appointees of the Synod of Texas of the Presbyterian Church, U.S., and of the Synod of Texas of the Presbyterian Church, U.S.A.

> . . . The discussions were frank and friendly and were carried

[11] *Ibid.*, p. 126.
[12] Minutes of the Faculty 1902–1914, May 4, 1907, pp. 161, 163.

on by both sides in the best of fraternal spirit. At the afternoon session, the following resolution was unanimously adopted: "the Special Committee on Seminary of the Synod of Texas, U. S. A. and U. S. is of the firm conviction:

"First, that a strong and adequate Presbyterian Theological Seminary in the Southwest is a vital need in order to realize fully our Presbyterian opportunity for the Kingdom.

"Second, that the Austin Presbyterian Theological Seminary of the Southern Presbyterian Church furnishes a nucleus of a strong and adequate Theological Seminary in the Southwest, such as is contemplated in the first part of this declaration."[13]

On May 13, 1942 the Board of the Seminary had endorsed this report in the following words: ". . . the Board express[es] its sympathy with the report of the Joint Committee of the U. S. and U. S. A. Presbyterian Churches on ownership and control of the Seminary. The Board earnestly hopes that the goals announced by the Committee will be realized."[14]

The above hopes were coincident with the effort to consummate a nationwide reunion of the two denominations. In 1938 the Presbyterian Church, U.S. had authorized the naming of its part of a Permanent Committee on Cooperation and Union.[15] For a number of years Dr. Currie served as chairman.[16] He noted that whereas conversations relative to reunion had not been wanting, no exact plan had yet been drawn up. This task the Permanent Committee assumed. The resulting Plan came to the attention of the two General Assemblies in 1943. One of the features of the Plan was the provision for strong regional Synods[17] such as actually came into being thirty years later in the Presbyterian Church, U.S. The Honorable P. F. Henderson, a member of the Committee, gave this estimate of Dr. Currie and his part in the work of the Committee.

My acquaintance with Dr. Currie has been in the work of the General Assembly's Permanent Committee on Co-operation and Union, in which we have been closely associated for more than

[13] Minutes of the Synod of Texas of the Presbyterian Church in the United States, Eighty-seventh Session, October 13–15, 1942, No. 3, pp. 136, 137.

[14] Minutes of the Board 1940–1946, May 13, 1942.

[15] Minutes of the General Assembly of the Presbyterian Church in the United States, A. D. 1938, p. 56.

[16] *Ibid.*, p. 13.

[17] *The Plan providing for the Reunion of the Presbyterian Church in the United States of America and the Presbyterian Church in the United States as the Presbyterian Church of the United States*, May, 1943. Printed for the use of the General Assembly of the Presbyterian Church in the United States, p. 2.

five years. From the same I can testify that he possessed not only "character, integrity, diligence and devotion to duty," but that he possessed learning, zeal, eloquence, perseverance, honesty of purpose, fairness of dealing, and a saving sense of humor. He brought many tense situations, in the serious and difficult efforts of the Committee to write a new Church constitution, to a happy conclusion by his ready wit.[18]

A development in the early Forties which provided a significant stimulus to the Seminary was the appearance of the Works Report.[19] Encompassing schools, colleges, and seminaries, this study grew out of the labors of the Executive Committee of Christian Education, the Presbyterian Education Association of the South, and the General Assembly's Advisory Committee on Christian Education, financed in part by the General Education Board of New York and the John Bulow Campbell Foundation of Atlanta and directed by Dr. George A. Works of Chicago. With respect to Louisville Presbyterian Theological Seminary, Columbia Theological Seminary, and Austin Presbyterian Theological Seminary, the recommendation was that they be merged in Nashville, Tennessee.[20]

In a more detailed paper concerning Austin Presbyterian Theological Seminary,[21] certain particular points were made. One was an adverse judgment on account of "a rigorously prescribed curriculum, centered on the biblical languages and the English Bible. There are no true electives. . . ."[22] Another criticism was the lack of "supervision of practical work done by the students."[23] Further, it was observed that there was a feeling of isolation from the cities in which the seminaries were located and from the centers of education and culture.[24] The Library was reported to have 16,000 volumes. The equipment and facilities were poor. There were insufficient reference books. While holdings in the field of philosophy of religion might be

---

18 P. F. Henderson letter to Samuel L. Joekel, n.d., in the Seminary Library Archives.

19 George A. Works, *Report of a Survey of the Colleges and Theological Seminaries of the Presbyterian Church in the United States* (Louisville, Kentucky: no publisher, 1942).

20 *Ibid.*, pp. 12–16.

21 George A. Works, "A Report on the Colleges and Seminaries of the Presbyterian Church in the United States made to the Executive Committee of Christian Education and Ministerial Relief," Section IV, The Seminaries of the Presbyterian Church in the United States. (Mimeographed.)

22 *Ibid.*, p. 5.

23 *Ibid.*, p. 5.

24 *Ibid.*, p. 8.

more nearly adequate, resources in other fields such as concerning the Greek New Testament were adjudged to be weak.[25] It was charged that "The Seminary faculty has made no serious effort to utilize the resources of The University of Texas, even for the undergraduate program."[26] It was recommended that a physical examination be given entering students and that a health fee be imposed which would be used to employ medical services as needed.[27]

Further, it was suggested that "the faculty should be more aggressive in establishing stimulating contacts with nearby educational institutions and with a wider circle of colleagues in the meetings of the various technical and professional societies."[28]

A minority of one on the Survey Study Committee, Dr. Henry Wade DuBose, held that Austin Seminary should not be asked to close or to be consolidated.[29] He noted that the rather large area west and south of Atlanta, Nashville, Louisville, Chicago, and Omaha and southeast of San Francisco was vast enough to require a Presbyterian Theological Seminary and to support one.

The Works Report had great weight but could be no more than advisory in nature since the ownership and control of Austin Seminary was vested in the four controlling Presbyterian U. S. Synods of Texas, Arkansas, Louisiana, and Oklahoma and the trustees appointed by each.

In the word from the faculty to the Executive Committee of the Board, the professors said they were unaware of complacency with respect to the deficiencies with which it had been charged. The faculty conceded the truth of criticisms concerning lack of opportunity for professors to take further academic work, failure of professors to be related to academic societies, want of adequate library, books, and facilities. After pointing out inaccuracies in the report, the faculty agreed on the validity of the indictment that the Seminary curriculum was centered on biblical languages and on the English Bible.

This we think is probably the most complimentary observation he makes touching us. We believe he could have truthfully added that we also emphasize in an intelligent fashion training for evangelistic and expository preaching. He is correct when he remarks that our emphasis on these things makes it hard for us

25 *Ibid.*, p. 9.
26 *Ibid.*, p. 13.
27 *Ibid.*, p. 21.
28 *Ibid.*, p. 23.
29 *Ibid.*, p. 28.

to find a place in our curriculum for studies in Sociology, Pastoral Counselling, general and personal supervision of students in field work.[30]

The paper adopted by the Faculty questioned the assumption of the Works report that the Seminary was a function of a well-established church rather than a necessary arm of evangelism in an only partly occupied territory.

Our confident conviction is that our Seminary is of indispensable value to the development of the Presbyterian Church in the states west of the Mississippi River. We believe that the presence of the Seminary in the Southwest encourages young men in this area to enter the Gospel ministry. We believe the Seminary is a useful agency in the evangelistic program of our church.

From the days of Daniel Baker back in the eighteen fifties, there has been an insistence that there ought to be a theological seminary in the great area known as the Southwest. Doctors Smoot and Dabney responded to the requests of the ministers in this area and started such a school in the closing decades of the 19th Century. At the opening of the 20th Century, the Synod of Texas requested Dr. T. R. Sampson to secure an endowment to make more stable such a school. In 1902 Dr. Sampson reported sufficient funds in hand to start the present school. On the basis of past experience in the Southwest, it seems that the persons who were responsible for the ongoing of our Church in this area have uniformly agreed that the presence of a training agency here is essential to the growth and stability of our Church.[31]

After noting the informal counselling program conducted by the Faculty with the students and defending the health program that Seminary students shared with the students of The University, the paper continues

We note with considerable surprise the statement of the committee . . . in which the faculty is adjudged as being content and complacent and satisfied to be isolated from centers of education and culture. Especially surprising is their conclusion as to the faculty's "failure to be concerned about adequate utilization of important educational resources in the immediate neighborhood . . . this is more striking in that those two schools (Austin and Columbia) are located in walking distance of strong institutions willing to cooperate."

30 Minutes of the Faculty 1940–1950, September 24, 1942.
31 *Ibid.*

As a matter of fact this is a definite misstatement of facts. The committee is evidently uninformed as to Austin Seminary's privileges and her established practices. Every student in Austin Seminary is registered in the University of Texas (the largest University in the South) and has been for more than twenty years. The catalogue of the Seminary outlines and encourages the taking of the M.A. degree from the University while in residence. . . .

. . . the committee, had it cared to establish the facts, might have noted in the reference to our own meager library, that the Seminary could easily add thousands of volumes offered daily at our disposal by the University in fields in which we are allegedly weak—New Testament Greek, etc. So close is the relation between the two schools in reality that we might reasonably report a working library for our students of more than 700,000 volumes, about 16,000 of which are housed in our own buildings.[32]

Dr. Currie had taught Bible for credit in The University of Texas for more than thirty years and Dr. Joekel for sixteen, their names appearing in the University official announcements. Dr. Penick's New Testament courses in the University and his name on the Faculty page of the Seminary bulletin are mentioned. The use by the Seminary of professors in the Modern Language Department and the Music and Fine Arts Department is noted.

The Board of Trustees of the Seminary responded to the proposal of the Works Report that Austin Seminary be merged with a new institution at Nashville at a called meeting January 20, 1943. The Board adopted the following minute: "It is the judgment of this Board that it will not be wise to proceed further looking to a merger of this Seminary and a relocation of the merged Seminary at some point east of the Mississippi River."[33]

The Works Report and the membership of the Seminary in the American Association of Theological Schools[34] were among the stimuli which prompted the further study of the curriculum of the Seminary with a view to making it more suited to the needs and abilities of each candidate. Language aptitude tests were suggested as a basis for predicting and arranging to deal with any special difficulty a candidate might anticipate in the study of Hebrew and Greek.[35] Formal conferences between students and faculty members,

32 *Ibid.*
33 Minutes of the Board 1940–1946, January 20, 1943.
34 Minutes of the Board 1940–1946, May 14, 1941.
35 Minutes of the Faculty 1940–1950, December 9, 1942.

individually, for counselling were provided for, as were more specific arrangements for the supervision of the field work of the candidates. The development of an elective course by each professor in his field was encouraged. These developments pointed toward the need for an academic dean.[36]

In support of the Assembly's Home Mission Emergency Fund Campaign, Dr. Joekel's study book, *While It Is Day*, was published in 1942. Thus, in this way, the Seminary was part of the effort to stir the denomination to greater efforts in the field of evangelism.

On November 10, 1942 the Seminary received a check in the amount of $5,534.62. This was the first eleven months' income from what to that point was the largest addition to the Seminary's endowment. It arose from a bequest of Mr. and Mrs. John Sleeper of Waco.

[36] C. Ellis Nelson letter, February 23, 1956, to T.W.C., Jr. and in the hands of the latter.

The Beginning of the Chapel
And the End of an Era

10

Chapel services at the Seminary for a number of years had been held five mornings a week in the northeast corner room of the first floor of Sampson Hall. This was a classroom without piano or other customary aid to worship. Dr. Gribble would ordinarily lead a hymn, and the Faculty would take turns week by week in bringing the meditation for the morning.

The desire to have a building more suited to worship, one which in its form and texture would proclaim the Gospel, one which would fix the casual eye upon Him to whom the Seminary would bear witness, this desire, after Dr. Currie's return full time to the Seminary, gradually changed from a dream to a determination.

The need for more adequate housing for the library was also apparent and the necessity for increasing the endowments was ever on the heart of the President. Hardly a day passed that the prayers he led in his own home did not include the petition for the men and the money that were needed for the Seminary.

A perusal of the minutes of the Board beginning in 1937 reveal unremitting efforts first in one direction and then in another to add to the financial resources of the Seminary.[1] Whether it was a Synod-wide campaign or an effort in a few selected congregations or an attempt on a wider scale, however, it seemed all hope was doomed to disappointment. In May of 1939 the Board noted about the library, ". . . Its location in the basement is known . . . and recognized to be a very inadequate place for the books for reading and for research. We hope that a suitable place can be provided for this purpose at an early date."[2]

Yet, if it came to a choice, the Board wanted the chapel first, and though it seemed that every normal avenue of benevolence was blocked, by 1940 the Board determined "that the President and

---

[1] Minutes of the Board 1932–1940, November 12, 1937, February 8, 1938, May 11, 1938, May 17, 1939, September 6, 1939.

[2] Minutes of the Board 1932–1940, May 17, 1939.

Executive Committee [should] proceed with plans for the construction of the proposed chapel and [make] every effort possible . . . for the proposed completed building and additional endowment. . . ."[3] Three weeks later Mr. Marvin Eickenroht of San Antonio was chosen as architect.[4] In another week the Executive Committee of the Board was convened at the cottage on Westminster Encampment in Kerrville where Dr. C. L. King was staying. Rev. Ernest Deutsch and Mr. Fred S. Robbins of Bay City met with the group.

A large period of time was taken up in an informal exchange of ideas touching the steps which ought to be taken at the time looking to the erection of a combination Chapel and Library Building on the Seminary Campus. Mr. Robbins told the Committee that he has in hand $10,000.00 to begin the erection of the Chapel, and intimated that he was anxious to see the building carried on to completion, once it is started.

On the basis of Mr. Robbins' informal statement to the group, a motion was made instructing Mr. Currie to advise Mr. Eickenroht that we are ready to proceed. Mr. Eickenroht is to be requested to draw the detailed plans for the Chapel, and to make sketches for the Library Building. . . . Mr. Robbins agrees that this shall be done, and the expense for this work is to be paid by him as the first charge against the $10,000.00 which are now available for the erection of the Chapel.[5]

A good many pictures and plans must have been studied by the members of the faculty and their wives, for there is a record in the Board minutes of a meeting which included "Mesdames Currie, Gribble, McLaurin and Kidd; and Messrs. Currie, McLaurin and Joekel." The following advice was offered the architect:

. . . the consensus of opinion in this meeting inclined toward the Gothic type of architecture as presented by Mr. Eickenroht some weeks ago; but with more delicate lines and submit complete sketches featuring this Gothic type with the further suggestion that he consider the rear tower of Canterbury Cathedral as a possible front tower for our Chapel.[6]

Despite the generosity of the pledge of Mr. Robbins, additional money had to be found. Finally it was decided to put on a campaign for funds in the city of Austin, so the services of a fund-raising firm

3 Minutes of the Board 1940–46, May 15, 1940.
4 Minutes of the Board 1932–1940, June 4, 1940.
5 Minutes of the Board 1932–1940, June 12, 1940.
6 Minutes of the Board 1932–1940, see paper dated June 17, 1940.

were employed with a view to securing $75,000.[7] The Faculty and students themselves were to be the solicitors and conduct the canvass. The bids for the Chapel were taken October 18, 1940. They were too high. A saving of $12,000 was made by omitting stone and substituting second-hand brick. On November 4, 1940 the Executive Committee of the Board met.

Dr. Currie stated that he and Mr. Frank R. Rundell (the successful bidder) had had an interview with Mr. Robbins regarding the erection of the Chapel. Dr. Currie was of the opinion that Mr. Robbins felt that the building contemplated in our plans would cost too much money. The bids on said building ran from $42,000.00 and up. Mr. Robbins was willing to place $15,000.00 at our disposal but seemed to be unwilling to go any further than that. After much discussion, Dr. Law made the motion that we proceed to erect a building on the basis of certain specified deductions which would bring the cost to within $35,000.00 and that Mr. Frank R. Rundell be employed to construct said building on the cost plus ten per cent basis. The motion carried unanimously.

Mr. Rundell agreed to undertake this work with the distinct understanding that construction would proceed only as far as we had the cash.[8]

The check for $15,000 from Mr. Fred S. Robbins to the Seminary was dated November 5, 1940.[9] The Faculty and students secured pledges just in excess of $20,000 in Austin. Toward the end of the effort, a gift from Arkansas assured that the Chapel would be completed. W. C. Brown, Jr. of Hot Springs, a member of the Board, and his sisters, Misses Jean and Josephine, each gave $2,500 for a total of $7,500.

Ground was broken for the Chapel December 2, 1940, with the first spade of dirt turned by Fred S. Robbins and brief addresses made by the Mayor of Austin, Tom Miller, the President of The University of Texas, Dr. Homer P. Rainey, and Dr. Currie.[10] This was followed by the "Kick-off" dinner in Lubbock Hall for the solicitors. Including all pledges and gifts, the total by the beginning of the new year barely exceeded $43,000. The cost of the Chapel had risen because of several revisions, and when the furnishings and

7 *Ibid.* See papers dated July 30, 1940, September 20, 1940.
8 Minutes of the Board 1940–1946, November 4, 1940.
9 *Austin Seminary Bulletin, The Theolog* LVIII (July 1942), 2.
10 Minutes of the Faculty 1940–1950, May 14, 1941, Paper "A."

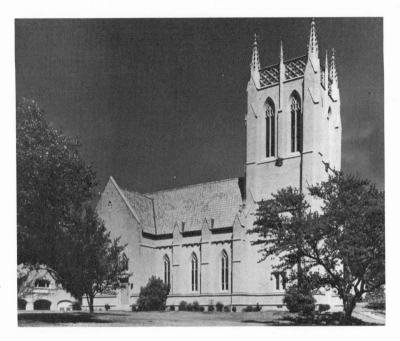

The Chapel

the rose window were added later, the total approximated $47,000. But various groups of the Women of the Church gave generously toward the pews, pulpit, and Communion table, and with other special gifts the cost of the building and furnishings was covered requiring, beyond gifts from all sources earmarked for the Chapel, only $3,361.83 from the current funds of the Seminary.[11]

The Chapel was an immediate source of interest from the time construction began. Before the tower was completed, groups were posing to have their picture taken in front of the building.

In May of 1941 the Cornerstone was laid.

Record is entered of the laying of the cornerstone of the new Chapel, May 15, 1941, 5:30 p.m., the program being as follows:

Invocation . . . . Dr. [Fred] Brooks (U.S.A. Church)
The Ritual . . . . Dr. Currie, President
The Address . . . . Dr. Caldwell, President of the Board

[11] Minutes of the Board 1940–1946, Audit dated May 8, 1943, Schedule 7, footnote.

Charles Turner Caldwell, Board Chairman 1923–1945

The Laying of the Stone..............Dr. R. F. Gribble
Benediction......Dr. C. T. Wharton (University Church)

Quite a good number were present, gathered before the Chapel, including members of the Board, out-of-town friends, Mr. Robbins and Mrs. Lewis (his sister-in-law), the Overseer, Mr. E. A. Crone, the Bricklayers, with Mr. Clawson, the head Mortarmixer, et al.[12]

During the summer of 1941 with construction still underway, an issue of the *Theolog* appeared which reported on the new Chapel.

Soaring high in the air, far above the roofs of surrounding buildings, the 80-foot Gothic tower on our new Seminary Chapel is destined to become one of the most interesting buildings in Austin.

[12] Minutes of the Faculty 1940–1950, May 17, 1941.

Interior of the Chapel

From the first day that ground was broken for the foundation there has been a constant flow of people watching its construction. This in itself has given untold advertisement to our Seminary and to its program of expansion. People who heretofore had given little thought to the only Southern Presbyterian Seminary west of the Mississippi, now find that this institution has a real place to fill in the work of our Church.

. . . Since the founding of our Seminary we have never had a suitable place for worship, and this, above all else, is needed in training young ministers. As yet, there is only enough money to complete the building, but with the aid of our many seminary friends we feel confident that by the time of its completion we can add the organ and the interior furnishings. Gifts in the form of memorials have been suggested . . .

The exterior of the building is resplendent with symbolical stone decorations representing the principles embodied in the Christian Church universal and in the Presbyterian Church as a separate denomination.

The interior will seat approximately 175 . . .

No matter how vivid the description of a new building may be, the real thing can never be accomplished through the medium of descriptive words. The spirit of worship and reverence must pervade the atmosphere and this is what we are looking forward to realizing.[13]

The Chapel was completed except for the furnishings about the end of January 1942. The Faculty notes an "urgent request," the harbinger of many to come.

The first wedding, by the bride-to-be's special urgent request, even before interior furnishings are installed, is to be held February 7th, 1942, the bride being Miss Montgomery, of Cuero, with her pastor, a former Professor in the Seminary, Rev. W. A. McLeod, D.D., officiating.[14]

By April 20 the Chapel was furnished.

A most impressive beginning was enjoyed at our Chapel. The Dedicatory Address, "We Give Thee Thanks," was given by Dr. Currie. The seminary faculty and their families, the students with their families and friends, and the colored help of the seminary and faculty families attended this Dedication Service.[15]

The Faculty record states:

This worship set a high mark for the Chapel and its contribution to the general life and spiritual tone of the Seminary. The Lord's Supper was under the direction of Professors Joekel and Gribble, with Messrs. Campbell and Nelson distributing the "elements." I Kings 8, Solomon's Dedicatory Prayer was read by Dr. McL.[16]

The next morning a prominent Jewish rabbi, Dr. Julius Freibelman of New Orleans, talked at the regular chapel service.

Two hours later that same morning Dr. E. Stanley Jones, the missionary to India, addressed the seminary and visiting ministers of Austin.[17]

The first student-preaching was on Tuesday night, April 21st, at which time the Rev. E. C. Williams conducted the worship.[18]

Doubtless it was not so planned, but a new era in the life and worship of the Seminary community began on an anniversary of Texas Independence, San Jacinto Day.

13 *The Austin Seminary Bulletin, The Theolog* LVI (July 1, 1941) , 5.
14 Minutes of the Faculty 1940–1950, February 6, 1942.
15 *The Austin Seminary Bulletin, The Theolog* LVIII (July, 1942) , 2.
16 Minutes of the Faculty 1940–1950, May 12, 1942.
17 *The Austin Seminary Bulletin, The Theolog* LVIII (July, 1942) , 2.
18 Minutes of the Faculty 1940–1950, May 12, 1942.

A great deal of study had gone into the Chapel, more than first might meet the eye. The effort to make it a picturebook of Bible stories and teachings beckoned again to art to become in stone the very handmaid of faith.

"This is a chapel of the PRESBYTERIAN CHURCH, therefore it is appropriate that there should be on the tower, high up on its three sides, the Shield of the Presbyterian Church: the Dove symbolic of the Holy Spirit; the Star, Jesus Christ; the Lamp, the Witnessing Church; the Burning Bush, the Indestructible Church; the Laurel Wreath, the Victory of the Church Triumphant. All this followed by the Motto, LUX LUCET IN TENEBRIS, Let the Light Shine in the Darkness.

"A little distance below this shield is a row of small stone plaques representing the Programme of the Christian Church: Teaching the ignorant; Feeding the hungry; Clothing the naked; Visiting the prisoner; Visiting the sick; Giving water to the thirsty; and Burying the dead. Immediately over the entrance to the Chapel are three symbols representing the Holy Trinity: the Hand of God; the Lamb; the Dove. On the Corner-stone, lower left-hand corner, is the symbol for I AM THAT I AM; and lower right-hand, the symbol for the abbreviation for the name JESUS.

"The Tower itself is patterned after the central tower of Canterbury Cathedral, and the inside is very like, in miniature, the inside of John Calvin's Church in Geneva.

"Within the Chapel there is much symbolism. Upon entering, one's attention is immediately caught by the beautiful Rose Window above the Reredos. This window is designed in geometric, Gothic forms and is mosaic in character. Like the great Rose Windows in the French Cathedrals it is an harmonious color pattern of primary and secondary colors thus creating a jewel-like quality reminiscent of the best work of the Middle Ages. To give added interest to the design a series of symbols is introduced in small medallions. In the center of the Rose is a large Cross (and Crown) symbolizing victory and reward. In the outer tracery pieces, beginning at the top of the Rose, there is a Shield which symbolizes Faith. To the right of the Shield is an Anchor symbolizing Hope; and then the Heart for Charity; the Oak for Strength; the Scroll for the Law; the Owl for Wisdom; the Lamp for Truth and Knowledge; the Scales for Justice; the Dove for Peace and Purity; and the Grapes for Unity. This Window was designed and executed by Wilbur Herbert Burnham in his studio in Boston. 126

"On the Narthex Screen, separating the vestibule from the nave, are thirteen hand-carved plaques of wood representing our Lord Jesus Christ and His twelve Apostles. The center plaque is the Agnus Dei and Book of Seven Seals (Rev. 5); the Greek Cross symbolizing St. Andrew; three money-bags, St. Matthew; three flaying knives, St. Bartholomew; a vertical saw, St. James the Less; an open Bible and a double-headed battle-axe, St. Matthias; two keys crossed, St. Peter; a serpent on a sword, St. John; a carpenter's square on a staff, St. Thomas; three escallop shells, St. James; a cross and a pilgrim's staff, St. Philip; a sailboat, St. Jude; two oars and a battle-axe, St. Simon the Zealot. On this 'Screen' just below the plaques are a number of conventionalized flowers symbolic of various things; on the pew-ends also, and on the pillars and the Reredos. The Fleur-de-lis, a symbol of the Annunciation; the Daisy, of the Innocency of the Christ-Child; the Gladiolus, of the Incarnation; the Bursting Pomegranate, the Resurrection; the Olive branch and Olives, 'the Grace of our Lord Jesus Christ which is able to give peace to the sorrowing sinner.' The Rose is a symbol of the Nativity and also of the Messianic Promise; Ivy Leaves, Faithfulness; the Glastonbury Thorn, the Nativity. The Vine and Branches is used much in the carving within the Chapel, symbolizing the one-ness of our Lord Jesus Christ and His True Church.

"On the Capital of each of the eight Pillars in the Nave are four Plaques; those on the pillars on the west side symbolic of the writers of the Four Gospels; and those on the east side, of the writers of the Four Major Prophets. St. Matthew is represented by the Winged Man; St. Mark, the Winged Lion; St. Luke, the Winged Calf; and St. John, the Eagle. A Saw is symbolic of Isaiah; a Cistern of Jeremiah; two Lions of Daniel; and a Turreted Gateway of Ezekiel.

"The NAVE represents the 'Church Militant' and therefore we find here the symbolism of those who DO the work of the CHURCH; THE SANCTUARY, or CHANCEL, represents the 'CHURCH TRIUMPHANT' where is found the INSPIRATION to DO the work of the CHURCH. Hence it is here that is found the Lectern, the Pulpit, the Communion Table, the Choir. Here is much symbolism. All around the Pulpit is carved the Vine and Branches, on the Lectern are carved the Heart, Cross, and Anchor. On the Communion Table are ALPHA and OMEGA, and the abbreviation of the name, JESUS.

"But the most significant of all the symbolism is that on the Reredos. On this are several of the conventionalized flowers, and on either side of the center panel the Vine and Branch carving reaches all the way to the top. In the center panel is the symbol of the supreme Work of our Lord Jesus Christ for the Salvation of Man, the symbol of the ATONEMENT, the Pelican-in-her-Piety. 'The Pelican is a touching symbol, reminding us that our Lord Jesus Christ has redeemed us, delivering us from all sin, from death and from the power of the Devil, not with gold or silver, but with His Holy precious blood and with His innocent suffering and death.' 'In times of famine the female pelican is supposed to tear open her breast and feed her young with her own lifeblood. She dies in order that they may live. In like manner our Blessed Lord died that we may live.'

(Quotations are taken from *Church Symbolism* by F. R. Webber.) [19]

This was the building that Dr. Currie had "loved" into being, and insofar as brick and wood and glass could ever be, it was the heart of the Seminary. Just over a year later, Dr. Currie's funeral was held in this chapel.

Dr. Currie presided at a meeting during the week of April 11, 1943, of the Committee on Cooperation and Union which met in Atlanta to give its final approval to the first draft of the Plan of Union which was distributed to the Commissioners of the General Assembly a few weeks later. He was put on the plane back to Texas by his good friend, S. W. Newell.

The system of priorities in operation during the War, especially for air travel, meant that often passengers who were not on errands of importance in the view of the government were "bumped" and had to give up their space to those with a higher priority. This was what evidently happened to Dr. Currie at Jackson, Mississippi. He seems to have caught a bus from Jackson to Dallas. At the terminal in Dallas the bus driver had to give him aid to make the transfer to an Austin-bound bus. By the time the bus reached Temple, Dr. Currie had slumped down in his seat and the driver felt impelled to get him off the bus. He brought him to the station. There the ticket agent recognized him, called the local Presbyterian pastor, Rev. Michael Mar Yosip, and they got him to the Scott and White Hospital. The stroke of paralysis from which he suffered, after two or three days, seemed to yield to rest and therapy, but a scant week after he had entered the hospital, a few minutes before midnight the night of April 22, Maundy Thursday, he died.

[19] *Austin Seminary Bulletin* LVIII (October 1942), 3. The use of the quotations from *Church Symbolism* by F. R. Webber is courtesy of F. R. Webber and J. H. Jansen.

Dr. Currie had been connected in some capacity with the Seminary from the time he entered as a student in the fall of 1908 until his death in the spring of 1943, almost thirty-five years.

The funeral service was conducted in the chapel by Dr. Gribble the Saturday before Easter.

The faculty entry reads in part

. . . As far as human strength and endowment were concerned he literally gave his life to this institution for the preparing of men to further the preaching of the Gospel of his Master. His heart was never lifted up above his brethren, but always by precept and positive example he led unselfishly in the work of this faculty.[20]

The Board on May 12 adopted the following:

God had richly endowed Dr. Currie's mind and heart with rare gifts which he cultivated until his value to the Church of Jesus Christ was recognized far and wide. He was a creative teacher, a unique expositor of the Bible, a constructive Christian statesman, whose vision included the whole Church; a man of sound, practical judgment; a counsellor whose wisdom was sought eagerly by his fellow ministers; a lecturer whose scholarship and originality brought eager crowds to his feet; a recipient of the highest honors that the Church which he loved and adorned could bestow, yet the noble simplicity of his bearing was never obscured by these tokens of the esteem of others; a friend, whose warm, sympathetic heart was ever open to the perplexed and distressed; a veritable "father" to his boys in the Seminary who found him a ready helper in the solution of their problems. Through the thousands who have been blessed with his friendship, heartened by his sturdy and rugged faith in God, inspired by the clarity and cogency of his teaching, "he being dead yet speaketh."

We, the Board of Trustees of the Austin Presbyterian Theological Seminary, express our gratitude to Almighty God for the life and leadership of Dr. Currie; and our sincere belief that when he stood before the Throne of Grace, the welcome words were addressed to him, "Well done, thou good and faithful servant, —enter thou into the joy of thy Lord."[21]

At the memorial service at the University Presbyterian Church that afternoon, the back of The Order of Worship carried words

---

[20] Minutes of the Faculty 1940–1950, April 26, 1943.
[21] Minutes of the Board 1940–1946, May 12, 1943.

that his friends found to be associated with the memory of Dr. Currie.

A life of unselfish service;
A willingness to die for the cause;
The spirit of non-resentment.
If any man will come after Me,
Let him deny himself,
And take up his cross
And follow Me.—Matthew 16:24[22]

To friends Mrs. Currie sent the following response to messages of sympathy:

Close the rank, and ride on! The banner he bore
For God and the right never faltered before.
Quick, up with it then, for the right, for the light,
Lest legions of men be lost in the night.[23]

[22] Order of Worship, 5:00 p.m., May 12, 1943, The University Presbyterian Church, Austin, Texas, in file of T.W.C., Jr.

[23] Acknowledgment card in file of T.W.C., Jr. The poem, "The Riderless Horse" is from *Mothers and Men* by Harold Trowbridge Pulsifer (Cambridge: Houghton Mifflin Co., The Riverside Press, 1916) , p. 32.

The Seminary and University Relations 11

Dr. Robert F. Gribble was made acting president at the meeting of the Seminary Board May 12, 1943[1] and a committee composed of B. O. Wood, chairman, C. L. King, and R. A. Law was named to nominate a person to be the next president.

The audit by J. G. Whitten showed a capital endowment as of April 30, 1943 in the amount of $486,389.35, a figure which included securities, endowments, real estate notes, personal notes, buildings and grounds.[2] The receipts for the year ending April 30, 1943 had been $37,726.24 and disbursements $35,312.68. The library of the Seminary had approximately 17,000 volumes.[3]

Recognition of excellence in academic studies by something more than grades and good conscience began when the Seminary Alumni made its first grant for a post-B.D. fellowship in 1943. The recipient was Robert Perry Douglass. The sum was $250. The award has since from time to time been increased and now bears the name of the David Stitt Fellowship. By 1976 the stipend had become $3,000. Other fellowships have been added subsequently: The Board of Trustees Fellowship, the W. P. Newell Fellowship, and the Janie Maxwell Morris Fellowship. These are for use after graduation.

The Martin G. Miller Scholarship is awarded part each year while the theolog is in the Seminary. The recipient must give promise of high potential in the pastoral ministry.

Second- and third-year students are eligible for the Mr. and Mrs. Sam B. Hicks Scholarships, the purpose of which is to provide incentive for exceptional work and maintenance of high standards.

There are scholarships for foreign students and for Christian leaders from abroad.

Of course, these fellowships and scholarships are in addition to the

---

[1] Minutes of the Board of Trustees 1940–1949, stated meeting, May 12, 1943, pp. 4, 5.

[2] *Ibid*. See Exhibit A.

[3] Minutes of the Board of Trustees 1940–1949, stated meeting, May 17, 1944.

Bertram Oliver Wood, Board Chairman 1946–1950. *Courtesy of B. O. Wood*

many work scholarships which have been and are available. It is probably true to say that few, if any, students who felt called to the ministry have been forced by the want of money to terminate their Seminary careers.[4]

It was during this interim period that the Board suggested an effort on the part of alumni to establish a foundation to support an annual lectureship.[5] From this impulse have come several series of lectures, known as the Mid-Winter Lectures or as Mid-Winter Ministry Colloquium. (See chapter XV). These lectures originated the first week of February in 1945.[6] One series, designated the Thomas W. Currie Lectures, was financed by the gifts of the Tom Currie

---

[4] *Austin Seminary Bulletin* 1975–1977, XCI, 1 (August 1975), pp. 78–81. 78–81.

[5] Minutes of the Board of Trustees 1940–1949, stated meeting, May 17, 1944.

[6] *Austin Seminary Bulletin* 1944–1945, LXI, 1 (April 1945).

Bible Class at Highland Park Presbyterian Church, Dallas. The E. C. Westervelt Lectures were made possible by gifts from Mr. and Mrs. Edwin Flato of Corpus Christi, and the Robert F. Jones Lectures were financed by grants from the Women of the Church of First Presbyterian Church, Fort Worth. Another series of addresses was called the Settles Lectures in Missions and Evangelism. These were begun in 1947, made possible by a gift of Mrs. W. R. Settles of Big Spring.

James I. McCord became Adjunct Professor of Systematic Theology in 1944 and C. Ellis Nelson who had been Associate Professor of Christian Education since 1940 assumed responsibility for Church History.

During the interim the advantages to students of the Seminary from its proximity to The University of Texas were emphasized by an article in the *Alumni Bulletin*: "Traditionally, theological education has been centered in, or adjacent to, a great University. As this is true historically, so today theological schools are found as a part of, or are located near, great educational institutions. This is a natural alliance. Universities are noted for their graduate study, research, and academic traditions of honest scholarship. . . ."[7] From the time of its move to 27th Street in 1907, Austin Seminary has had a cordial relation with The University of Texas. These close ties stem from 1884 when they were personified in Robert Louis Dabney and in those who studied in both schools.

The physical distance between the campus of The University, which began with forty acres bounded on the north by 24th Street, and the Seminary, whose property extended north of 27th Street, diminished as The University added to the size of its campus. Other ties were revealed when The University persuaded Robert Ernest Vinson to be its president in 1916.

A number of Seminary students while engaged in their theological pursuits also studied in The University. Beyond the courses in Greek some of them earned Masters degrees and some, as, for instance, James I. McCord and Sam Lanham, became teachers at The University (McCord in Philosophy and Lanham in Law). While he was teaching at the Seminary, Eugene W. McLaurin earned a Ph.D. at The University.

Extracurricular activities were not totally barred to theologs. The

[7] "Supplementing Theological Education," *Austin Seminary Bulletin, Alumni Edition* LVIII (January 1943), 4.

Looking north over The University of Texas campus toward the Seminary

tenor lead of William M. Logan was heard from the stage of The University of Texas Light Opera Company in the middle thirties and David L. Stitt had the title role in Gilbert and Sullivan's *Mikado*.

One of the connections between The University and the Seminary was to be found in the courses offered for credit by Seminary professors for University undergraduates. The first man to come to the University community as full-time teacher of religion to undergraduates was Dr. Frank L. Jewett who arrived in 1905 to occupy the Texas Bible Chair of the Disciples of Christ. Dr. Sampson and Dr. Vinson were concerned in this field and began to take an active part in such instruction shortly after the Seminary moved to 27th Street. The matter of accreditation was dealt with as early as 1908.

Led by Dr. W. J. Battle (Professor in the Department of Classical Languages, sometime chairman of that department, sometime acting president of the University) the University began by granting credit to students who took one (of Dr. Jewett's) courses and made application for credit after completing the course . . . It was for a course in the Life of Christ, 1908. The Austin Presbyterian Theological Seminary had been offering Bible courses at the graduate level, of course, for many

134

years. Dr. T. R. Sampson of the Seminary faculty cooperated with Mr. Jewett and Dr. Battle to define the basis on which credit would be granted students making a grade of C or better in the Bible courses offered by Texas Bible Chair and The Austin Presbyterian Theological Seminary. Other church groups came. This made a forum of religions, something like that envisioned by Thomas Jefferson for the University of Virginia, a reality.[8]

The brochure from which the above is taken credits the Presbyterians with having begun instruction for undergraduates in 1910 with Dr. Sampson and Dr. Vinson having been responsible for the classes. Dr. Currie began to teach in 1911 and continued for more than thirty years. Dr. Joekel taught from 1926 when he came to the Seminary until his death in 1954.

It was Dr. Sampson who organized the Association of Religious Teachers in 1913 and served as its president until his death in 1915. This Association certified to The University that incoming A.R.T. courses and instructors were up to the academic standards of excellence of the College of Arts and Sciences. In effect, the Seminary has been the Bible Chair at The University of Texas for the Presbyterians of the Southwest.

Dr. Joekel's study book, *Fitly Framed Together*, gave in broad outline his approach to the Bible as a teacher. His concern was with the total message of the whole volume, almost never with the historical and literary development of any portion. Here was not the scholar but the town crier. He was not one to dissect but to herald.[9]

Among the correspondence courses offered through the Division of Extension of The University of Texas was a series on Bible which was organized and graded under the direction of Dr. Currie, and, through this little noticed means, the Seminary reached many homes with its Bible study program. In this course, in lecture, outline, and question, one can find clues to his interpretation of the Scripture. A favorite word was "metanoia." This was understood to be change of mind, character, nature that attended one's conversion to the Christian faith. Another idea upon which continual stress was laid was the conquest of Christ in men's hearts and over men and na-

8 "Religion at The University of Texas." A brochure published by the Association of Religious Teachers, University of Texas (May 17, 1956), pages unnumbered. In the Seminary Library.

9 Samuel L. Joekel, *Fitly Framed Together* (Richmond, Virginia: John Knox Press, 1948).

tions. One was never allowed for long to be unaware of the racial prejudice that rent society. One question the student was required to answer was, "Is our present race prejudice defensible from a Christian point of view?"[10]

The Seminary by its proximity to The University was continually exposed to the skepticism or to the searching challenge of scientific and secular points of view. Theologs, with the aid of Seminary professors, had opportunity to forge weapons with which to battle contemporary paganism.

The Alumni *Bulletin* of January 1943 deals with other advantages to the Seminary arising from its location.

. . . Theology not only fits into the atmosphere of scholarship, but Theology as "Queen of the sciences" embraces every field of human learning and is concerned with every new discovery of truth.

Presbyterian leaders have been aggressive in advocating this policy. John Knox, when he outlined an educational system for Scotland after the establishment of the Presbyterian Church, proposed that the theological schools be a part of the Universities. Knox went further and indicated that the salaries of the theological professors should be twice the salaries of the professors in other professional schools because theology teachers ought to be the most able and gifted men obtainable.

The Austin Presbyterian Theological Seminary is uniquely situated to follow in this tradition. Located two blocks from The University of Texas, the Seminary can utilize to the full the magnificent opportunities of that great educational institution. The University of Texas is the largest University in the south, one of three in the south which are members of the Association of American Universities; and it contains a graduate school which ranks among the best in the nation. . . .

With rare exception, the students in the Seminary are enrolled in The University of Texas . . .[11]

This issue of the *Bulletin* includes a picture of a first edition of the King James Bible from the Bible Collection of the University, a picture of a scene from the Curtain Club's production of "Family Portrait," and a picture of "Old Man Malakaff," the oldest piece of sculpture in the Western Hemisphere, one of the attractions in

10 Thomas W. Currie, "The Life and Teachings of Jesus." Mimeographed. (Austin, Texas: The University of Texas, Division of Extension, Extension Teaching and Field Service Bureau, Course Number: Bible 301, n.d.), p. 21.
11 *Austin Seminary Bulletin, op. cit.*

the University Museum. There is also described the fashion in which the students share in the health program provided for University students and in the intramural athletic events. Not the least of the advantages comes from the libraries.

Education is dependent on a good library. In addition to the Seminary library of 19,000 volumes of religious and philosophical books, a student has access to the 700,000 volumes at the University. The University library includes the Wrenn, Stark, and Aitken rare book collections, about 30,000 volumes of manuscripts and early copies of rare books. These rare books contain much material on the great religious controversies of history and, therefore, are a first-hand source of information to the theological student. Also at his disposal are the State Library of 206,795 volumes and the Supreme Court Library of 40,884 volumes. Such library resources are found in few places in America.

As a graduate student, the Seminary student can obtain a pass key to the classical library on the twenty-seventh floor of the University tower. Day or night he has at his finger tips all the reference books necessary for classical studies and a beautiful private library room for study.[12]

[12] *Ibid.*

David Leander Stitt Becomes President 12

On May 2, 1945, the Board, on the recommendation of the committee to nominate a president, unanimously voted to extend a call to David Leander Stitt to become the fourth president of the Seminary.

David Stitt was a native of Fort Worth, Texas, where his father, William S. Stitt, and his mother were members of Broadway Presbyterian Church. His father was a patent attorney and served for some years as Clerk of the Session of Broadway (later St. Stephen) Presbyterian Church. David studied three years at T.C.U. He took his fourth year at Austin College from which he graduated with a B.A. in 1933. After earning a B.D. conferred by Austin Seminary in 1936, he was ordained and installed by Fort Worth Presbytery in First Presbyterian Church, Haskell, Texas, June 28, 1936. In 1938 he went to Westminster Presbyterian Church, St. Louis, as assistant to Dr. William Crowe, and succeeded the latter as pastor the following year.

David L. Stitt and Jane Wilkinson Dupuy were married in Greensboro, North Carolina, September 10, 1940, and to this home were born four sons and two daughters. In 1942 the Synod of Missouri elected David Stitt its moderator and Westminster College of Fulton, Missouri, conferred on him the degree of Doctor of Divinity.[1]

Jane Stitt, in addition to her duties as wife and mother, was to become the gracious hostess for many Seminary events. She was active in the University Church where on occasion she taught a college class. She earned a Ph.D. at The University of Texas. But none of her many and varied activities in the community diminished her contribution to the welfare of the students, faculty, and members of the Board and their families.

---

[1] Rev. E. D. Witherspoon, Jr., Compiler, *Ministerial Directory of the Presbyterian Church, U.S., 1861–1967* (Doraville, Georgia: Foote & Davies. Published by order of the General Assembly, 1967), p. 534.

The new era that began for the Seminary with the coming of David Stitt coincided with radical changes in world and national affairs.

The five-year-old Second World War that roared onto the beaches of Normandy June 6, 1944 came to a conclusion the next summer in the Pacific.

Franklin Delano Roosevelt had offered a prayer on the occasion of the invasion of Europe:

God of the free, we pledge our hearts and lives today to the cause of all free mankind.

Grant us victory over the tyrants who would enslave all free men and nations.

Grant us faith and understanding to cherish all those who fight for freedom as if they were our brothers.

Grant us brotherhood in hope and union, not only for the space of this bitter war, but for the days to come which shall and must unite all the children of the earth.

We are all of us children of the earth—grant us that simple knowledge. If our brothers are oppressed, then we are oppressed. If they hunger, we hunger. If their freedom is taken away, our freedom is not secure.

Grant us a common faith that man shall know bread and peace—that he shall know justice and righteousness, freedom and security, an equal opportunity and an equal chance to do his best, not only in our own lands but throughout the world.

And in that faith let us march toward the clean world our hands can make.[2]

Perhaps that prayer summarized aspirations for which much life and wealth were sacrificed. The challenge to march on toward "the clean world our hands can make" was answered in part by the convening April 25, 1945 in San Francisco, thirteen days after Roosevelt's death, of those who would form the United Nations.[3]

On July 15, Harry S. Truman arrived in Potsdam to confer with Winston Churchill and his successor, Clement Atlee, with the Russians and with others concerning sequels to the defeat of Germany. "The clean world our hands can make" began to resemble a modern, sophisticated, hideous counterpart of the tower of Babel. Truman's accommodations for the Potsdam meetings were on Lake Griebnitz

[2] W. Averell Harriman and Elie Abel, *Special Envoy to Churchill and Stalin 1941–1946* (New York: Random House, 1975), pp. 443, 444.

[3] George E. Delury, Managing Editor, *The 1973 World Almanac and Book of Facts* (New York, N.Y., The World Almanac, 1973), p. 626.

David Leander Stitt, President 1945–1971, Professor of Pastoral Theology

in a villa called Babelsberg. It was there on July 16 that a coded message was received which read,

Operated on this morning. Diagnosis not yet complete but results seem satisfactory and already exceed expectations. Local press release necessary as interest extends great distance. Dr. Groves pleased. He returns tomorrow. Will keep you posted.[4]

Alamagordo had seen the Manhattan Project explode the first atom bomb. On the way home on the *Augusta* August 6, Truman was handed the message:

Big bomb dropped August 5 at 7:15 p.m. Washington time.

141   [4] Harriman, *op. cit.*, p. 489.

First reports indicate complete success which was even more conspicuous than earlier test.[5]

On August 14 Japan capitulated.

Stitt came to the presidency of the Seminary during the summer of 1945, having been elected in May of that year when the era of the Great Depression was a fading memory. The noise and the slaughter of war were coming to an end. Reconstruction efforts typified by the Marshall Plan were in the offing. Pent-up consumer demand was giving added impetus to industrial prosperity. The world had entered the age of nuclear fission, and the weight of a new and terrible knowledge lay heavy on the consciences of Christians everywhere. The summer of 1945 was not a time of triumph, of rejoicing in victory, but a sober turning to the tasks of peace—tasks which now presented unguessed and frightening dimensions.

After the war, the Seminary prepared itself to receive candidates who would arrive in the normal course of their studies and also those whose arrival had been delayed by their service in the armed forces. This entailed keeping the faculty pulling together as a team and adding new teachers as needed. It meant giving attention to augmenting the library books and equipment. It meant arranging accommodations for faculty and students. It meant kindling and cultivating generosity on the part of those whose gifts could bring reality to glorious dreams. It meant challenging both the young and the more mature who might feel called to become ministers of the Gospel to study at Austin Presbyterian Theological Seminary.

All the above concerns had to be handled, of course, while the day-to-day teaching and learning and worship of the Seminary community proceeded. And in the midst of it all the president discovered that the endowment funds on hand had not been untangled from the days before World War I. In the matter of working through to a solution of the endowment puzzle, he had the support and assistance of a C.P.A. from Pine Bluff, Arkansas, Glenn A. Railsback, who wrote:

> I came on the Board of Trustees the year after Dr. Currie's death and during the second year of Dr. Gribble as acting President of the Seminary. My first meeting attended was in 1944. Shortly after that meeting Dr. Gribble wrote me asking me to write a letter to David L. Stitt asking him to prayerfully consider accepting the position as President of Austin Seminary.

[5] *Ibid.*, p. 493.

142

This, through the grace of God he agreed to do and my first meeting with him after the inauguration was the annual meeting of the Board in 1945. At that time the Seminary had very few permanent records and they were quite sketchy. A single entry record book was used to record receipts and disbursements of cash from both the operating and endowment fund. This cash was not separated and was spent for whatever was necessary. There was no cash available for operation and no independent audit had ever been made of the Seminary books. The first positive step taken by the new President was to employ the firm of R. A. Moore and Company, Certified Public Accountants, of Fort Worth, Texas, to make an exploratory audit of such records as were available to establish two things; the integrity of the endowment fund and a list of and the cost of the assets making up the net worth of the Seminary and which of them belonged to the endowment fund and which to the operating fund. Mr. Moore delivered two audits to the Seminary simultaneously. One covered the year from May 1, 1945, to April 30, 1946, and the other covered the period from May 1, 1946, to April 30, 1947. The result of these two audits was to show that the operating fund had used $128,135.99 of endowment money. When this matter came before the Board of Trustees there was quite a bit of consternation and steps were immediately taken to repay in cash to the endowment fund the amount of the overdraft. This was done and was paid in full to the endowment fund in useable funds so that the integrity of the endowments was re-established.[6]

The R. A. Moore Audit Report, dated April 30, 1946, summarized the way in which the operating account had come to be obligated in an "ultra vires" indebtedness to the endowment funds:

> With the approval of the Synod of Texas, the Austin Presbyterian Theological Seminary was incorporated under the laws of the State of Texas on October 24, 1899, with no capital stock and for a term of fifty years. It was stated in the minutes that the incorporators held assets for the benefit of the corporation "of the estimated value of $10,000.00." This obviously represented the assets of the Seminary's predecessor, the Austin School of Theology, which were conveyed by deed of that institution to S. B. Campbell, et al., Trustees on October 19, 1899.
>
> From the minutes of the Trustees, dated October 9, 1902, we quote from their report to the Synod: "—that about $102,-

---

[6] Glenn A. Railsback letter to T.W.C., Jr., October 3, 1975, and in the hands of the latter.

000.00 have been added to the assets of the Seminary since the last report to the Synod—."

"Sarah C. Ball Fund	75,000.00
Scholarship Fund	17,000.00
General Funds	10,000.00
	102,000.00"

[Note: from the minutes, it is obvious that the scholarships were the A. A. Alexander $12,000.00, and the Pattie Bennett $5,000.00 funds.]

With the approval of the Synod of Texas, the Austin Presbyterian Theological Seminary was formally opened during October, 1902.

Subsequently, the Bonny Castle, Bungalow and Cunningham properties were purchased at a cost of $7,100.00, according to the minutes. Stuart Hall, acquired from the predecessor, was shown in the minutes at a value of $6,000.00. During May, 1908, these properties were sold for $14,000.00. The Board of Trustees in the minutes of March 20, 1907, authorized the purchase of the present Seminary site of 5¼ acres, which was done at a cost of $5,029.00. During the fiscal year April 30, 1908, Lubbock Hall and Sampson Hall were constructed for the ascertained costs of $8,159.00 and $37,504.28 respectively, as shown on the balance sheet submitted herewith. During the fiscal year April 30, 1909, faculty residences Nos. 1 to 4 were constructed at an ascertained cost of $25,626.15. Faculty residence No. 5 was acquired from Sampson and Vinson for an ascertained cost of $11,449.85. Included in this cost was the value of the lots in the sum of $1,600.00, which was a gift from Dr. Vinson. The chapel was constructed during 1941-2 at a cost of $48,549.15, and its pews, costing $5,500.00, were provided out of special funds raised for those purposes.

SCOPE OF WORK

Because of the generally known fact that during the prior years, distinction between the Endowment and Operating (or Available) funds, both corpus and income, had been neglected, we were engaged to determine the true status of all endowment funds at April 30, 1946, and to properly account for the income from Endowment funds investments to that date.

Without comment or criticism, we submit quotations or excerpts from the minutes of the Board of Trustees, beginning in 1902, which should afford an accurate picture of the situation.

Minutes of October 9, 1902:

"In view of the present peculiar conditions and exigencies of the Seminary: Resolved: that, until otherwise ordered by

144

this board, the Treasurer is authorized and instructed to pay from any money in the treasury (of either the General or Endowment fund) all expense authorized by this board, and that money so used be charged to the fund to which it is applied, and returned to the fund from which it is taken, when the funds are in hand."
Minutes of May 13, 1904:
"Investment committee reported no investments made during the year."
Minutes of May 12, 1905:
"That in view of the existence of rumors—with regard to Endowment Fund, we advise that steps be taken to show that this fund is intact if it be so, and if not, to restore funds to this account."
Minutes of May 15, 1908:
"—In view of furnishing suitable residences for the members of the faculty, there seems to be no reason why a portion of the Endowment funds should not be used therefor, and to that end recommend the erection of 3 or 4 residences —to range in cost from $4,000.00 to $6,000.00, and that such houses be rented to said members of the faculty at such yearly rental as will yield 6% net upon their respective costs."
Minutes of May 10, 1910:
"Ascertained cost of 4 residences, $25,626.15." Recommendation: "That total cost of each residence be charged to permanent funds as follows:
#1 to Lutcher Fund
#2 & 3 to Ball Fund
#4 to Allen-Johnson Fund
Minutes of May 11, 1911:
"We have no means whatever of knowing what the original Lutcher fund amounted to, and therefore cannot say what relation the above figures have to the original amount subscribed."

* * * * * *

"It should be stated Dr. Sampson and President Vinson have given their personal obligation to the American National Bank for about $16,000.00, used the money from this note to finish and furnish the dormitory, and pay debts of the concern, and have been permitted to rent rooms—to meet interest—, but the obligation for $16,000.00 is in reality the obligation of the Seminary, and should be paid off out of monies received by it out of the $250,000.00 fund— by the Committee of Ten."

145

"That the investment committee be authorized to acquire in whole or in part the obligation of Sampson & Vinson to the American National Bank for $16,388.48 and to invest therein permanent funds of the Seminary, if they deem it advisable."

Minutes of May 8, 1912: from Rob't E. Vinson, Annual Report:

"(12) I recommend that the Treasurer be directed to pay $150.00 to Mr. Milton Morris for opening a new set of books."

> Our note: See subsequent quotation from minutes of May 12, 1920.

Minutes of May 6, 1913, Auditing Committee:

"We recommend: That the President of the Seminary be directed to execute notes to the Treasurer of the Board in favor of the respective funds from which money has been applied to the building of professors' houses, equivalent to the amounts so used. Further that these notes bear each an interest which shall be equal to the amount of the annual rent received from the houses so built. These notes will then appear in the annual report of the Treasurer as part of the permanent funds of the Seminary."

Minutes of May, 1914:

"The Investment Committee would report that it has examined into the affairs of the Seminary as exhibited by the Treasurer's books and accounts and recommend first, the full professors of the Seminary be given house-rent free for the current fiscal year, and second, that each such professor be granted an additional $500.00 in salary—."

Minutes of May 12, 1915:

"We have employed Mr. Milton Morris, an expert accountant, who has examined the Treasurer's books, vouchers, etc., and has stated same to be correct as stated in the Treasurer's report."

> Our Notes: Did not locate report referred to. See subsequent quotation from minutes of May 12, 1920.

Minutes of October 11, 1916:

We do not quote but suggest that you read these minutes in their entirety. They deal with the election of Neal L. Anderson, as President, and the frank discussion of the Seminary's financial affairs.

Minutes of November 9, 1916: Special Committee on Ways and Means, report—adopted:

"—and also such plans as the Board may adopt for the restoring the Endowment and enlarging the assets of the institution."

"In view of conditions which make it impossible for the Board to adopt, at this time, any specific plans for improving the general financial situation of the Seminary, that the Executive Committee be authorized to devise and execute such plans as may seem best to them, co-operating if possible, with the Executive Committee of Schools and Colleges of the Synod of Texas; that the President of the Board and the President-elect of the Seminary be instructed to present to said Executive Committee of Schools and Colleges not only the current needs of the Seminary, but the necessity for restoring the funds diverted from the Endowment—."

Minutes of March 20, 1917:

Being the President's report to the Synod's Committee on Schools & Colleges: Quotation from Letter 12/18/16: "By a recent examination of the Seminary's financial status there has been disclosed a state of debt which puts the very life of the institution in jeopardy—. But the erection of these buildings and the paying of its teachers has created a debt which at the close of the last session in May, 1916, aggregated $100,000.00."

" (1) —this debt is of a nature which has cut the ground from under the institution's life by destroying the corpus of its trust funds, so that we have no resources with which to continue the Seminary."

" (2) Until now this condition has not been known to us. —unless it is very wisely and promptly handled, it contains the possibility of destroying the confidence of the people in our administration of trust funds."

Quotation from Synod Executive Committee to Synod at Dallas: "The committee unanimously signified its willingness that the Synod direct its Executive Committee to assume the $106,000.00 due to the trust funds of Seminary, to be paid at such time and in such amounts as may be possible out of available funds, and to pay interest on this amount to the Seminary at the rate of 6% per annum, which would have the effect, so far as the income of the Seminary is concerned, of immediately replacing its Endowment Fund."

Quotation from Dr. Anderson's report, 3/20/17: "Neither the other members of the faculty, who share these views, nor the acting President, have felt it to be wise to give them publicity—."

"It is inevitable, however, that people asked to give money,

will ask questions, and the problem created by those questions is to be found in the plan itself."
Minutes of December 3, 1918:
Our note: Board rescinded order of 10/9/02 permitting use of permanent funds, to be subsequently replaced.
Minutes of May 12, 1920: From report of T. H. Williams, Treasurer:
"Following your instruction, I have employed Miss Ray Perrenot at a salary of $300.00 per year to keep the books of the Seminary."
Our note: On October 5, 1946, through your Seminary Secretary, Mrs. Kidd, inquiry was made of Miss Perrenot as to the books of the Seminary that she might have taken over upon her employment. Miss Perrenot's statement was that there were *no books—only bank statements and cancelled checks*, at the time she assumed her duties.

Upon initiating our work the latter part of May, 1946, it was at once apparent the books of the Seminary from its inception would be needed for reference. Following is a list of the books of record found to be on hand and the beginning dates of each:

Ledger, Beginning June 1, 1923
Cash Book Beginning December 1, 1921
Journal Beginning October 1, 1924

Of the above named books of record, the following were missing and never found:

Ledger, May 1, 1927, to April 30, 1934
Journal, May 1, 1927, to April 30, 1933

There were no books of record prior to the beginning dates stated above. Fortunately, the annual audit reports from February 15, 1922, to April 30, 1946, were available.

To preclude any erroneous inference, there was no transaction examined that in the least indicated personal dishonesty on the part of anyone.

Our audit was restricted to the determination, as accurately as possible, of the actual costs of all assets reflected on the books, the determination and setting up the costs of assets not reflected on the books; the determination of the actual amounts received in cash or its equivalent for all endowment and permanent or non-available funds; the determination of the annual total balances of funds and the annual totals and net endowment investments income. The audit reports submitted, beginning with February 15, 1922, through April 30, 1946, were evidently performed in a manner that generally assured the integrity of the recorded financial transactions and presented accurate statements of both endowment and operating income and expenses,

148

with a minimum of confusion of the two types of income.[7]

The Board and the new administration gave high priority to the matter of restoring the integrity of the endowment funds from excess of income over expenditures in the operating funds from year to year. In summary, as Mr. Railsback wrote, "the integrity of the endowment funds was re-established."[8]

---

[7] *Op. cit.*, pp. 1–5 of Section 1: Covering letter.
[8] See also Minutes of the Board of Trustees 1940–1949. May 18, 1949, p. 3. Minutes of the Board of Trustees 1950–1959. May 23, 1951, pp. 4, 5.

Additions to the Facilities 13

When David Stitt came to the Seminary, the only additions to the original 5¼ acres at 27th Street and Speedway were the property east of Speedway purchased in 1913 for the faculty home at 2621 Speedway and in 1924–1937 for married student housing in what came to be known as "The Leper Colony."

As mentioned in chapter IX, the Works Report had found the Seminary deficient in so many areas that it had recommended the school be moved and consolidated with other institutions. The Board had refused to close or move. Rather, it took steps to remedy the deficiencies.

The Board agreed in 1945 "that an adequate library building is perhaps the most pressing unmet need of the Seminary."[1] But this required money, more money than had ever been available to the Seminary for a building. And the cost of a library was only the beginning.

The prodigious labors of Dr. Stitt and the Board with respect to finances are suggested by a comment from Glenn A. Railsback.

> . . . I think that a Seminary to be vigorous must of necessity be well financed and from the time that David Stitt came to the Seminary as President up to the present time the finances have been improving and becoming more stable. As an illustration, in 1950–51 the Seminary received 45% of its income from Synod Benevolences, 36.8% from investment earnings and 18.2% in tuitions, rent and miscellaneous items. The members of the Seminary Board and faculty were convinced that even though this ratio of income source was inadequate, in the years to come it was bound to get worse. To offset this, efforts were made to build investment earnings to a larger percentage of Seminary requirements. The latest figures I have on the result of this effort is for the fiscal year 1971–72. Only 26.6% of income came from Synod Benevolences and 61.4% from investment earnings. I

[1] Minutes of the Board of Trustees 1940–1949, May 2, 1945, p. 5.

The "Leper Colony" (1925)

think that the recognition of the need for adequate financing and the ability and effort necessary to produce it naturally leads to a well equipped school. As far as physical equipment is concerned, above all it must be well guided. When David L. Stitt became President of the Seminary in 1945, that leadership was apparent from the time he came on the field. He had a wide range of acquaintances and numerous friends in places of responsibility and ability to be of great financial assistance to the Seminary. Dr. Stitt was able to contact these people and convince them of the need of the Seminary and adequate financing. Through these efforts he was able to increase the net assets of the Seminary from 1945 to May 31, 1952, as reflected by the audit report to a total net worth of $1,647,110.47 and this net worth has increased every year to a total on May 31, 1972, of $10,752,814.15. During that period there was only one year in which the annual net increase was less than $200,000.00 and that was for the year 1963–64. I hope this will give you some idea of what I think the Seminary means to the kingdom of God.[2]

The growth in assets of the Seminary over·the quarter-century of the Stitt administration can be appreciated by a glance at information supplied by John W. Smiley in his final report as treasurer August 16, 1971.[3] (See Chart, page 153). For a chronological list of property acquisitions and disposals, see Appendix III.

[2] Railsback to Currie, October 3, 1975.
[3] John W. Smiley letter to Board of Trustees, August 16, 1971. Copy in hands of T.W.C., Jr.

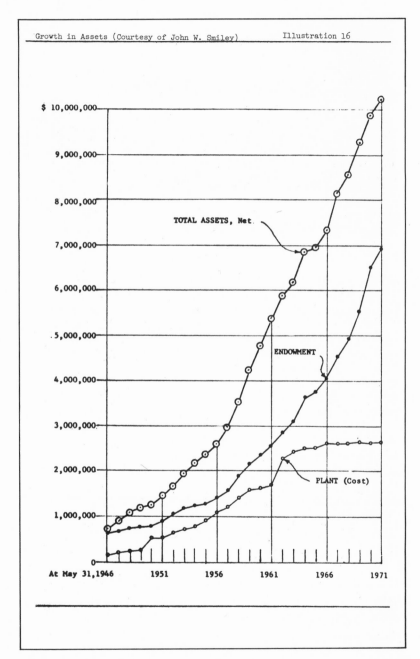

Growth in Assets (Courtesy of John W. Smiley)   Illustration 16

TOTAL ASSETS, Net

ENDOWMENT

PLANT (Cost)

$ 10,000,000

9,000,000

8,000,000

7,000,000

6,000,000

.5,000,000

4,000,000

3,000,000

2,000,000

1,000,000

0

At May 31,1946   1951   1956   1961   1966   1971

153   Growth in Assets. *Courtesy of John W. Smiley*

The Library

The library was erected and furnished at a cost of approximately $225,000. For its dedication May 23, 1950, an address was delivered by the distinguished student of American church history, Dr. William Warren Sweet. He defended the conviction that "a library is the powerhouse of an educational institution."[4]

The library which at first seemed commodious had a basement with a small auditorium equipped for audio visuals and provision for safekeeping of archive materials. On the first floor were the loan desk, display cases, and card files. Stacks occupied parts of the first, second, and third floors. There were carrels in the stacks and typing rooms. One classroom was soon converted to additional stack space as was the basement auditorium. The approximately 10,000 volumes housed at the time the building was erected had by 1977 increased to more than 100,000.

Featured at the entrance to the Library are two crests. On the left is that of Augustine of Hippo, a heart shot through with arrows of

[4] Minutes of the Board of Trustees 1950–1959, May 23, 1950, p. 3.

154

Married Students' Apartments (1952 and 1958)

sorrow for sin but aflame with zeal for Christ. On the right is that of John Calvin. When he finally acceded to the calls to return to Geneva he wrote Farel, "My heart as offered up to God I present in sacrifice." And so the crest pictures a hand offering up a heart aflame. In the porchway can be seen a symbol of the Apostle Paul: Spiritus Gladius, the open Bible with the upright sword. Also there is the open Bible with the text: "The fear of the Lord is the beginning of wisdom" flanked by a lamp on one side and a chalice on the other.

The reading room at the north end of the first floor is handsomely appointed. At the entrance from the loan desk there is on one side a serpent carved in stone and on the other a dove reminiscent of the admonition to be wise as a serpent and harmless as a dove.

On the ceiling there are two inscriptions: "In the beginning God created" (Hebrew) and "And the Word became flesh" (Greek). There are six shields, one for Abraham, one for the decalogue, one for the prophets, one for the church, a reproduction of the Celtic cross, and the Lamb of God.

The names high on the walls speak eloquently of the Reformation: Wycliff, Huss, Cranmer, Olivetan, Luther, Calvin, Zwingli, and Knox.

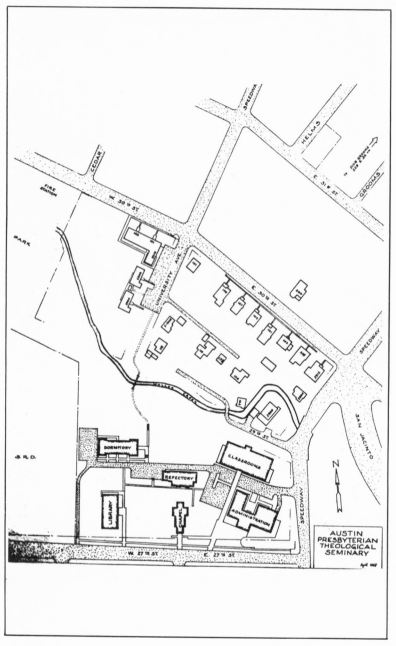

The Campus. *Courtesy of John W. Smiley*

Single Students' Dormitory (1955)

In 1951 contracts were let for the building of apartments for married students. These apartments were built facing University Avenue, south of 30th Street.[5]

In 1947 the property adjoining Sampson Hall on the west, including the Whitis House, was acquired leaving only one lot between the Seminary and Scottish Rite Dormitory. But this one lot accommodated the home of the President of The University of Texas and was owned by this institution. Inquiries revealed that The University often acquired but seldom, if ever, released property near its campus. Nevertheless, by skillful perseverance and through the timely generosity of Toddie Lee Wynne, this parcel of land was bought in 1954.[6] The house was used to accommodate students who were studying toward a degree in Christian Education. In 1955 the single students dormitory was erected. Two years later the married student apartments facing 30th Street materialized.

In 1951 the committee of the Board on Seminary Development had heard the results of a study by Professor C. Ellis Nelson which

[5] Minutes of the Board of Trustees 1950–1959, January 26, 1951.
[6] See Appendix III.

Trull Administration Building (1962)

projected future growth of the population and of the needs for ministers. Using the trends from 1900–1950, as a base, he indicated that the demands on the Seminary might be greatly increased.

I. Growth of our controlling Synods 1900–1950

	Population	Numbers	Ministers
1900	6,532,290	52,823	390
1950	14,504,210	124,648	559

Projected for 1970 the figures would read:

	17,500,000	165,000	725

In case of the reunion of U.S.—U.S.A. churches, current figures would read:

	14,504,210	205,153	957

In case of reunion the projected figures for 1970 would read:

	17,500,000	261,500	1,225

II. The growth of the Seminary is dependent on these factors:
   1. The area served
   2. The quality of instruction
   3. The reputation of the faculty
   4. The field work opportunities for students
   5. The physical equipment
   6. Underlying the above: the financial resources necessary to attainment.[7]

In line with this view of future needs, the Board moved toward the replacement of Sampson Hall with an administration-classroom building and toward the acquisition of the property west of Speed-

[7] Minutes of the Board of Trustees, 1950–1959. Committee on Seminary Development, March 20, 1951.

McMillan Classroom Building (1962)

way and south of 30th Street. The property had to be bought in parcels as available. The Trull and McMillan administration and classroom buildings were erected in 1962 with funds supplied from generous grants from foundations.

About the time Sampson Hall was razed, fire brought such damage to the Wynne House in 1962 that it too had to be demolished. The lay school which it housed was integrated into the theological degree program of the Seminary. The loss of Wynne House, however, was not the main factor affecting the decision to bring the work of the lay school into the regular theological degree program. Perhaps the most important reason was the decision to allow for the ordination of women. The first woman to be ordained to the ministry in the Presbyterian Church, U.S. was Dr. Rachel Henderlite, who was ordained by Hanover Presbytery May 12, 1965, and came as professor to Austin Seminary that same year.[8]

8 Witherspoon, *Ministerial Directory of the Presbyterian Church, U.S., 1861–1967, op. cit.*, p. 239.

The Faculty: 1945-1970 14

The teachers at the Seminary in the fall of 1945 in order of seniority were Robert F. Gribble, Samuel L. Joekel, R. D. Campbell, Eugene W. McLaurin, C. Ellis Nelson and James I. McCord, plus those who were taking up their work there for the first time, E. A. J. Seddon, Jr., instructor in the Spanish-speaking Department, Gus J. Craven, Director of Field Work and Instructor in Christian Education, and David L. Stitt, President and teacher of Pastoral Theology. Daniel Allen Penick was listed as Instructor in New Testament Language and Exegesis although he was a professor at The University of Texas and unpaid by the Seminary. He continued his work with the Seminary till 1957.

The catalogue number of the Seminary *Bulletin* for April 1946 announced that the Seminary had begun to offer a program of study leading to a Master of Theology degree. A student would be able to take a major under a Seminary professor and a minor in the Graduate School at The University of Texas.[1] This study was to include residence at the Seminary for several six-week periods that were to include January and early February. First candidates for the Th.M. degree to matriculate were Ernest F. Deutsch, J. Kelly Neal, Leslie Lee O'Connor, Henry W. Quinius, Earl Raitt, George M. Sullivan, and Joseph V. Kieft. Thus began the efforts of the faculty in the area of on-campus continuing education for ministers leading to a degree. J. Kelly Neal was the first to receive a Th.M. under this program in 1948, the title of his thesis being "The Relationship of Kierkegaard's *Stages on Life's Way* and the Characters of *The Brothers Karamazov* by Dostoevski."

The new administration faced a tension in the faculty. The points of view of those who were open to the considerations arising from the streams of Biblical criticism and those who were, at best, reluctant to study, much less teach, the elements and the fruits of modern critical scholarship put a strain on faculty policy and relations. In

[1] *Austin Seminary Bulletin* LXII, 1 (April 1946) , 47, 58.

the spring of 1947 the Board had before it the resignation of Dr. Gribble.[2] For him, any tendency to doubt the Mosaic authorship of the Pentateuch was a step toward denying the inspiration of scripture. However, when the Board declined to accept the resignation, Dr. Gribble stayed on. But he and Dr. Joekel continued to hold views that were considered passé by the newer additions to the faculty. It was a tribute to the devotion of all to the mission of the Seminary that these tensions were contained within their mutual Christian commitment.

With Eugene W. McLaurin in New Testament Greek, C. Ellis Nelson in Christian Education, James I. McCord in Theology, T. Watson Street in Church History and Missions, R. F. Gribble in Hebrew, Samuel L. Joekel in English Bible and James A. Millard in Homiletics, the faculty was both versatile and increasingly appreciated by the church at large as well as by the students.

McCord, Street, and Nelson gave new breadth and intensity to the study program at the Seminary. Nelson's quiet practice of personal and group dynamics led students toward a greater appreciation of resources available through Sunday school and youth and adult work in the church. Street insisted on getting to original sources in ancient, Reformation, and modern church history, and by word and example brought new vistas of missions into the purview of his students. McCord, as well as Street and Nelson, expected the theologs to do academically acceptable work and more of it than the Seminary had theretofore required.

McCord became the most exciting, challenging, sometimes awesome, personality on the campus. What Stitt did for the Seminary in the field of administration and finance, McCord did in scholarship. The two worked as a team. McCord, by reason of his own classes and because his duties as Dean kept him closer to the day-to-day life of the faculty and students, made a deeper impression on many.

Further, McCord often supplied the pulpit of the University Presbyterian Church and called on the sick and other members of that congregation. His pastoral heart, his memory for names, and his wise and gracious spirit made him a widely sought after and highly prized friend whether on the Seminary campus, in the supporting synods, or beyond.

Toward the end of the fifties the picture changed. Dr. Nelson in 1957 went to Union Theological Seminary, New York, New York,

2 APTS Minutes of the Board of Trustees 1940–1949, May 21, 1947, p. 2.

and later became president of Louisville Presbyterian Theological Seminary, Louisville, Kentucky. In 1958 Dr. McLaurin retired. In 1959 Dean McCord became president of Princeton Theological Seminary, Princeton, New Jersey, and Dr. Millard became Stated Clerk of the General Assembly of the Presbyterian Church in the United States. In 1961 Dr. Street became Executive Secretary of the Board of World Missions of the Presbyterian Church, U.S., Nashville, Tennessee.

The Committee on Program of Study of the Board, without being able to foresee more than a part of the need for new leadership, recorded in its minutes: "The committee was deeply conscious of the fact that the future of the Seminary for a generation to come will be determined to a large extent by these . . . appointments and expressed its determination to seek the best qualified persons to fill these places on the Seminary teaching staff."[3]

With this ideal in mind Henry W. Quinius became Associate Professor of Church Administration and Director of Field Education in 1955, John R. (Pete) Hendrick was instructor in Bible, primarily for university undergraduates (1956), and James A. Wharton began as Assistant Professor of Bible (1956). In 1957 Edward B. Paisley for one year became Visiting Professor of Christian Education. The next year John F. Jansen became Professor of New Testament Interpretation and Dietrich Ritschl became Visiting Professor of Biblical Theology. In 1959 new teachers included Lena Lea Clausell and Paul Calvin Payne in Christian Education, J. Rodman Williams in Systematic Theology, Don Marvin Williams in Homiletics, and Prescott H. Williams, Jr. in Old Testament Languages and Archeology.

The decade of the 60's began with addition in 1961 of Stuart D. Currie in Church History and W. Walter Johnson and Charles L. King in Homiletics. Nineteen hundred sixty-four brought George S. Heyer, Jr. in the History of Doctrine, Jorge Lara-Braud in Missions, and W. Eugene March in Old Testament Languages. Dr. Ernest Trice Thompson retired from Union Theological Seminary, Richmond, Virginia, and in 1965 began his five-year stay at Austin Seminary teaching Church History. The same year Rachel Henderlite came to the chair of Christian Education. Calvin C. Klemt came as Librarian in 1966. The next year brought Ross D. Dunn to teach Christian Ethics and to be in charge of continuing education. The

[3] APTS Minutes of the Board of Trustees 1950–1959, meeting of the Board May 21, 22, 1956, p. 3.

decade closed when Edward Dixon Junkin succeeded Dr. E. T. Thompson in Church History.

The 70's witnessed the addition in 1971 of Robert M. Shelton in Homiletics. William C. Spong of the Episcopal Theological Seminary of the Southwest began in 1973 to teach Pastoral Care. Merwyn Johnson came to Austin Seminary in 1974 to teach Theology, and the next year saw J. Carter King come as Visiting Professor of Ministry and Director of Supervised Practice of Ministry. Carl Siegenthaler at the same juncture began to teach in the area of Urban Ministry, and David Ng began his courses in Church Program and Nurture, while John E. Alsup became Visiting Professor of New Testament.

To telescope the comings and goings of teachers over a period of thirty years into a few paragraphs may tend to give the false impression of instability. Although David L. Stitt was remembered once to have observed that Austin Seminary seemed to be a training ground for teachers who went to other responsible places, it was more than that. True, Nelson and McCord became presidents of other seminaries, Street went to be Executive for the Board of World Missions and Millard to be Stated Clerk of the General Assembly of the Presbyterian Church, U.S., but David L. Stitt spent more than a quarter of a century as President. Henry W. Quinius was at the Seminary for twenty years before going in 1975 as pastor of Hope Presbyterian Church, a congregation in northwest Austin related to the Cumberland as well as to the United Presbyterian Church of the U.S.A. and the Presbyterian Church, U.S. When Robert F. Gribble retired in 1960, he had been with the Seminary thirty-seven years. The responsibilities of Thomas W. Currie at the Seminary spanned thirty-two years and of Samuel L. Joekel twenty-eight years. Though such length of service was unmatched more recently, those who served a decade or more included Eugene W. McLaurin (1938–58), C. Ellis Nelson (1940–57), J. I. McCord (1944–59), T. Watson Street (1947–61), John F. Jansen (1958–   ), Prescott H. Williams, Jr. (1959–   ), James A. Wharton (1956–75), Stuart D. Currie (1964–75), Eugene March (1964–   ), and Calvin Klemt (1966–   ).

From 1955–1958 Dr. Carlyle Marney, pastor of Austin's First Baptist Church, taught at the Seminary in the field of homiletics. He offered some flashbacks after he moved to North Carolina.

While using library materials in preparing for Rauschenbusch lectures at Chicago, I noted all the works of Walter Rauschenbusch were from private library of Dr. Tom Currie, and bore the underscoring of at least four readings which I judged to be his markings.

Chapel—the way Jim McCord could literally cause worship to start with "Let us worship God!"

Faculty luncheons—the way spinach and potatoes and corn-bread and meat tasted in that company—best "School food" I ever ate.

The perfect courtesy and fraternity extended me by a pair of choice, older, very conservative professors who knew my heresies all along.

The privilege of teaching where Ethics was properly related to Theology—indeed, Ethics was an offering in the Department of Theology.

Dave Stitt with a huge office full of plans and mock-ups for new buildings.

Richard Niebuhr stepping off the train into 14 inches of snow in Austin, complaining mildly that he had thought to leave all that in Connecticut.

University Church filled for lectures the year Krister Stendahl and I were there for the spring convocations.

A veteran faculty member remarking to me after Stuart Currie had corrected a visiting authority on his use of a Greek source, "We have a new King in Israel." And Stuart's office, in the mid-60's with at least a dozen books left open to some particular passage he was using.

Seminarians and wives (and sometimes Stitt) scattered through my Sunday night congregations downtown.

One of Stitt's boys showing up at my study door to enlist help in finding the copperhead that had killed a neighbor cocker spaniel. The boy was nine years old, barefooted, armed with a water pistol.

Ernest Best using an Irish liturgy for Holy Communion—featuring interminable prayers—Frank Young leaning over to whisper—"is this Holy Communion or an Irish wake?"!

Meeting one of last year's seniors back in registration line, I asked, "What are you doing here?"—Answer, "I preached those four sermons on race relations that you said I'd be back taking a Master's degree if I used in Arkansas my first summer."

The professor of Old Testament who would neither sit nor kneel during prayer. He always *stood*—no matter where.

Jim Wharton's honors the Commencement he graduated.

The obvious respect and mutual regard between President Stitt and Dean McCord.

The intense theological excitement of the years and the students 1948–58 when so much was happening.

McCord, badgered in a World Council Committee as to why he would not seek Episcopal ordination and thus give an example on how WCC could approach the problem of order—swelling to full size and answering "I have been ordained to the whole ministry of the Gospel of God—why should I consider a lesser ordination?"

Outlining my "Structures of Prejudice" on an envelope at lunch—University Tea Room—ten years to write it out.

Student regard for faculty and the camaraderie of the reunions and alumni lecture series.[4]

Perhaps the most prolific writer and publisher on the faculty is John F. Jansen. His affiliation with the United Presbyterian Church, U.S.A. has added breadth to the relations of the Seminary. His careful scholarship and winsome empathy with the students added a much appreciated dimension to the faculty. The summary of his attitude was, "I love this school." He continued

When some years ago an accrediting team from A.T.S. was here, we were asked to describe the seminary. As we all reached for short descriptive phrases, Stuart Currie said it best—for us all. He described the seminary as a "community of the Word." And I've always remembered those words because they say it for me. I suppose at every seminary—and almost every year, whether during opening retreats or during times when students hit the "slough of despond" the question is asked whether indeed we are truly a community. But whenever some particular illness or sadness or crisis faces us, I've found that we all discover anew what community means. And what kind of community? What binds the academic and the personal concerns together is the Word. I've been through several curriculum changes here, but always it is the Word that is seen as central. This is far more than a "departmental" conviction but one that binds us all together—as much in the teaching of homiletics, etc. as in the biblical field per se. I'm persuaded that this has made for the quality of faculty comradeship in our common effort as well as for the quality of our whole life together as a seminary. Of course "community" is never a finished achievement—but it is a gracious reality.[5]

Jansen noted the widespread use of Seminary teachers to write for

---

[4] Carlyle Marney letter to T.W.C., Jr. received November 21, 1975, and in the hands of the latter.

[5] John F. Jansen letter to T.W.C., Jr., October 19, 1975, and in the hands of the latter.

the Sunday school curriculum of various branches of the Presbyterian Church and for devotional and other publications. In addition to the assumption by many teachers of denominational responsibilities, Jansen and Wharton were representatives to the World Alliance of Reformed Churches, North American Area.

While the Seminary was no less an institution of the Presbyterian Church in the United States than ever, it broadened its interests in several directions. One was by offering housing to the Office of the Hispanic American Institute of which Jorge Lara-Braud was the first director, succeeded by Ruben P. Armendariz. Another was being linked with the United Urban Council of Austin, whose missioner, Carl Siegenthaler, became Adjunct Professor. A cordial relation was established with the Episcopal Seminary of the Southwest located only a few blocks to the east. This was expressed in accommodation of library policies and reciprocal faculty relations. The Seminary shared in the work of The Institute of Religion in the Medical Center in Houston and in its clinical pastoral counselling training program.

The call of the pastorate and of other important denominational posts made itself heard again and again. Sometimes even in the case of tenured professors the call became irresistible. "David Stitt often said that he did not want anyone on the faculty who did not from time to time struggle with the call of the pastorate."[6]

One of the integral persons of the Seminary, although not a teacher, is someone Dr. Jansen calls an unforgettable personality.

I take this occasion to pay particular tribute to Catherine Sautter, our Registrar. She came the year before I came and was McCord's secretary. She helped me in ever so many ways during my three years as acting dean. And as Registrar:

She is an amazingly careful and able administrator who has brought all student records—before and since her time as registrar—into excellent shape.

She has every student record at her finger tips.

She combines this with a warm personal interest in and sensitivity to student needs. I would guess that she does as much "pastoral counselling" or more than any of us. When alumni return to the campus, they immediately seek her. She carries on a wide correspondence with them. Students and alumni appreciate her candor and interest—and often ask to use her name as reference.

6 *Ibid.*

Her warm humanity expresses itself particularly in helping our ecumenical students to feel at home. When Clement and Joyce Janda came from Uganda, Cathy went out of her way to see that the apartment was "home," the refrigerator full, etc. She corresponds at least annually with our ecumenical students, and knows where they are presently, what they are doing, etc.

She is as much a member of the faculty as of the administration—in ever so many ways.[7]

Another member of the Seminary staff was a particular model for John B. Spragens.

Jack Hodges was never recognized as a member of the faculty, and yet students learned more about Christian living from his example of cheerful service than from all their classroom lectures and discussions.[8]

Not only was the Seminary a beneficiary from the proximity to The University of Texas. The reciprocal elements in the relation were evident in courses offered for university credit and other activities by Seminary teachers. Prescott H. Williams, Jr. taught courses in archeology. Stuart D. Currie, Gene March, and John Jansen taught Bible courses for credit. Ross Dunn was the Presbyterian in a course offered by the Law School in which The Episcopal Seminary also shared. George Heyer was occasional guest curator at The University's Art Department, directed exhibits, and delivered lectures jointly sponsored by the Art Department and the Seminary.

Some courses at the Seminary were advertised as being of community interest. John Jansen recalled an incident one evening at one of his lectures. "I usually teach an evening course that meets once a week. A Baptist lady took several of these courses. One night she put an envelope on my desk while I was talking to another student after class. When I opened it I found a letter expressing appreciation for what the seminary meant to the community—and a check for $500 toward student aid!"[9]

If John F. Jansen brought gifts to the Seminary from the United Presbyterian background, W. Eugene March brought treasures from a life nurtured by the Presbyterian Church in the U.S. As he reflected on the significance of Austin Seminary to him, he wrote,

---

[7] *Ibid.*
[8] John B. Spragens letter to T.W.C., Jr., September 3, 1975, and in the hands of the latter.
[9] John F. Jansen letter, *op. cit.*

". . . I think if I had only two things to say about all Austin Seminary has meant to me, I would link them together under the general rubric of "A Christian Lifestyle." And what are the two components I would single out? Intellectual integrity and commitment within God's people. But, and very important so far as I am concerned, the way I came to these insights was through the people who made up Austin Seminary."[10]

While careful, thorough, and honest study was inspired by Mc-Cord, Street, Ritschl, McLaurin, Wharton, and Prescott Williams, Gene March found further light from another quarter.

> At the same time the quest for intellectual integrity was in progress, the other side of the Christian life was constantly being laid upon us. For me, the call to commitment within God's people was first clearly identified at the Seminary with the person of David L. Stitt. His commitment to the institutional church with all of its failings was obvious and contagious. Anyone can throw rocks at the church, but only a few, it seems, are willing to throw themselves at the church and to be informed and reformed in the course of the struggle. David Stitt, it seems to me, has always been willing to do that. He taught me that it is foolish to have an illusion of a perfect church, but far worse is the cynical retreat from the particular, frail community where God is praised, sought, and called upon to display his presence. David Stitt's enthusiasm for this strange institution called the church was infectious. My own understanding of the church was to benefit greatly from a continuing relationship with David Stitt after I joined the faculty of the Seminary, for we were in the same Presbytery for a number of years. I frequently found myself disagreeing strongly with the position taken by David Stitt, but his own tolerance for views that were different from his and his conviction that the correct views would finally prevail because Jesus Christ was Lord of this strange institution was most instructive.[11]

A significant event of the early sixties was the coming of W. Walter Johnson to the Seminary to teach in the field of homiletics. A native of Shreveport, Louisiana, he was an alumnus of Centenary College and of Union Theological Seminary of Virginia. His two pastorates had been in West Helena, Arkansas, and Northridge, Dallas. His rapport with the students was cordial. But what im-

10 W. Eugene March letter to T.W.C., Jr., October 1, 1975, and in the hands of the latter.
11 *Ibid.*

pressed the Seminary community most about him was the valor and the winsome Christian spirit with which he faced the increasing pain of a lingering malignancy to which he finally succumbed March 7, 1970.

The first two professors to come from outside the Presbyterian, U.S. denomination were J. Donald Butler and John F. Jansen in 1958, who both maintained their connections with the United Presbyterian Church in the U.S.A. In 1971 Robert M. Shelton arrived and continued his affiliation with the Cumberland Presbyterian Church. Shelton notes the beginnings of his connection with the Seminary.

"My first awareness of Austin Presbyterian Theological Seminary was when I was a doctoral candidate at Princeton Theological Seminary and read a book by Dietrich Ritschl entitled *A Theology of Proclamation*. I was very much impressed by the substance of the book, even though I strongly disagreed with parts of it, and I decided APTS must be an exciting place to be if such thinking was going on as I encountered in that volume. Very soon after that I met Walter Johnson who was a member of the faculty of APTS and a doctoral candidate at Princeton as was I. We became friends and he talked frequently about APTS. During my written comprehensives I spent several nights with Walter and Marjorie Johnson in their apartment at Princeton, since I lived over seventy-five miles from Princeton at the time. The support they gave me during my comprehensives was much appreciated. It was beyond the wildest thought of either one of us that in less than ten years after our experiences together in Princeton Walter would be dead following a painful bout with cancer, and that I would succeed him as Associate Professor of Homiletics at APTS.

"One Sunday evening in December of 1970, David Stitt, whom I had never met, phoned me while he was in Memphis, Tennessee, visiting his daughter Sally, who was a student at Southwestern. He identified himself and asked if it would be possible for us to have breakfast together the next day. I picked him up at his hotel, we ate breakfast together and we talked continuously about theological education and the task of teaching homiletics. I was at that time serving as pastor of the Park Avenue Cumberland Presbyterian Church in Memphis, and also teaching one or two courses a term at Memphis Theological Seminary, the only seminary operated by the Cumberland Presbyterian Church.

"Our conversation excited me very much, and he too seemed to

170

enjoy very much our time together. He explained to me in our time together that APTS was looking for someone to come to teach homiletics. However, when I left him at the airport, he indicated that he did not know whether or not the faculty at APTS would want to interview me.

"I did not expect anything to come of the meeting, so I was most surprised when I received a telephone call from him approximately two months later during which he asked if I would be willing to come to Austin for an interview, with no obligation on my part or on the part of the seminary. I said I would. He asked me when I could come. I checked my calendar and found I had a very full schedule. He said I should make it at my convenience. I stated that an appropriate date for an interview with me would be April Fools Day. He laughed and said he agreed. I told him I would inform him relative to my flight schedule. He said he was looking forward to seeing me. I had received the call at the home of a parishioner where I was engaged in pastoral counselling. It was after 10:00 p.m. David Stitt had spent some time that evening running me down.

"David Stitt met me at the airport early in the afternoon of April 1, 1971. I arrived on a Braniff flight approximately one hour late. David asked me if I had eaten lunch. I had not. He asked if I wanted to eat before going to the seminary to meet with members of the faculty. I said I preferred to get started with the interview. He then drove me to the campus and took me directly to the office of Professor Stuart Dickson Currie. He introduced me, then left. I had no idea what was expected of me. I told Professor Currie that I brought greetings from one of his former students, a minister in Memphis, expecting I suppose that we would chat a bit about Memphis and his former student. He smiled and asked me: "What do you understand Søren Kierkegaard's view of preaching to be, and what in your judgment is significant about the position?" I swallowed hard, tried to recall everything I had read by Kierkegaard, paused to compose an answer to the question and then made a stab at it. He picked up on my response and the hour flew by. I had never in my life encountered a person with such a perceptive mind. From that first interview until the last hour I had with him on the handball court, I continually learned from Stuart Currie, "the most unforgettable character I have ever met."

"Following that initial interview the day and evening and next day simply flew by, chocked full of individual and group interviews. I left thinking that the faculty had certainly looked me over from

171

every angle.

"Approximately a month later David Stitt phoned again to say the faculty wanted to obtain my permission to nominate me as Associate Professor of Homiletics. I gave my permission and the election took place at the meeting of the Board of Trustees in May, 1971. I moved to Austin in August."[12]

Ernest Trice Thompson who remembered his years at Austin (1965–1970) as "among the most satisfactory" of his teaching career wrote:

> When I think of the Seminary I guess I think first of people. The school will always be associated in my memory with [Thomas W. Currie], certainly one of the greatest leaders our church has ever possessed. Stuart [D. Currie] was the outstanding personality during my teaching regime—a man of amazing versatility, brilliant in so many areas. I was impressed with the fine relationship that existed between faculty and students, and between faculty and board . . . I thought Catherine Sautter as Registrar was a tremendous asset to the institution. She took such a personal interest in every student and sort of toned up the whole atmosphere.[13]

James A. Wharton, who entered the pastorate in 1975 after spending most of his life close to or on the campus of Austin Seminary, says of the Seminary:

> What the Seminary meant to me: quite simply, the place where the grandeur of the Christian Gospel in its universal, global, and historical dimensions was opened to me . . . Through the years of working with students, and with colleagues, Austin Seminary has pressed me to concentrate on the endlessly profound simplicities of faith that can be shared by all followers of Christ, without relinquishing the sheer fun of trying to think faith through to its farthest frontiers . . . What excited me most as a student and later as a teacher at Austin Seminary was the possibility that The Seminary could be a place where all the concrete realities of the church in the Southwest could be reflected on, worked at, explored, discovered, prayed about—in order that resources might flow back into the churches for greater fidelity and effectiveness in mission.[14]

12 Robert M. Shelton letter to T.W.C., Jr., December 18, 1975, and in the hands of the latter.
13 Ernest Trice Thompson letter to T.W.C., Jr., February 28, 1976, and in the hands of the latter.
14 James A. Wharton letter to T.W.C., Jr., October 13, 1975, and in the hands of the latter.

Dr. Edward Dixon Junkin came to the Seminary as assistant professor of Church History in 1970 succeeding Dr. E. T. Thompson. Dr. Junkin initiated the novel manner of concentrating a survey course in Church History for first-year theologs in a few weeks at the beginning of the fall and gave leadership in bringing to completion a number of curriculum studies begun when Dr. Williams was Dean. It was in 1976 that Dr. Junkin became Professor and Dean of the Faculty.

The Seminary community was shaken by the resignation of David L. Stitt in 1971 to become Minister of Christian Education at First Presbyterian Church, Houston. Dr. Stitt's twenty-six years of leadership of Austin Seminary were fruitful in many respects. The financial resources of the Seminary grew as did the extent of the campus and the new buildings. Stitt built an excellent faculty and kept them working in harmony. He faced the unabating challenge to the youth of the church to consider the ministry of the Gospel as a possible calling. He continually pursued the task of keeping the mission of the Seminary fresh in the minds of those of the Seminary community, the courts of the church, and the communicants in four states.

Though a review of the minutes of the Board revealed no such formal action until May 18, 1974, Henry W. Quinius reported that

> . . . in 1945–46 . . . the Board of Trustees at Austin Seminary made the decision that the Seminary must be operated without debt and that in any capital construction there must be matching dollars for endowment. . . . This meant that if a project cost $400,000, at least $800,000 would have to be raised before the project could be built. This did not allow Austin Seminary to expand quite as rapidly during the 1950's as some educational institutions, but in the 1970's [this] has assured Austin Seminary . . . a financial stability that many other educational institutions do not enjoy. It would seem to me that much of the wisdom for this policy may be attributed to Dr. B. O. Wood, Dr. Charles L. King, both of these men being on the Board of Trustees, and [to] Dr. David L. Stitt . . .[15]

In reflecting on the work of David L. Stitt at the Seminary, T. Watson Street said, "One of my deepest impressions is of him as the presiding officer of the seminary. The faculty, though technically different from the administration, governed the seminary. And the president trusted the decisions of the faculty. I have no recollection

---

[15] Paper from Henry W. Quinius accompanying letter from same to T.W.C., Jr., March 1, 1976, in the hands of T.W.C., Jr.

of any time when I felt he pressured the faculty to accept his own judgment or to arrive at a pre-set decision. Faculty meetings were informal and democratic. Each member of the faculty gave his input. The president said very little. He allowed the faculty the freedom to arrive at the decision the faculty deemed best. I would be surprised if this were not difficult at times for David Stitt, for sometimes the faculty—in the long ago 1950's—would champion some stand or resolution on an issue that was controversial, and this, I am certain, did not make the president's task of money raising any easier in those days.

"The president was a money-raiser. He had to be. The seminary had a small campus and a few old buildings. New construction had not been possible in the 1930's and early 1940's. So funds were needed for new construction. In addition funds were badly needed for endowment. David Stitt worked tirelessly to secure funds. Perhaps some time he will give us an estimate of how many miles he drove those old Chevrolets. Day and night he kept at promoting the seminary. He always kept post cards in his pocket to send from various places to friends of the seminary, to keep them informed and reminded of the seminary. And he would make detours to drop by for brief visits. In spite of his incessant work at seminary I never received the impression that David Stitt was tired. At least he never talked about it, and he always appeared fresh and vigorous.

"David Stitt's strength was his relationship with people. I always associated this fact with three strengths in his character. For one thing he had an inner security and hence an inner strength. He could accept himself. In many ways he was outshone in the seminary community, and by reputation outside of the seminary community, by "theological giants" on the faculty. I never sensed that he felt insecure or jealous. He could be himself. Second, he had sensitivity to people. Far quicker than most people he could sense the other person's needs and stresses and moods. So you would find him coming up to you, giving you a heavy pounding on the shoulders, and saying, "Let's go get a hamburger for lunch." Soon you would be sharing, and he would be "draining your neuroses," and you would not realize that the lunch had been set up just to give you an opportunity to talk. Third, he accepted the other person and would allow that person freedom. I don't believe a student or faculty member felt that David Stitt pressured him theologically, personally, or any other way. David Stitt related to people in a genuine way.

"One secret to David Stitt's contributions was his ability to relax.

174

He could work hard till late afternoon, then become for an hour a terror on the tennis court or handball court. Periodically, in fact frequently, he would take a two or three day excursion for hunting or fishing. At conferences or meetings of Church assemblies, he would relax at the bridge table. While he carried some substantial volumes for reading, he frequently included a mystery book or two and would thus get away from heavy responsibilities for an hour or two.

"One other strong impression I have of David Stitt is his love for the institutional Church, in all its parts, and his positive and hopeful attitude toward the Church. He never joined the chorus of those debunking the Church. This is one reason he helped to build Austin Presbyterian Seminary into a great institution of the Church."[16]

No clues have surfaced that give a hint as to the secondary reasons that may have had a bearing on the decision of David L. Stitt to leave the Seminary and re-enter a pastoral relation. Perhaps none are to be found save the primary fact: that he was convinced of the authenticity of a call that came to him to go to a different post of service. In every measurable way he left the Seminary stronger than he found it.

At the time of the announcement of Dr. Stitt's resignation as President of the Seminary, the supporting synods took note of his monumental importance to the church while in that office. They noted his service on the Board of World Missions since 1964 and as chairman since 1967. They noted his influence upon the lives of the more than nine hundred students from thirty-three states and twenty-two nations who had studied at the Seminary during his administration. They noted that the library had increased its holdings from 7,000 to more than 93,000 volumes and that the assets of the Seminary had grown from $300,000 to more than $10,000,000. They paid tribute to the splendid faculty which had been assembled and the freedom it enjoyed.[17]

One of the resolutions read as follows:

> WHEREAS, David Leander Stitt, a son of Texas, was called by the Lord twenty-six years ago to come out of the wilderness of Missouri to assume the presidency of Austin Presbyterian Theological Seminary; and,

[16] Paper from T. Watson Street, unsigned, undated, received by T.W.C., Jr., March 23, 1976, and in the hands of T.W.C., Jr.

[17] Synod of Louisiana Seventieth Stated Meeting, Broadmoor Presbyterian Church, Shreveport, Louisiana, May 18, 19, 1971, vol. 8, no. 6, pp. 84, 85.

WHEREAS, with ready obedience he heeded and answered this call; and

WHEREAS, his fidelity for more than a quarter of a century has issued in unparalleled benefits both for Austin Presbyterian Theological Seminary and for this Synod; and,

WHEREAS, in the discharge of his office he has embodied our Lord's injunction to combine the wisdom of a serpent with the innocence of a dove; and,

WHEREAS, like the heroes of Scripture, he has prevailed over adversaries both on the right and on the left, and,

WHEREAS, he has lavishly shared with us the fruit of his faith, sometimes to admonish, sometimes to encourage, but always to speak the truth in love; and,

WHEREAS, he has once again heeded the call of the Lord and now goes to pursue his ministry in the largest city of this Synod; and,

WHEREAS, we esteem him as friend, guide, and fellow-servant in the cause of the gospel of Jesus Christ;

THEREFORE, BE IT RESOLVED that the Synod of Texas of the Presbyterian Church in the United States, meeting in solemn session June 8–10, 1971, on the campus of Trinity University in San Antonio, declare to God its gratitude for the grace bestowed upon this man in his boundless talent and tireless labor; and that this Synod assure David Leander Stitt of its continued prayers and good wishes in the work that lies before him; and that it express its joy over the knowledge that he will remain a member of this fellowship.[18]

The Alumni Association announced that the fellowship annually awarded to graduated seniors for further study would be designated the Stitt Fellowship.[19] The Board of Trustees named the library "The Stitt Library" and ordered a suitable plaque in recognition and appreciation of the service of David and Jane Stitt.[20]

[18] Minutes, One Hundred Sixteenth Session Synod of Texas, Presbyterian Church, U.S., Trinity University, San Antonio, Texas, June 8, 9, 10, 1971, volume XIV, 1971, no. 2, p. 226.

[19] *Austin Seminary Bulletin* LXXXIX, 1 (August 1973), 80.

[20] Minutes of the Board, June 21, 1971, p. 3.

Beyond the Classroom: Lectures and Publications

15

The Seminary community, especially since the early twenties, had welcomed lecturers to the campus. This custom received added emphasis beginning in the forties, when visits by denominational executives and missionaries on furlough were supplemented by a more organized program of lectures.

In February of 1945 a conference on Christian Basis for World Order was arranged with lectures delivered by Dr. G. Baez-Camargo of Mexico, Dr. Ernest Trice Thompson of Richmond, Virginia, Rev. E. T. Cornelius of San Antonio, and Dr. Homer P. Rainey, President of The University of Texas.[1]

The first series that went under the title "Mid Winter"—a lecture series which is still an integral part of the life of the Seminary— occurred the first week of February 1946. The featured speakers were Professor Joseph Lukl Hromadka of Princeton Theological Seminary, Dr. Felix B. Gear, Pastor, Second Presbyterian Church, Memphis, Tennessee, and Dr. W. A. Benfield, Jr., Vice President of the Louisville Presbyterian Theological Seminary.[2] Ministers from the supporting synods received cordial invitations to come to these lectures. President Stitt often offered, on request, to suggest to sessions that the church grant time and money to encourage pastors to attend.

The lectureship which was first assured of permanent financing was the Settles Lectures. Mrs. W. R. Settles of Big Spring, Texas, in 1947 pledged $10,000 to establish this series to be offered each January. The subject of the Settles Lectures would alternate year to year between missions abroad and missions at home. The initial lecture was delivered by Dr. James F. Hardie on home missions in 1949. The first on world missions was a series, 1950, by Kenneth Scott Latourette of Yale Divinity School.[3]

The Mid-Winter Lectures encompass three series. They take place

[1] *Austin Seminary Bulletin* LXI, 1 (April 1945), 9.
[2] *Austin Seminary Bulletin* LXII, 1 (April 1946), 10.
[3] *Austin Seminary Bulletin* LXV, 4 (May 1949), 11.

during one week, usually at the beginning of February. The earliest to be established were the E. C. Westervelt Lectures, made possible in 1949 by the gift of Mr. and Mrs. Edwin Flato in honor of the parents of Mrs. Flato. The same year the Women of the Church of First Presbyterian Church, Fort Worth, began an annual gift that made possible the Robert F. Jones Lectures in Christian Education. The Thomas White Currie Lectures were established beginning in 1952 by the Tom Currie Bible Class of the Highland Park Presbyterian Church, Dallas, Texas. The class cared for the annual cost plus making a contribution toward the permanent endowment of the lectureship.[4]

The Hoxie Thompson Lectures, occurring from time to time during the course of the academic year, were begun in 1961 by the late Hoxie H. Thompson of Trinity, Texas. Gifts from his family and friends augmented the original donation.[5]

Some of the able ministers and teachers in the life of the church were invited to the Austin Seminary campus with the Presbyterian and Reformed tradition most emphasized. Others who delivered series were Paul Scherer (1947) and Warren A. Quanbeck (1968), Lutherans; D. Elton Trueblood (1948) and Douglas Steere (1956), Friends; Charles Johnson (1956), Albert Outler (1962) and James Glosse (1970), Methodists; Theodore Wedel (1950) and A. T. Mollegaen (1951), Episcopalians. Carlyle Marney, a Baptist, became for a few years a part-time teacher of homiletics.

The ethical imperatives laid upon the church and the particular opportunities arising from its being in the midst of society were dealt with by H. Richard Niebuhr (1949), John Coventry Smith (1951), Waldo Beach (1959), Marshal L. Scott (1966), Robert McAfee Brown (1966), Lyle Schaller (1972), and John R. Hendrick (1973).

Fruits of recent Biblical studies were brought by Ernest Wright (1951), A. G. Wehrli (1954), James Muilenburg (1956), Dietrich Ritschl (1965), Balmer Kelly (1966), John Bright (1971), and James A. Sanders (1976).

The series of lectures of two laymen were outstanding. In 1964 Roland Mushat Frye delivered five lectures on the religious values to be found in Shakespeare's tragedy of Macbeth and in 1972 W.

---

[4] *Austin Seminary Bulletin,* 1957–58, Catalogue No. 5, LXXIII (February 1958), 6, 7.

[5] *Austin Seminary Bulletin,* 1961–62 Catalogue, No. 5, LXXVII (February 1962), 28.

Page Keeton, then Dean of the School of Law at The University of Texas, spoke on some of the ethical issues in the area of our legal system.

A number of the well known preachers delivered addresses. These included William M. Elliott (1954), John A. Redhead (1955), James T. Cleland (1958), George M. Docherty (1959), Warner L. Hall (1961), David H. C. Read (1962), and Edmund A. Steimle (1971).

Those interested in counselling and chaplaincy services benefited by the lectures of Granger E. Westberg (1968), Edward E. Thornton (1962) and George A. Benson (1975).

A continuous emphasis on Christian Education was assured. Among the speakers in this field were Lewis J. Sherrill (1952), Seymour A. Smith (1958), H. Shelton Smith (1961), Rachel Henderlite (1964), William B. Kennedy (1971), Harry Smith (1973), Sara P. Little (1975), and John H. Westerhoff, III (1976).

Men who were or who became presidents of other seminaries came as lecturers: John A. Mackay (1952), Henry P. Van Dusen (1956), Carl Ellis Nelson (1959), and Donald Shriver (1970). In 1946 David L. Stitt was the alumni lecturer as was James I. McCord in 1947.

The number and variety of those who lectured on the campus on some other basis than one of the major lecture series was extensive. For instance, in 1961–62 the following, among others, spoke for the Society of Missionary Inquiry: Eugene Daniel, Donald Bobb, Jack McClendon, Bakatushika Pierre, Mukeba Andre, Tshisungu Daniel, William Ross, M. S. Dickerson, Malcolm Carrick, Clarence Prince, and John Stout. Eight countries were represented. Fourteen other visiting lecturers included H. H. Farmer, Leroy G. Kerney, George A. Buttrick, Michael Testa, Wayne E. Oates, and Wallace M. Alston.[6]

Each year there were from eight to twenty or more occasional addresses by visiting ministers or missionaries or others who kept the students in personal touch with the denominational clergy leadership and with many currents of church world affairs.

Thus a steady stream of some of the most vigorous thought continued to be presented to those in the Seminary community and to ministers and laypersons who wished to participate.

In addition, the teaching of Austin Seminary reached beyond the classroom and beyond the campus. The faculty as well as the stu-

6 The above information about the lecturers may be found in the bound copies of the Seminary Bulletins in the Stitt Library.

dents supplied pulpits and counselled in and spoke to various conferences and other gatherings. Professors were in demand as lecturers at other theological institutions. The list of publications by the faculty became extensive. A number of the Settles and Mid-Winter Lectures were to be seen in print.

Moreover, in the mid-fifties there began a series of faculty bulletins which came in whole or in part to be used across the supporting Synods, not only by alumni for whose particular benefit they were initiated, but also by officers, Sunday school classes, and other students of the current events and issues in the life of the church.

> The Alumni Association, meeting during the Mid-Winter Lectures February 1955 requested the faculty to consider the publication of a bulletin for ministers that would reflect the intellectual and spiritual life of the Seminary. The faculty concurred with this request, and this publication is the first in a series designed to share more fully Seminary life with the ministers of our church.[7]

Since understanding the Bible was primary to the Seminary's existence, the first faculty edition contained an address by President Stitt in which he gave an overview of trends in Biblical criticism:

> The past few years have seen a radical change in Bible study. One generation ago and less, radical higher criticism was pulling Scriptures apart. It found no intrinsic unity in the Bible, but . . . [set], for example, the religion of Paul over against the supposedly quite different religion of Jesus. The result was the fragmentation of the Bible . . . A great change has come. Schweitzer's devastating criticisms in *The Quest for the Historical Jesus* and Barth's emphasis on the Word of God revealed in *Der Römerbrief* were largely instrumental in halting the old direction and pointing a new way. The current emphasis is on the unity of the Bible, an inherent unity which is found in Biblical proclamation.[8]

Any view of the Bible emerges from the academic into the practical when one seeks to be a preacher and helping prepare those who felt called to be preachers was, in the view of the president, one of the primary concerns of the Seminary. "One who truly preaches," he said, "is one 1) who is called and commissioned by God, 2) who is

---

[7] *Austin Seminary Bulletin* LXXI, 2 (October 1955), 1.
[8] David L. Stitt, "Toward a Biblical Concept of Preaching," *Austin Seminary Bulletin* LXXI, 2 (October 1955), 3, 4.

given a function to perform, never a position to fill, 3) who is given power to perform this function. The message to be delivered is 1) a message revealed by God, 2) a message for the salvation of man-under-judgment, and therefore a joyous message, 3) a message to be delivered to all men everywhere without restriction."[9]

This same theme was elaborated the next year by Charles W. Ransom, General Secretary of the International Missionary Council, in his 1956 Settles Lectures. He emphasized the missionary meaning of the Covenant and the pattern of redemptive purpose in the Scripture and in addition, the beloved community as the instrument of mission.[10]

The place of the Bible and of the living Saviour in a theologian's or in a Christian's view of history and of life was illuminated in an article by a visiting professor, Dietrich Ritschl. He held that

The proclamation of the church is primarily teaching history. The history book and the newspaper belong in the hands of Christians as much as the Bible does. No one beside Christians can have the courage to face the full reality of sin because only they know the power of forgiveness.

The understanding of history requires some very concrete steps . . . . We should teach at least one foreign language to our children, we must study and teach in our schools the naked facts of history instead of talking about "the meaning of history." We must study where the fear of communism or of intermarriage with Negroes comes from instead of having conferences on "Kierkegaard's concept of fear." We must study the history of God with His people so that we are able to trust in Him, instead of tolerating our nation's trust in military power while having weekend retreats on "faith." Obedient theological work challenges our beliefs and judges us. It is, in itself, part of the history to which we belong. It is the humble repeating and observing step by step of the way Jesus Christ wants us to go with him.[11]

This plea by Dietrich Ritschl for disciples to deal not only with doctrines but with contemporary realities did not fall on barren soil. Members of the student body sensed that sometimes the academic

[9] *Ibid.*, p. 16.

[10] Charles W. Ransom, "The Biblical Basis of Christian Mission," *Austin Seminary Bulletin* LXXI, 10 (June 1956) , 5.

[11] Dietrich Ritschl, "The Theological Significance of History," *Austin Seminary Bulletin* LXXV, 6 (April 1960) , 27.

surroundings insulated them from events rather than training them to deal with the crucial issues of modernity. If they were being prepared to be preachers they must develop an empathy for those who were in quandaries and agonies in the pews and beyond.

On Reformation Sunday October 25, 1959, twelve theses were affixed to the door at the entrance to the Chapel. Eight students had signed them: George Boyd, Lewis L. Wilkins, Jr., Dick Junkin, George Herrscher, Charles Taylor, Michael Parsons, Harry Paschall, and Michael Murray.

After noting the creative and sovereign activity of God and the fallen state of man and society the theses continue

4. The Word to whom the Church is witness is the word of reconciliation, who alone provides the possibility of and power for authentic human life in the midst of the power conflicts of a fallen world.

5. The task of the Church is not to relate the Word to these power conflicts, but to see with the eyes of biblical faith those points of conflict in which He is calling us to participate with Him in obedient trust in the work He is already doing there. As a seminary we are not being the Church in that we are not seeing the world to which we are called as the Church to minister.

6. The unique place of the seminary in the life of the Church demands that it must not only prepare people for a future participation in the ministry of Jesus Christ but that by its very existence it must give its own authentic witness now to what He is doing in the world.

7. The seminary can do this because it represents a unique concentration of resources of mind, concern and the heritage of the Church and its fathers.

8. But to do this it must take seriously and try to understand the world as it is with its fallenness and its conflicts and as it has been reconciled by God in Jesus Christ.

9. It must be free to hear and to speak the Word of God and to defend this freedom for the ordained ministry of the Church.

10. It must be free to take the risk of faith in thinking daring thoughts, ultimately trusting in the providence and forgiveness of God, rather than in the providence and approval of its financial supporters.

11. We do not find in our academic curriculum nor in our common life that Austin Presbyterian Seminary is thus uniquely serving the world as the obedient arm of the body of Christ.

12. Not only the faculty and board of trustees are responsible for our past failures but each student must share with them in

confessing our sins and trusting in God's grace as we seek together the way of renewal.[12]

A forum was held November 10 at which a paper was presented elaborating on the theses and making suggestions as to how by participating in faculty and board discussions and decisions students might participate to a greater degree in development of Seminary policies. There was expressed the need for those at the vortex of social conflict to share in seminars and for the seminary community to study and make deliverances to synods and others concerning burning contemporary issues.

One sequel of this posting of the theses was that students' views became part of the consideration of the faculty and board through committees on which students served. Another was a broadened view of the suitable content of theological education. Clinical pastoral education assumed a larger importance, as did community understanding. The former concerned ministry to the sick and to their families. The latter put students in touch with police, legal, and social agencies and with those they meet and seek to control or to serve.

Another sequel might be illustrated by Rachel Henderlite's recollection:

> Another January . . . was a traveling seminar with Jorge Lara-Braud to study "Ministry in the Southwest." This was even more widely interdenominational, involving one faculty member and up to ten students from each of four seminaries, adding Perkins and Bright to the Episcopal and Presbyterian. We spent two weeks in San Antonio with Tom Cutting serving as guide along with Jorge. We interviewed the city fathers, and mothers. We talked with Anglo and Chicano pastors, social workers, directors of welfare agencies and schools and we visited a wide variety of activities and institutions.
>
> And then we moved to the Valley for a week and had some remarkable experiences with Valley Farm Workers and with the farm owners and political leaders of the community. There we had several local priests to help Jorge steer us and to interpret for us.
>
> Before the course began, we read carefully selected articles and books about the life of the Mexican family. We had various discussions on the way. We lived together in churches and hostels for three weeks, and nowhere were we separated from the prob-

---

[12] Mimeographed paper, dated Austin, Texas, 25 October 1959, placed in the hands of T.W.C., Jr., October 24, 1975 by Dean E. Dixon Junkin.

lems presented to the church by the worker and by the owners and employers. Our last week we spent in teams working on possible approaches to ministry in this area of the church's life. And here again I found myself concluding that this was education for ministry at its best.

In the sixties our students, like students throughout the country, were social activists and protestors against the status quo whatever that might be. Racial and economic injustice and the Vietnam war were on everybody's front burner. My first year it was the United Farm Workers and their march from the Valley to the Capital. The university, which adjoins our campus, had a volatile group of faculty and students too, and we often made common cause with them in the struggle for justice for the Mexican-American farm worker.

We had a great bunch of students, not only social activists but rebels against the ineptness of the church in dealing with social injustice. They were open to every human need and unafraid to try out new ways of working. Some left the church and went into other agencies that seemed more effective change-agents. Others have taken their freedom and their indignation with them into the church—to its great benefit.[13]

In 1961 the Seminary faculty took note of the appearance of the New Testament part of the New English Version of the Bible.

"The Preacher and the Bible" was an answer by John Frederick Jansen to the question, "What is the Bible to us and what should it be?"

> When we have been faithful to the Bible's witness, when we have brought to the text the best we have of brain and heart then as James Stewart puts it, "something else remains: 'Stand back and see the salvation of God.' The sermon does not harness the Word. Rather, the living Word can be trusted to use the sermon because God is free to be Himself: free to speak in Jesus Christ."[14]

Dr. Prescott H. Williams, Jr. pleaded with ministers to share with laymen the fruits of modern Biblical research openly, frankly, rev-

---

13 Letter from Rachel Henderlite to T.W.C., Jr. received January 7, 1976 and in the hands of the latter.
14 John Frederick Jansen, "The Preacher and the Bible," *Austin Seminary Bulletin* LXXVII, 3 (November 1961), 13.

erently.[15] An extensive study of one word and its derivatives was a condensation of the Ph.D. dissertation of Professor Eugene W. Mc-Laurin. He chose the word luō and elaborated on its two chief meanings, to loose or release, and to destroy, especially as illustrated in the New Testament.[16]

In connection with the discussion of Jürgen Moltmann's *Theology of Hope* by W. Eugene March in the April 1969 *Bulletin,* there was a study of "Hope in Its Biblical Settings" by Stuart D. Currie.[17]

The theme of hope and of the meetings of the World Council of Churches at Frankfurt, Uppsala, and Bangkok were the subject of the Settles Lectures by T. Watson Street in 1974.[18] He spoke of the mission of the church to proclaim liberty to the captive and then he raised the question, ". . . does God only liberate? Is there danger of . . . proclaiming liberation as the only dimension of salvation and the only dimension of God's activity?"[19]

There is a comment that has at least an oblique bearing on the above question in an article by W. Eugene March on the first chapter of Jeremiah.[20] He points out that God's people have never been certain they were being obedient before they acted. Only after the fact is a degree of certainty possible. "The problem is to learn to live with the suspense . . . God's word of assurance to his prophet . . . 'I am with you to deliver you' does not have anything to do with personal 'success' . . . [God's] deliverance means that he offers us security in our relationship with him. But being in relationship with God places all else in jeopardy."[21]

One *Bulletin* was given over to Biblical studies for a seminar on Sexuality and the Human Community, a series of studies presented by Stuart D. Currie at Perkins School of Theology, Dallas, at the request of the Committee on Continuing Education, Synod of Texas, United Presbyterian Church.[22] This seminar was scheduled because

15 *Austin Seminary Bulletin* LXXVII, 3 (November 1961), 29.

16 Eugene W. McLaurin, "Redemption or Deliverance: A Study of 'Lutron' and Its Derivatives," *Austin Seminary Bulletin* LXXIII, 8 (June 1958), 3–11.

17 *Austin Seminary Bulletin* LXXXIV, 7 (April 1969), 40–56; 29–39.

18 T. Watson Street, "Salvation Today," *Austin Seminary Bulletin* LXXXIX, 7 (April 1974), 5–25.

19 *Ibid.,* p. 18.

20 Wallace Eugene March, "Jeremiah 1: Commission and Assurance; A Study of the Form, Compilation, and Some Theological Implications of Jeremiah 1," *Austin Seminary Bulletin* LXXXVI, 1 (September 1970), 5–38.

21 *Ibid.,* p. 30.

22 *Austin Seminary Bulletin* LXXXVII, 4 (November 1971).

of interest aroused in connection with the report on Sexuality and the Human Community presented to the 182nd General Assembly of the United Presbyterian Church in the United States of America in 1970. After examination of a number of passages in the Old Testament, notably Judges 19–21, and in the New Testament, especially I Corinthians 6 and four dominical words from Matthew and Mark, the author offers a section on preaching from the Bible about sex. The concluding paragraphs read:

> Proper love of self and proper love of neighbor are derivative from and aspects of that unreserved commitment and unqualified allegiance of embodied creatures to their Father and Maker who has graciously appointed that his everlasting love should be figured in that bond because of which a man leaves father and mother and cleaves to his own wife.
>
> It is the Good News of his chastity, courtesy, and commitment which leads us to pay serious attention when Jesus of Nazareth says: "This new commandment I give you: that you love one another as I have loved you." (John 13:34) [23]

The prospect of launching the Covenant Life Curriculum in the Presbyterian Church, U.S., in October 1963 brought forth studies by the Seminary faculty on facets and aspects of the concept of Covenant.[24] Prescott H. Williams, Jr. held that

> The people or church or congregation which would claim covenantal belongings to our Lord as its own,
> —recognizes a sovereign claim,
> —receives a Deliverer's call,
> —stands in a Presence that says, "Decide,"
> —strives for obedient life,
> —knows a judging deliverance,
> —expects a delivering judgment,
> —lives a possessed life,
> —serves a world also possessed,
> —recites a holy history,
> —moves toward obedience in community,
> —hopes in a living Lord,
> —becomes the "you" to whom the "I" makes promises,
> —enters an awesome covenant with the saving Judge,
> —accepts a call to move from natural unity toward political and social unity in responsive responsibility.[25]

[23] *Ibid.*, p. 55.
[24] *Austin Seminary Bulletin* LXXVIII, 6 (March 1963), 3.
[25] *Ibid.*, p. 51.

When Dr. Ernest Trice Thompson came to Austin Seminary in 1965 as Visiting Professor of Church History, he shared with the community an authoritative compendium of information and a lifetime of experience that added new dimensions to the faculty. Not only did he have the twentieth-century sweep of church history at hand, but he put into publishable form his studies concerning Presbyterians in the South which has appeared as a three-volume work.[26]

In the spring of 1968 there was published in the Seminary *Bulletin* an article, "Southern Presbyterians and the Race Problem."[27] Two years later the Th.M. candidates and others who had heard four of Dr. Thompson's January lectures on continuity and change in the Presbyterian Church in the United States[28] became so excited about what they had heard that the schedule for the *Bulletin* was revised and these fascinating lectures published. They noted areas of stability and areas of metamorphosis in theology and especially in the doctrine of the spirituality of the church, "In Regard to the Negro," and "In the Mission of the Church."

In looking forward Dr. Thompson held that

> The new mission of the church will include word and deed, each for its own sake, neither merely a stepping stone for the other. For the mission of the church is not merely to go out and win converts to the church for the sake of the church, nor to bring men to Christ for the sake of their own spiritual wholeness and ultimate redemption; its mission is to serve the world, to meet the needs of men, to seek to bring the whole of society as far as that is possible under the Lordship of Christ.[29]

As early as 1963 it was possible to find the faculty studying and writing about the Holy Spirit in Scripture and in the life of the church.[30] The prayer, "Veni Creator Spiritus," was the theme of the Alliance of Reformed Churches Holding the Presbyterian System meeting in Frankfurt, Germany, in August 1964.

In his inaugural address published in the fall of 1966[31] J. Rodman Williams announced, "We stand on the verge of a new theological

---

[26] Ernest Trice Thompson, *Presbyterians in the South*, vol. I (John Knox Press, 1963); vols II and III (John Knox Press, 1973).

[27] Ernest Trice Thompson, "Southern Presbyterians and the Race Problem," *Austin Seminary Bulletin* LXXXIII, 7 (April 1968), 5–28.

[28] *Austin Seminary Bulletin* LXXXV, 7 (April 1970).

[29] *Ibid.*, p. 84.

[30] *Austin Seminary Bulletin* LXXIX, 3 (November 1963).

[31] J. Rodman Williams, "A New Theological Era," *Austin Seminary Bulletin* LXXXII, 3 (November 1966), 37–47.

era . . . the focus of the new era will be the doctrine of the Holy Spirit."[32] The spreading interest in glossolalia had prompted a deliverance on the subject by the 1965 General Assembly of the Presbyterian Church, U.S.[33] By 1967 the issue as to whether, or the degree to which, tongue-speaking was a legitimate and an authentic expression of the work of the Holy Spirit had become a matter of concern, not only in the church at large but also in the Seminary community. The most extensive treatment[34] of the subject omits any contribution by J. Rodman Williams, Professor of Theology. Members of the Biblical Department survey Jewish pneumatology, review Jesus and the Spirit in the Gospels, and analyze speaking in tongues as viewed in First Corinthians and in Acts. The findings may be summarized in the final sentence from the article on the Gospels by Stuart D. Currie: "The records carefully examined leave little room for supposing [Jesus] created the impression of a wonder-worker, and even less that he was remembered as the paragon of all pneumatics."[35] Thus the faculty as a whole gave its support to the deliverance of the General Assembly minimizing the value of glossolalia and finding it to be one of the least of the gifts of the Spirit, if indeed any support for it in Scripture is warranted. Professor Williams found himself in the position of supporting an interest in glossolalia as an evidence of the work of the Spirit when the balance of the faculty saw it as, at best, unnecessary, and, at worst, an aberration.

The Plan of Union between the Reformed Church of America and the Presbyterian Church in the United States engaged the attention of the two denominations. It was approved in 1968 and referred for votes by the classes and the presbyteries in 1969. The faculty saw no reason for not consummating the union.[36] However, the plan did not receive the necessary support in the Reformed Church for it to go into effect.

Contributions to the *Bulletins* by W. Walter Johnson and Robert Shelton on preaching and by Stuart D. Currie and John F. Jansen on New Testament studies and by James A. Wharton and Eugene March on Old Testament were instructive and illuminating. Rachel Henderlite wrote on the Covenant Life Curriculum and on the Mis-

---

[32] *Ibid.*, p. 37.
[33] Minutes of the One Hundred Fifth General Assembly of the Presbyterian Church in the United States, Montreat, North Carolina, April 21–26, 1965, part I, pp. 174–78.
[34] *Austin Seminary Bulletin* LXXXIII, 3 (November 1967).
[35] *Ibid.*, p. 41.
[36] *Austin Seminary Bulletin* LXXXIV, 3 (November 1968).

sion of the Church of Christ Uniting,[37] Ross D. Dunn discussed a film depicting racial riots and disorders in Omaha and the attitudes of Christians there,[38] George S. Heyer, Jr. sought to help the church face the inescapable fact of change.[39] The discussions of glossolalia and the Plan of Union evoked supplementary orders and reprints of the Seminary *Bulletins* dealing with these matters, but in demand more than any of the rest was the issue in the fall of 1974 on The Declaration of Faith and The Book of Confessions being written by an ad interim committee of the General Assembly named in 1969 and chaired by Albert C. Winn.[40] In this issue of the *Bulletin*, Albert C. Winn explained the process by means of which the committee arrived at its first draft and was dealing with the more than twenty-two hundred responses and suggestions received from individuals and groups. Stuart D. Currie, in pithy, laconic descriptions, characterized the documents composing the Proposed Book of Confessions. James A. Wharton, a member of the committee, reflected on the form of The Declaration of Faith. George S. Heyer, Jr. examined some theological issues while Ross D. Dunn noted some ethical implications and Robert M. Shelton set out some liturgical values he saw in the proposed Declaration of Faith. So great was the call for extra copies of this bulletin that a price had to be imposed on supplementary orders.

The same was true with respect to the *Bulletin* the next spring[41] which brought into focus A Plan for Union which was being hammered out with a view to enabling the Presbyterian Church, U.S., and the United Presbyterian Church in the U.S.A. to vote on becoming a single denomination. Contributing to this issue were J. Randolph Taylor, co-chairperson of the Joint Committee on Presbyterian Union, together with Seminary faculty members: Edward Dixon Junkin, Merwyn S. Johnson, Carl Siegenthaler, Henry W. Quinius, Jr., and John F. Jansen.

In these two concerns of the church the points of view espoused by the Seminary were generally favorable to the adoption of The Declaration of Faith and Book of Confessions, with George Heyer expressing some reservations; and enthusiastically, on the positive side, with respect to union. Thus, the *Bulletin* contributed not only

[37] *Austin Seminary Bulletin* LXXXII, 7 (April 1967), 7–34.
[38] *Austin Seminary Bulletin* LXXXIII, 7 (April 1968), 47–57.
[39] *Austin Seminary Bulletin* LXXXI, 7 (April 1966), 4–12.
[40] *Austin Seminary Bulletin* XC, 4 (November 1974).
[41] *Austin Seminary Bulletin* XC, 7 (April 1975).

to answering the request of the alumni for reflections from the intellectual and spiritual life of the Seminary, but in many instances offered light on certain important issues before the church at large.

The Board of Trustees   16

Dr. Charles L. King, pastor of the First Presbyterian Church, Houston, and long-time member of the Board and chairman from 1951 to 1960, recalled the devotion and faithfulness of the members of the Board, both ministers and laymen. He noted that the attendance at Board meetings was uniformly good, and in his judgment the members were forward looking and ready for new adventures in theological education.[1]

One of the responsibilities of a member of the Board is the ability and inclination to interest ministerial candidates to study at Austin Seminary. Even though Dr. King was an alumnus of Union Theological Seminary of Virginia and a native of Georgia, he was able to say, "I have never advised a student to go elsewhere than to Austin."[2]

Barton W. Freeland, a rice farmer of Crowley, Louisiana, in reflecting on memories for which he is grateful writes,

> I place at the top of this list of the happy experiences my association [as Board member] with our Austin Presbyterian Theological Seminary. The people here that teach, learn, administer and contribute financially are, without a doubt, the salt of the earth. . . . The outstanding blessing that I received during my tour of office was my personal acquaintance with a large number of students. To see young people, dedicated and with a feeling that they had been called, spend three years of intensive study and preparation, then go out to their chosen field and become spiritual leaders in many parts of the Kingdom; to me, this is what the Seminary is all about. It has been my pleasure to follow the progress of many and I say with pride, "I knew him when he was in Seminary."[3]

[1] Charles L. King letter to T.W.C., Jr., October 14, 1975, and in the hands of the latter.

[2] *Ibid.*

[3] Barton W. Freeland letter to T.W.C., Jr., October 13, 1975, and in the hands of the latter.

Charles Leonidas King, Board Chairman 1951–1960

In considering the function of the Board, Bart Freeland continues,

The Board of Trustees consists of twenty-four men and women that are truly dedicated and interested in the education of the students that enter the seminary. They come from the Synod of Red River, selected because of their dedication to the proper operation of the seminary. Their main function is to make policy, make and approve budgets, assist the administrative officers, approve the acquiring of new faculty members and the investment of endowment funds. This latter committee has done an excellent job over the years and made it possible for the institution to operate in a business-like manner, providing all of the expenses involved in such a large institution plus keeping the tuition fee at the lowest of our Presbyterian Seminaries.

The Red River Synod is blessed by having hundreds of unselfish, generous and far thinking people that, over the years, have given of their worldly goods for the ongoing of the seminary. This group, alone, kept the seminary financially strong, making it possible to obtain the best faculty, housing, aid to students and maintenance of the entire campus. Without the above group, I feel that the seminary could not survive in these days of inflation.

To those that have given cash, stocks and bonds, oil royalties and real estate and enjoy the results, I say "Thank God for your interest and love for Austin Seminary." I pray that many more will sense the financial needs of the seminary and will add their names to the list to replace some that have left this earthly scene.

I praise the memory of those that have included the seminary in their wills. Their thoughtfulness is and will continue to serve the many needs of this institution. As I look back almost three quarters of a century, I wish to give my parents the credit for instilling in me the reasons why I should tithe. They believed in it; they practiced it because it was Biblical. At an early age I was told of great business men that were tithers and the good that came from their giving. At no time did they indicate that financial rewards followed or that there was tax advantage to be considered. It was right and proper for a Christian to tithe and that was it, as well as the good feelings that come from giving a portion of my income gladly.[4]

Rev. Shirley C. Guthrie began his service on the Board in the forties. He writes,

My first Board meeting left me bewildered. That was in 1945. The Seminary had no President, the student body was under twenty in number, the War had not ended but was near the end. No one was sure just what to do about anything except one, we voted to call David Stitt as President. I'm glad I got on the Board in time to vote to call him. We talked, we planned, we dreamed and we prayed, and left that meeting feeling that we were on the march.

The coming of Dr. Stitt, his adroit leadership, his vision, his seemingly unending energy, his personal relationships throughout the four Synods, were to mark the next number of years. Our problems were the problems that always had been; students, accommodations, and money. Each one of these problems was faced with reality and assurance. Things began to happen, a strong faculty was gathered; enrollment began an upward climb; plans were made for new and much needed buildings; money was sought and people were challenged. Looking back after all

4 *Ibid.*

Shirley Caperton Guthrie, Board Chairman 1961–1962.
Courtesy of Shirley Guthrie

these years it seems that things moved unbelievably fast, but
during those years [the pace] seemed so slow.

The whole face of the Seminary plant changed or was in the
process of changing during the seventeen years I served on the
Board. Not only did the physical plant change but the heart of
the Seminary was changing, effectiveness was growing, the learning process was heart warming and hope-giving. Too much
credit cannot be given to the President and Faculty of the Seminary. The warm relationship between Board and Faculty stands
out in my mind. The unanimity with which decisions were
made, after long and heated arguments at times, on the part of
both Board and Faculty was a beautiful thing and paved the way
for a bigger and better Seminary.[5]

5 Shirley C. Guthrie letter to T.W.C., Jr., December 22, 1975, and in the hands
of the latter.

From the ranks of the lay members of the Board, another of the able and dedicated leaders was Glenn A. Railsback, a CPA of Pine Bluff, Arkansas. He was one who was asked by Dr. Gribble to get in touch with a young pastor in St. Louis and press upon him the needs of the Seminary. Thus began the close association between Glenn Railsback and David Stitt. Mr. Railsback recalls,

> I had the privilege of traveling all over the State of Arkansas on behalf of the Seminary with David Stitt. We had lots of fun and made lots of contacts for the Seminary. My love of David has never waned. He is the same today as he was the first day I met him when he came to Texas from Missouri. His wife, Jane, is a great helpmate and a wonderful person whom I also love. To me the highlight of my time as Trustee of the Seminary is punctuated with the association of men of great spiritual discernment and accomplishment, good to work with, wonderful to know and valuable men to the kingdom of God through the Seminary. John Smiley was called as business manager of the Seminary and served the balance of his active career in that capacity. He was a man of deep discernment, understood figures and finances and their association with the operation of an institution like the Seminary and was an excellent accountant, a most lovable person.[6]

Tom Sealy of Midland, Texas, could write, "my membership on the Board during the 50's was one of the most interesting and challenging assignments I had ever received. . . ." He proceeds to pay tribute to Dr. Stitt as "an outstanding administrator and leader" who helped make "this Seminary . . . one of the better known and most respected seminaries of any denomination throughout the nation."[7]

One of those who studied at the Seminary and also served on the Board was Don G. Shepherd, minister at St. Luke Presbyterian Church, Amarillo, Texas. He felt that " . . . my reception and the terrific concern for helping me on the part of every one of the faculty, administration and staff will remain with me always. I found it to be not only an academic institution offering the highest degree of excellence in theological education, but even more importantly, a group of Christians banded together to train, pastor, counsel, assist

[6] Glenn A. Railsback letter to T.W.C., Jr., October 3, 1975, and in the hands of the latter.

[7] Tom Sealy letter to T.W.C., Jr., December 22, 1975, and in the hands of the latter.

in every way every person regardless of former education or qualifications. This, I believe, was, is, and always will be a strong characteristic of Austin Seminary."[8]

President Stitt was ever on the alert to acquire for the Seminary the land it needed and the means to pay for it. A word from one of those who was in position to know reveals how this sometimes worked. As he reviewed his Seminary file, Robert B. Trull wrote

> Letter dated September 29, 1970 indicates the B. W. Trull Foundation sent $1,000 to help purchase the Osborne property on 29th Street. David called me on the phone to ask if I would contribute $1,000 toward buying this property. I reminded David that the Seminary had set up a fund to buy any property which might become strategic to the Seminary and located close by. He said he was aware of the fund but thought maybe I would like to donate for this particular project. This will give an idea of David's fund raising ability in that he knew people would contribute to a specific project. In this case he probably called a number of people and raised the money without having to dip into the amount that had been set aside for this purpose.[9]

One way of looking at the responsibility of a member of the Board is that he should support the President in his labors to challenge young people to consider whether they are called to be ministers of the Gospel and to engage their interest in studying at Austin Seminary, to support and supplement the efforts of the President and faculty in choosing teachers and operating the school, to release funds and develop the liberality of those by whose generosity the needs of the Seminary can be met. In short, the Board must support a president or fire him and choose another. It is doubtful if any other act of the Board is so crucial to the life of the Seminary as the choice of a president.

Dr. B. O. Wood, long-time pastor at First Presbyterian Church, San Angelo, Texas and member of the Board from 1928 to 1957, recalled that in 1943

> A committee of three had been appointed to nominate to the Board a new president. After two years search and much prayer they nominated Dr. David L. Stitt. He was a young man with

---

[8] Don G. Shepherd letter to T.W.C., Jr., December 19, 1975, and in the hands of the latter.

[9] R. B. Trull letter to T.W.C., Jr., October 13, 1975, and in the hands of the latter.

John William Lancaster, Board Chairman 1962–1972. *Courtesy of John Lancaster*

no experience as president of a seminary. A prominent pastor of one of our city churches asked the writer this question: "What were the qualifications of Dr. Stitt for this position?" The answer was: "Ask me ten years from now and I will tell you." He never did ask again. Dr. Stitt proved himself to be what the Seminary needed at that time. World War II ended. Many young men came out of the military service with the determination to invest their lives in service to mankind through the ministry of Jesus Christ. They came to the Seminary in large numbers. The need for new buildings and equipment and a larger faculty was very great. Dr. Stitt had the unusual ability to persuade people to make an investment in these needs of the Seminary. The buildings needed were gradually erected. The endowment of the Seminary was increased very greatly, and the

197

Seminary became what it is today. We rejoice in these accomplishments and look forward to greater ones in the years ahead.[10]

One member of the Board recalled a Board meeting that occurred when it seemed as if the annual budget of the Seminary could not possibly be completed without a splash of red ink. He wrote, "One time when the Seminary was pressed to meet the budget [one of the board members] wrote out a check for $10,000."[11] This degree of continuing radical and costly commitment on the part of members of the Board had been no small element in the story of the financial survival and progress of the Seminary.[12]

[10] B. O. Wood letter to T.W.C., Jr., October 8, 1975, and in the hands of the latter.

[11] Marion A. Boggs letter to T.W.C., Jr., August 18, 1975, and in the hands of the latter.

[12] See Appendix II for the Roster of Members of the Board of Trustees.

Alumni Recollections   17

The impact of a school on its alumni is often hard to measure. In the case of Austin Seminary alumni, some of the former students themselves have evaluated and shared their impressions of their seminary experience.

One of those who was graduated soon after Dr. Stitt became President was William H. Arnold. He wrote:

> I will always be deeply indebted to Austin Presbyterian Seminary . . . for the ministry.
>
> I entered [the] Seminary in September 1943 . . . I came by bus to Austin as most Seminary students did in those days, without having even a thought of owning an automobile. Austin Seminary made every effort to make the new students feel at home, and I certainly did.
>
> In October of my first year I became Student Minister at the Hyde Park Presbyterian Church in Austin. It was a kind of training ground for students a good number of years and helped me greatly in the practical aspects of the ministry, preaching every Sunday, doing some pastoral work, and aided me in making a livelihood. I started receiving $50.00 per month as the Student Minister at the Hyde Park Church and remained serving the church until I graduated. By the time of graduation, the salary had gone up to $85.00 per month. It was a happy experience for which I will always be grateful.[1]

When Leonard R. Swinney and his wife came to the Seminary, there were more married students than could be housed in Seminary facilities.

> Ethel and I arrived there in late October, 1945, with all our earthly belongings on a truck we saved when we closed our dirt-moving business, R. E. Swinney & Son of Baton Rouge. . . . Dr. Gribble was . . . in charge of student housing and nothing was

[1] William H. Arnold letter to T.W.C., Jr., December 23, 1975, and in the hands of the latter.

available when we arrived, so we bought a house out on 44th Street—away from the Leper Colony.

I started out the day with chapel at 8:30, then English Bible under Dr. Joekel 9:00–9:50. But then we had baby Greek at UT at 10:00, and classes often ran overtime. There was a huge grandfather clock out in the hall, but it only said tick-tock—no bells— in fact not always tuned or synchronized with the UT tower clock. Frequently I was late to Greek. I always liked to be punctual. After Dr. Stitt took over as President, I talked with him about a bell system. Of course it cost money, but I had a friend in First Presbyterian Church of Baton Rouge named Douglas McIver. . . .[2]

His may not have been a unanimous sentiment, but Earl Wiggins remembered

. . . Mrs. Green and her delicious meals in the refectory. I remember some of the characteristics and gestures of the faculty: McCord with his booming voice and rotund figure with arms held high to make some affirmation. I remember his phenomenal photographic memory, too. Or, Dr. Joekel making a point of emphasis by reaching to the top of his head for hair, where there was no hair. I remember that familiar leaning of the head by Dr. McLaurin and his gentle spirit. I remember Dr. Gribble with his machinegun-like speech giving a sermon or talk which he had memorized. He told of a time during a worship service one evening when the lights went out. It did not phase him. He went right ahead and finished his sermon, because he had committed it to memory. I remember Dr. Penick in his penthouse office and classroom at the top of the University tower building. I remember a week-end preaching trip to east Texas with Dr. Stitt. He carried along a couple of shotguns with which we shot at crows on the way down; and at jack rabbits on the way back at night. Drs. Street and Nelson brought a fresh new spirit to campus also. I remember that for a while Street and McCord required more reading and written work than all the rest of the faculty put together.[3]

Attesting to the camaraderie, Prentice H. Barnett (1950–1951) was filled with warm feelings and appreciation for the students, fac-

---

[2] Leonard R. Swinney letter to T.W.C., Jr., November 23, 1975, and in the hands of the latter.

[3] Earl B. Wiggins letter to T.W.C., Jr., December 16, 1975, and in the hands of the latter.

ulty, and staff who made the atmosphere much more of a family fellowship than that of an institution of brick and mortar.[4]

Few were in better position by first-hand experience and by reason of denominational overview than James William Newton to see what the Seminary did to staff small churches as well as medium and large congregations, and, not least, to be instrumental in organizing new churches. Evangelism and missions continued to be central emphases —indigenous leadership for local opportunities. Born in Maysfield, Texas, an alumnus of Austin College as well as of the Seminary, he served as pastor of churches in Lott, and of Llano and its larger parish in Texas. He was on the staff of the Board of Church Extension for a time, and, later, he was Associate General Presbyter in North East Texas and Covenant Presbyteries. Few in recent times have had a hand in organizing more new congregations or in aiding and inspiring more small ones, both rural and urban. He wrote

It is true that today Austin Seminary graduates hold pastorates, high administrative positions in Seminaries, Colleges and religious institutions and on church court staffs all over our General Assembly and in other Reformed Churches around the world. However, the greatest contribution—the fulfillment of Dr. Daniel Baker's dream of 130 years ago "raising up preachers among ourselves," is producing ministers native to the Synod of Red River, trained in our Seminary to know and effectively translate the Gospel of Jesus Christ to the people of the Southwest.[5]

An alumnus of the early fifties, Gerald H. Slusser, who later became a professor at Eden Theological Seminary, Webster Groves, Missouri, recalls how Austin Seminary, for a time, arranged to supply vacant pulpits some distance away.

"Sometime in 1950, Austin Seminary began a most interesting outreach program. It had many colorful names, one of which was 'The Gospel Airlift.' One of the students, Leslie Webb, a middler in the Fall of 1950, owned an airplane, a small four place Stinson as I recall. I had been an airline pilot with Braniff until I resigned to enter the ministry. Hence, between us, we had a natural combination.

"Several churches in northern Louisiana were in need of supplypreaching and willing to help bear the cost of getting us there by

[4] Prentice H. Barnett letter to T.W.C., Jr., December 17, 1975, and in the hands of the latter.

[5] James W. Newton letter to T.W.C., Jr. dated December 30, 1975 and in the hands of the latter.

private plane. The Gospel Airlift was off and running. Soon Leslie felt the need for a bigger and more weather-capable airplane. He went to Arizona and traded his plane for a WWII surplus twin-engined Cessna. Now we were really in business.

"For the next two years, except for the summer, we operated a regular flight service every weekend from Austin to Monroe, La. We also supplied some towns in southern Arkansas. Sometimes only two of us went up, but usually it was three or four. We even acquired another airplane and another pilot. A friend of the Seminary in Southern La., in fact I think he was a member of the Board of the Seminary, heard with interest of our project and recalled his old large four place Stinson gull wing. It was then in storage in an old hanger, more of a barn, on a small airfield. He decided to give the plane to the Seminary, and we agreed to take it.

"The plane hadn't been flown for some time, perhaps several years. Several of us went over to pick it up. We finally got the plane started, ran it a good while on the ground, and finally test-flew it. It stayed up! After a short test flight with everything of essential nature for a daylight flight working, I agreed to fly it back to Austin. Except for a few anxious moments in which the engine faltered, probably due to dirt in a fuel line, the flight was uneventful.

"We now numbered four pilots, having added Joe Slicker and Arthur Strickland. Having two planes allowed us to expand our sights and many weekends we had six or even eight people going the 300 to 400 mile trip to Northern La., and Southern Ark. I was the only weather rated pilot, so in poor weather, we could only fly the one plane. I can't imagine just how we solved the logistics, but I do recall having to drive instead of fly on many weekends.

"For the flight, we left Austin early Saturday afternoon, as soon as was feasible, after the end of Saturday classes. In those days, we went to school six days each week. We usually arrived in Monroe by four in the afternoon, or a little later. Then followed ground trips by car, courtesy of the local churches, to our preaching points. This was at least another hour, sometimes more. On Sunday, after church services, we all scurried to snatch a hasty lunch and return to the airport for the flight back.

"Ellis Nelson recalls one flight very vividly. His son was accompanying him on that trip. I flew him and his son to Shreveport, where he was to preach that Sunday. The weather was right poor, as I recall. He remembers it as being terrible. We had thunderstorm conditions, with rain and gusty winds and low clouds, so that an in-

202

strument approach was necessary. My two passengers had never seen what happens in the cockpit during such conditions and found it almost more exciting than they had bargained for. Needless to say, we landed safely. I waited for some improvement in weather and proceeded on to Monroe.

"I think that every person who made this flight, even once, will recall it, and the regulars have more memories than we can easily write. One of the funniest trips was not to La., but to South Texas. This must have been some special supply request, but only two of us were going down. One to a small town between Corpus and Alice, and I was to preach at McAllen. David, my passenger, was young, inexperienced and nervous.

"To land him as near as possible to his destination, I elected to put him down on an abandoned military field. We circled a couple of times, saw no action on the ground and proceeded to land. David deplaned and I taxied back out and took off. A few minutes later, as David was walking down a road toward the outside gate, he was stopped by two MP's. They had neither seen nor heard our airplane and could give no credence to David's story. To them he was an invader without a pass on a military airbase. The airport was in fact closed, but there was still an active military contingent there, and the base was under guard. For more than an hour poor David sweated and fretted, facing incarceration in the base jail, until at last he was able to reach a local contact who assured them that David was in fact a Presbyterian minister and that they were expecting him to fly in.

"The Gospel Airlift produced a lot of such hairy stories, provided a half dozen churches with regular supply preaching, and doubtless exerted a life-long effect on many of the young men who participated in it. It gives meaning to an old cliche, 'those were the days'."[6]

One of the later pilots was Ralyn C. Parkhill who had a narrow escape.

> . . . the guys at Seminary had been asking me to buzz that old Stinson airplane, which we flew on weekends to services to attend churches in the Monroe area in Louisiana, down between the chow hall and the chapel. The day that I did this the buzzing was a very big success. I pulled the old airplane up and over and dove down. I never did go back up, I stayed down between the trees and went over to the airport and landed. All of which

[6] Gerald H. Slusser letter to T.W.C., Jr., December 2, 1975, and in the hands of the latter.

is against the law and contrary to any regulation which we were supposed to observe. It happened on that day that the Regional Inspector for the Southwest for the Civil Aeronautics Administration was coming down Red River at the time that I put on this demonstration. He sent for me at the airport and had a few words to say. I told him that I had to go to class and could I meet with him at 2:00 that afternoon and he cooled down enough to say that would be appropriate. I went back to Seminary and said that I would not be in class that day. And I took off for San Antonio to get my Airman's certificate which I was supposed to have with me when I flew and fortunately he had forgotten to ask for it. I flew to San Antonio by Chrysler and back and managed to make it in time to get with him. In the meantime, he had talked to different people at the airport, Dr. Stitt and others who managed to bail me out, although he was still very unhappy about the incident. . . .

What really meant most to me was the comradeship of the whole Seminary family and the high caliber and high privilege of the Seminary experience. It had been my privilege to be on some winning football teams where comradeship and team spirit are extremely meaningful. Also I had experienced the strange comradeship men know in combat and the trust and the oneness that are in men who fly together and who fight together. . . . The seminary peer group experience in the men and the faculty is an irreplaceable experience.

The reflections of things of lasting value are the purpose of learning together that a rich oneness of faith may be shared and exhibited in the most amazingly different forms of life style. We each had to learn that deep faith comes packaged in the strangest externals, this was both richly rewarding and highly disturbing to us from time to time.[7]

A son of missionary parents, J. Allen Smith, has preserved several Seminary scenes of the 50's in his memory.

"I remember the custodian, known as Monroe, and his proclivity for White Owl cigars. He would shuffle up and down the halls, sweeping up to the doors of the rooms and perhaps a little bit in the middle of each room. One room he would never attempt was ——'s room because the floor was always about three inches deep in pecan shells and wood shavings (—— was a whittler). Dr. Joekel said that —— was sweeping his room one day and in the trash found an unabridged dictionary. . . .

[7] Ralyn C. Parkhill letter to T.W.C., Jr., November 11, 1975, and in the hands of the latter.

". . . on one occasion David Parsons was criticized for letting the dorm get too cold. (His work scholarship was to keep the furnace stoked.) David took offense at this criticism and stormed down to the basement and spent several hours stoking the furnace. The furnace got red hot—the steam for the radiators backed up into the cold water pipes so that any faucet that was opened emitted live steam—including commodes, urinals, cold water faucets, etc. . . .

"My over-riding memory is the sense of community that existed at the Seminary. There was a bond, a closeness, that permeated the entire life of the community. We were indeed 'one in the Spirit, one in the Lord.' As students we felt close to the faculty, and this closeness was not programmed or organized. It was simply there. I remember the occasion of my first funeral—held in Valley Mills where I was doing 'field work'—I went to Dr. 'Mac' and he gave me counsel, support, and exegetical material for the service. It was so natural for me to turn to him—and his help was so authentic, practical, and supportive. 'The funeral' was a subject covered in class, but Dr. Mac's personal help was in some measure in a different dimension. And that relationship was characteristic of the life of the entire community.

"One of the long term highlights of my life at the Seminary was my work in the dining hall. I lived at the dorm during my undergraduate years, so I waited tables for six years. Much of that time I worked with my roommate, Ed Robertson. On one occasion, Aunt Emma (Mrs. Thomas L. Green) called on us as her most experienced waiters to serve the table for the Board of Trustees who were on campus for a meeting. Everything went smoothly until we came to the dessert. Ed was removing the plates while I came right behind him with the 'fried egg dessert'—the name we gave to apricot shortcake. There was a slight accident and the 'fried egg' landed on top of the head of one of the baldheaded trustees. His fringe of hair kept the cold juice from running down on his clothes—but he did indeed look ridiculous with a fried egg on his head. Aunt Emma was mortified! There were many experiences connected with the dining hall: On one occasion we put root beer in a beer bottle, shook it up so that there would be 'foam' and served it with flourish. This was for the benefit of a visitation group of 'pre-theologs' from Austin College who were eating in the dining hall. We wanted to impress the 'pious God-squad from the church college' how worldly we were at the Seminary.

"I remember that the coffee at the Seminary was notoriously bad.

The common saying was that it was boiled in one of [the cook's] socks. It was indeed boiled in a bag but as far as I knew, it was not a sock. Ed Robertson and I poured half a bottle of Worcestershire Sauce in the coffee pot one morning, hoping to cause some consternation. The joke was on us when no one noticed!

"We had a very efficient crew in the dining hall. During one period Jim Wharton was the dishwasher while Ed Robertson and I were the waiters. Lunch was served at 1:15. We would serve lunch, clear the tables, wash and wipe the dishes by hand (for about 50 people) and set the tables for dinner—all of this in time for Jim, Ed and myself to attend our Greek 405 class at The University at 2:00 p.m. We were so fast that newcomers were warned to keep their left hand on their plates at all times and never to put down their forks! . . .

"I am proud of Austin Presbyterian Theological Seminary. I am proud of the training I received there. I have done work in graduate education since my Seminary days—in Scotland and in California—and I have always felt that my background was equal to that available anywhere else in the world. I am grateful for the people, the life and faith examples, the support and concern available only in a community where the spirit of Christ is clearly evident."[8]

William I. Boand recalled, "Dr. Ernest Best, Guest Professor, 1955–57, was called 'The laughing Irishman.' He had a ball buying books for the library—the Administration having given him the right to buy anything and everything the Biblical Department needed. . . . It was reported that he read Greek each day except Sunday when he read Hebrew! He is now William Barclay's successor at The University of Glasgow, Scotland."[9]

A man of many gifts who studied at the Seminary in 1956 was John Gillies. He served the church in Brazil, Atlanta, Georgia, Elkhart, Indiana, and later came to the State Department of Public Welfare in Austin. He wrote

> I am grateful for the expansion of intellectual frontiers, primarily through the influence and goading of Drs. Street, Wharton, and McCord. My college major had been music, then speech (radio/TV, in my case) —with a minor in history. Dr. McCord's Systematic Theology forced me to take a freshman course in philosophy at UT, just to keep my head above water.

[8] J. Allen Smith letter received by T.W.C., Jr., December 26, 1975, and in the hands of the latter.

[9] William I. Boand letter to T.W.C., Jr., received December 11, 1975, and in the hands of the latter.

A happy happenstance, somewhat related to the Seminary, was sharing a graduate course in Mass Communications at UT with Dr. James Millard. We later compared our evolving convictions growing out of that course in Sao Paulo, Frankfurt, and in Atlanta.

I thank God for the joy of the chapel services. It was there I first learned to sing *Be Thou My Vision*—and how it was sung in those days! I also became acquainted with the split pages of the Scottish *Psalter*, by way of the occasional evening get-togethers Dr. McCord arranged in his home.

I felt then a common commitment to share the Good News, to do this with relevance, integrity, and joy. It seems to me that that commitment was felt and shared by the entire community, which extended far beyond the seminary.[10]

Tailoring theological education to the calling of a particular student was the work of the Seminary in the experience of one candidate, Ben F. Gutierrez, who later went to an administrative post in The Program Agency of The United Presbyterian Church in the U.S.A. He wrote

Serious theological doubts, while at The Austin Presbyterian Theological Seminary, made my student days there the most difficult, and in some ways, most rewarding. So intensely had I questioned some of the basic tenets of the Christian faith, that during my middler year I decided to leave the seminary. Besides, I also had serious doubts as to whether an Anglo-middle-class theologically oriented education would, in the long run, prepare me to serve the Latin American Community in the United States.

The day before leaving I decided to inform Dean McCord of my firm decision. After a lengthy discussion with him, I felt that I had encountered a different person from what I had imagined. Instead of the stern, demanding person, I found one whose understanding was beyond my expectations. Far from reproaching me for my doubts, I was challenged to seek the truth regardless of the consequences. I never felt that he was really able to understand the extent of my anguish in my search for ways to reconcile what I was learning with the reality of the marginated [*sic*] minorities I would be serving after graduation; however, I did find someone who was sensitive to my predicament.

Encouraged by what I considered to be a most positive and

10 John Gillies letter to T.W.C., Jr., November 23, 1975, and in the hands of the latter.

crucial encounter with him, I challenged my other professors to help me in complementing what I considered to be a somewhat limited preparation. Dr. James Millard agreed enthusiastically to my continuing studies at the University of Mexico the summer following my middler year, and at the same time, relating to the local Presbyterian Churches in Mexico City. Dr. Henry Quinius made special assignments and took a real interest in my fieldwork, gearing it to my needs as well as those of the churches. Dr. Watson Street's classes in history and mission and chapel services were a special inspiration to me, thus preparing me, in many ways, for my present assignment as Liaison with Latin America and the Caribbean of the United Presbyterian Church in the U.S.A.

Bringing all these and other able persons together for the benefit of the student body was its friendly and athletically inclined President, David Stitt, whose interest in the student body, the faculty, and for the Church as a whole, was always evident.[11]

William R. Jarvis, who later became pastor at Falfurrias, Texas, in reviewing the faculty of the fifties could observe, "It took a great Board of Trustees to enlist these Godly men." He continued

The students had ideal facilities in Library, Chapel, and Classroom Buildings . . . on the edge of The University of Texas campus. . . .

[Then there was] the time I could not go on my field trip [because] my wife was sick. Dean McCord came down to the Leper Colony with a $25.00 check just to help out. We had no money and no food. Jim McCord gave me a suit of clothes that fit me perfectly. The students teased me that McCord's mantle had fallen on me. . . . One night each week, we had student preaching with Faculty Evaluation. After the service, one Faculty member said, "More fire should be put into the sermon." But when Dr. Joekel got up, he said, "More sermon should be put into the fire."[12]

One of the most dynamic men who came from a business career to study at the Seminary was Jack K. Bennett, later to be pastor of First Presbyterian Church, Galveston. He was impressed with ". . . the giant personalities that made up the administration and faculty during my years of '55–58. What I appreciated most at the time was

11 Ben F. Gutierrez letter to T.W.C., Jr., January 8, 1976, and in the hands of the latter.
12 William R. Jarvis letter to T.W.C., Jr., December 12, 1975, and in the hands of the latter.

being able to sit intellectually and spiritually at the feet of men who were at the same time good friends."[13]

The three years Jack Bennett spent at the Seminary were but the beginning. "A source of great pleasure for me has been my continuing relationship with the seminary community over the years. Because it has been a major source of my continuing education, because friendships emanating from those earlier years have deepened and because I have been associated with so many of the students of later years, the Seminary has been a real hub of my activity in the ministry."[14]

Fred L. Campbell also left a business to study for the ministry. "As for a personal experience that I would not take anything for, it has to be the welcome and encouragement that Dr. Eugene McLaurin gave to me and my wife the first day we went to look over the seminary in the summer of 1956. He gave me strength—and the daily trips to the third floor of the library where the classes were then held —all became possible, even with crutches."[15]

Preaching on "the circuit" gave students practice and sometimes had other results as remembered by John H. McCord:

> Student preaching at Austin Seminary seemed to be about eight parts terror and two parts trouble. The terror involved the criticism of truly masterful preachers who were also faculty critics for student preachers, and the trouble involved manuscript preparation. However, one of the deeply satisfying experiences I had at seminary had to do with the weekend preaching assignments.
>
> A departure in the dark on an early Sunday morning put me on my way to a church in the coastal area southeast of Austin. An early arrival furnished plenty of time for pacing the floor of a recently vacated pastor's study once I had arrived at my destination. A good elder briefed me on the order of service and blessed calm came with the beginning of the service. The sermon on Isaiah 6:1–8 went well and soon the service was over.
>
> A most interesting twenty minutes with the elders then transpired. There were questions. Had I been informed of any particular difficulty the church had had?
>
> "No."

13 Jack K. Bennett letter to T.W.C., Jr., December 2, 1975, and in the hands of the latter.

14 *Ibid.*

15 Fred L. Campbell letter to T.W.C., Jr., November 20, 1975, and in the hands of the latter.

Was there any special instruction given me for preaching the sermon I had preached?

"No."

The sermon had been just what was needed for them that day.

"You'll have to thank the Holy Spirit for that, I just preached a sermon prepared for student preaching and faculty criticism."

The return trip to Austin was short in the winter afternoon. Home again in the dark, I still did not know the problem I had spoken to nor the particular word of help and encouragement I had uttered. The Holy Spirit had used the word and the words to bless the church. He blessed me, too. From that time, student preaching was only four parts terror and one part trouble.[16]

William E. Pryor had a vivid memory from the fall of 1956.

McCord was lecturing one morning and gradually turning green. He became more ill. We were on the 3rd floor of the library, and I was organizing the troops in my mind to haul him down that winding stair when he collapsed. I was picking out the biggest bruisers we had in the class because James I. was about 280 at that point. Joel Lucke, Dick Lamp, Bob Baxter— I even had us assigned to particular points alongside the carcass. But, thank goodness, he didn't need our transportation. He got down under his own power.

Men who meant the most to me: I was there at a great time in the history of the faculty, we had great people. They meant— each in his own way—unique perspectives and prisms of the whole—Dr. McLaurin, saintly gentleness who always had time to listen—Ellis Nelson, brilliant and competent—Dr. Gribble, from whom I learned little Hebrew but much wisdom—McCord, profound and impressive and dramatic—Dr. Ernest Best, probably the finest New Testament scholar I've ever encountered—Dave Stitt, warmth and good humor—Dr. Millard, a churchman from his toenails up—and probably most impressive to me—Carlyle Marney. Marney would be my model if I could choose one man like whom I could think, write and speak. He had and has no peer.

As one thinks about those three years, '56–'59, there is a collage of colors running together and tripping over themselves— coffee breaks that lasted late into the night—the quiet of a library carrel—friends made who are still friends—chapel—a few

---

16 John H. McCord letter to T.W.C., Jr., received December 4, 1975, and in the hands of the latter.

210

lectures become vivid—some books we had to read—papers we had to write—but generally a blur of good feelings about those years on pilgrimage.[17]

Alan Farquhar could not forget the interest and concern Dr. Mc-Laurin showed to all his students.

The circuit rides and early morning rising to drive to preach at pastorless churches and always being well received and encouraged. On one particular Sunday morning while driving to Rocksprings my old Mercury broke down at Mountain Home, it was 7:00 a.m. and there was only one service station and a few summer cottages. I awakened the owners who let me use their phone. Upon overhearing my conversation over the phone, they fed me breakfast, and drove me to Rocksprings in time for Church School (which I led as the teacher didn't show up that Sunday), they attended worship, we shared lunch together and they returned me to Mountain Home and the broken-down car. The Good Samaritans—Revisited. A warm memory of days that were filled with books and requirements and little time for reflection.

The bleak times when there was no money for food and no preaching assignment and opening the mailbox to find that God had worked through some gracious person to give money for the children's necessities.

The three years passing so rapidly that upon graduation one is struck with the enormous task that awaits him as he is to be thrust into the life of a congregation with all this new-found knowledge and vast amount of ignorance.[18]

Joseph L. Turner had a kaleidoscope of impressions:

As a student, 1958–61—
entering with keen expectation, as a sponge eager to soak up every experience and opportunity afforded—
encountering the Christian faith in an unexpected way through Old Testament Introduction and James A. Wharton
7 classes and 23 hours in class my first semester!
James I. McCord, the only man I have known who thunders a whisper
the unbelievable scholarly grasp, competence, teaching skills,

[17] William E. Pryor letter to T.W.C., Jr., December 10, 1975, and in the hands the latter.

[18] D. Alan Farquhar letter to T.W.C., Jr., December 3, 1975, and in the hands of the latter.

and transparent faith of the faculty

on or about Reformation Sunday certain members of my class nailing to the chapel door "ninety-five theses," challenging the faculty to a debate on certain matters—and the faculty accepting the challenge—and the reading room of the library filled to capacity with students and faculty engaging in lively and enthusiastic debate!

T. Watson Street, after hearing students month after month speak of their concern for "the world"—"the world"—"the world," one morning in the midst of Church History stated "you people couldn't locate the world, even if you had a telescope," closed his notes, walked out of class—leaving us to ponder his quip and our rhetoric—

numerous conversations in faculty homes, most notably in the homes of John Jansen and Dietrich Ritschl, sometimes including a meal or dessert—but always featuring the finest theological conversation and personal interest I have known—

picnics, retreats, student-faculty softball games, student touch football games, living on a shoe-string (which is another fun game!) —

my entering class, the largest in the history of the Seminary, with so many sharp minds, with such diverse experiences, with vastly different theological perspectives—whose influence upon my theological growth is second only to our faculty

a visual image of *loyalty*, David L. Stitt, toward the Seminary, the faculty, the students, the Church—

visits to the campus by internationally known theologians and churchmen—

an instructor by the name of John Thomas, who began our first class in Pastoral Care by writing in large letters on the board—CARE—pressing into my mind the significance of this word for ministry—

To sum up, Austin Presbyterian Theological Seminary was a tremendous experience for me as a student. I believe that the Seminary was the single most important factor in encouraging me to be a lifelong student, a lover of learning, a discoverer. There faith took shape; discipline and caring became companions; and I wish that profound an experience for every theological student.[19]

As a former plasterer, James Andrew Beverley recalled repairing

---

[19] Joseph L. Turner letter to T.W.C., Jr., December 11, 1975, and in the hands of the latter.

the statue of the Greek goddess, Diana, in order for it to appear on campus April 1, 1960. The inscription in Greek and Hebrew being translated read, "Much study is a weariness of the flesh."[20] Beverley's plastering experience was later put to use on Dr. Gribble's retirement home near Leander. But Beverley recalled another impression from his days on campus, "Dr. Jansen had the deepest effect on my preparation for the ministry. His solid scholarship and deep piety impressed me greatly. I am a better man, and I trust a more effective minister because of having studied under him."[21]

In addition to the academic program the chapel and the Leper Colony provided the setting for some memories as recounted by G. R. M. (Bob) Montgomery, Jr.

"Just as the chapel structure dominated the campus architecturally, so did the daily morning chapel worship services make a major impression on my Seminary life. It put the whole day's work in a meaningful perspective to worship God at 8:30 a.m. with fellow classmates, faculty members and other members of the Seminary community. I recall that most professors were there every day. Not all students participated regularly but a majority did.

"Some random chapel related memories include: Dr. Gribble always rising for prayer from his left front pew no matter what the rest of us did; the tell-tale noise of the front door closing behind a tardy worshiper whose only hope of being undiscovered lay in slipping quietly upstairs into the balcony; the spine-tingling impression of the predominantly male voices singing with gusto such favorite hymns as: 'I Greet Thee Who My Sure Redeemer Art,' 'A Mighty Fortress Is Our God,' and 'God of Grace and God of Glory;' our five year old son, Scott, sitting with me through chapel service before crossing the street to his morning kindergarten class at the Episcopal church.

"For many years the most colorful segment of married student housing was that unique circle of old frame structures fondly known as the Leper Colony.

"Betty and I and our son, Scott, came to live in the most distinctive appearing house in the Colony, a high-roofed, long, narrow old building situated at the base of the hill below the two-story brick

[20] George A. McCall letter to T.W.C., Jr., December 3, 1975, and in the hands of the latter.
[21] James Andrew Beverley letter to T.W.C., Jr., December 2, 1975, and in the hands of the latter.

home which had housed Dean McCord before he moved to take up his duties as president of Princeton Seminary. We lived two years in this old building except for the summer intern work spent at Crowley, Louisiana.

"Our second son came into the world during our second year at the Seminary, so it was to the Leper Colony that we brought Steve home. Bringing babies home to the Colony became so frequent that there were all sorts of rumors about the drinking water.

"The Leper Colony always had an interesting student population. For example, during 1959–1961 there were couples from Mexico City and from the Philippine Islands in addition to two future Seminary professors: Dick Junkin and Gene March.

"But to me, our most unforgettable Leper Colony neighbors were David and Monica Hadden, who lived in the cottage just to our north. David hailed from Northern Ireland, Monica from London. Often in his thick Irish brogue David would tell she was the only Englishman he could ever stand, so he just married her.

"She was at that time a strict vegetarian. In fact, the smell or sight of cooking meat made her ill. David didn't share those sentiments so we'd have him over to share some bacon or hamburger.

"Their customs and idioms reminded us that God's people don't come from the same pattern. For example, neither David nor Monica could tolerate prolonged exposure to gas heating. They just weren't accustomed to much artificial heat at all. So, no matter how brisk the winter air, they always had a window or two open. You might see Monica washing dishes in front of her open kitchen window bundled in layers of sweaters topped by a heavy overcoat. As the day warmed up she would shed her coat and sweaters.

"And you might hear an Irish tenor voice from the darkness of the yard beckoning for Monica to 'bring the torch' (flashlight) so he could find their kitten.

"Life in the Leper Colony drew student families together: around the common clothes dryer, watching the children play on the swing set and in the grassy central yard area, visiting for a moment on the way home from classes, and sharing a barbequed chicken. Colony classmates baby-sat for each other, talked theology or just socialized over a cup of coffee and borrowed first-aid supplies and advice from each other when a child suffered an injury.

"Wives often got up an evening bridge game that would last until the husbands trudged home from the Episcopal Seminary Library at 11:00 p.m. (It got a lot of Presbyterian business because it stayed open an hour later than the Presbyterian Seminary Library)."[22]

Ecumenical students studied at the Seminary. One of these was José Cruz-Antonio from Mexico and, with him, his wife, Alejandrina Navas de Cruz. At one time, when Mrs. Cruz was sick, "Dr. T. Watson Street came to our home which was situated in what was then called 'The Leper Colony.' . . . He brought us groceries and proceeded to cook our supper for us."[23]

D. C. M. Gardner of England remembered a lecture of Dr. C. L. King which highlighted some of the temptations of a pastor to "whine, shine, and recline." He thought a particular contribution of the Seminary was "an ability to adapt to changing times without departing from a base of orthodox Biblical theology. . . ."[24]

From the Sudan came Clement H. Janda, who "enjoyed every bit of my stay and study. Academically speaking, Austin Seminary was one of the best staffed institutions I have ever attended. The scholarliness of the faculty was very excellent."

Wherever I went in other parts of the USA I was always asked the question whether I would rank Austin Seminary among the "conservative" or "liberal" schools. My observation, without pretending to know what conservative and liberal really mean, is that Austin strikes a real balance between the two. A good illustration can be found in the denominations that send their students to Austin Seminary. At my time there were Methodist students, Disciples, Church of Christ, Baptist, Episcopal (like myself) and, needless to mention, Presbyterians both Southern and Northern!

The faculty-student relationship was one of the best I have ever experienced in my life. The relationship was not that of "inferior-superior" but that of fellow seekers, fellow learners of the Gospel. The President, Prescott H. Williams, Jr. was a very understanding person, easy to approach and to talk to. He really influenced my life very considerably. The simplicity of professors like Eugene March, John Jansen, Merwyn Johnson, Dick Junkin, to name but a few, was a factor in the excellent relationship between students and faculty.

As ecumenical people on the campus of Austin Seminary my wife and I had the privilege of being the focus of the Seminary

22 G. R. M. Montgomery letter to T.W.C., Jr., received December 6, 1975, and in the hands of the latter.

23 José Cruz-Antonio letter to T.W.C., Jr., December 17, 1975, and in the hands of the latter.

24 David C. M. Gardner letter to T.W.C., Jr., November 21, 1975, and in the hands of the latter.

community. In most things that were done in the Seminary it was made sure that we were involved. In that way we were able to contribute to the life of the school, and in a small way to the life of the Kingdom of Christ. I think it is significant to say that one of the unique contributions of Austin Seminary is its role to foster inter-denominational dialogue. . . .

The one thing I hope Austin Seminary will give more attention to is its ministry to minority groups.[25]

Michael F. Murray, will never forget "the day Dietrich Ritschl talked about being bombed in Germany—only to discover that John Albrecht, one of his students, had flown in that raid." Another memorable event was the trip aboard the private plane supplied by Toddie Lee Wynne to see the agencies of the General Assembly at Nashville, Richmond, and Atlanta. Further, Murray told of, "the awareness, which grew out of talking with students from other seminaries, that what I received at Austin was very solid, basic and historical."

Judging from others reporting on McCormick and others, their studies tended to focus more on Theology and Modern Literature or the Sociology of Religion. I perceived these students from other seminaries to be lacking in a solid historical study of the church and theology.

The care and concern of John Jansen, my advisor, when my wife was ill.[26]

The responsibilities of Henry W. Quinius for summer field work supervision did not go unappreciated by George A. McCall.

Dr. Quinius' efforts as Director of Field Work may not always have been as greatly appreciated as they ought to have been. I recall that in my first summer of field work, while serving as a student assistant pastor at Westminster Church in Port Arthur, Dr. Quinius' visit was a very important and supportive occasion. I wonder how many seminaries then or now provide for their students the kind of encouragement that he provided as he traveled around every summer to visit each and every student engaged in field work. I wonder also how many students must have heard Dr. Quinius' pre-summer speech which always had in it a list of all the terrible perils that we would certainly fall into

---

[25] Clement H. Janda letter to T.W.C., Jr., December 4, 1975, and in the hands of the latter.

[26] Michael F. Murray letter to T.W.C., Jr., December 23, 1975, and in the hands of the latter.

in the ensuing months. The speech had as a constant refrain "I know you're going to do it—they do it every year!" My recollection is that the summer experience when we all gathered back at seminary the next fall and reported was such that this prediction of recurring catastrophe was never different from what actually had happened.[27]

On the afternoon of Tuesday, April 15, 1975, a doubles game was just beginning on the Seminary handball court. Dr. Currie, one of the four, who seemed perfectly fit, collapsed. No first aid, no emergency measures on the way to or in the hospital, availed. At the peak of his powers he died.

Two days later in a special edition of *The Forum*, a senior, Ray Maxwell, wrote: "I do not believe it is possible to say all that could be said concerning the man, Stuart Currie, and what he has meant to so many people in so many different ways. But suffice it to say that in many ways we know that we have been torn by a sudden sense of separation from someone truly unique in the lives of most of us who were acquainted with him. This is true not only for those who have known him for many years—for many of whom he was 'Stuart'—but also for those who have known him for only a short time—to whom he was always, 'Dr. Currie' and we were 'Mr., Miss, or Mrs. _____.' The phrase, 'Whence comes such another,' rings in my ears as I remember the man: kind, strong, brilliant, compassionate, insightfully humorous, awesome, challenging, encouraging, questioning, overwhelming, humble, and courteous. Courteous. It is a word I have heard him use on more than one occasion, and, while I never have been able to fathom all that the idea of courtesy meant for Dr. Currie, I knew that he mentioned it often in the hearing of myself and of others, not by accident: one shoe dropped, one clue given, one avenue suggested. At present, as I try to come to grips with what I remember about courtesy from his lips, I find it has to do with that appropriate attitude which one human being takes when approaching another, that deference to others which one adopts, not as strategy, but as appropriation of consideration for the neighbor that one must adopt when one sees in the mirror of scripture the image of Jesus, the lowly servant, in whom the exalted Lord resides, and considers alongside it, one's own self-image.

"There are hundreds of stories, anecdotes, remembrances of this man, who will take umbrage with us should we try to idolize him,

[27] George A. McCall, *op. cit.*

but whose own lifestyle, which forms the content of our memory of him, will mostly work against that. We will, nonetheless, remember— each in our own particular way—and we will share our memories in this APTS community which always has far more 'togetherness' than we often realize, speculate about our failings as we may.

"I have my own memories, of course, and I will share a couple of them now.

"There was the day that I, a racketballer, decided to see what this game of handball was all about and attempted to propel the ball around a little bit with a fellow student who was warming up in preparation for a foursome of which Stuart Currie was a member. The other three members of the foursome soon arrived, and I, already red-handed, left the court, and said something to the effect that I didn't think my hands were intended for handball. I received the reply, 'There are some folks for whom that might be true . . . like surgeons and concert pianists.'

"There was the time I turned in my first late paper at APTS. It happened to be the first section of Mark exegesis. I apologized when I turned it in, and was told, 'Well, I try not to grade them before I get them.'

"That was the first paper I ever turned over to Dr. Currie. The last I turned in, ironically, I found returned to me in my mailbox, Tuesday, April 15. In it I had tried to wrestle in sermonic discourse with I John 1:5–2:2 (One-Eyed John), and tried to get my mind wrapped around the idea of the church as a fellowship of forgiven sinners. I received from Dr. Currie this notation on my sermon, (along with a tiny, almost imperceptible, but highly prized 'S') :

'Maybe it goes like this—
Are you a sinner?
    Well, yes & no!
Come again?
    Well, I was, I will be, but I am not.
Are you sure?
    Maybe I should say, I am: I wasn't; but thanks to him
I know I was—but then couldn't have known what I was.
But though I am, I need not be.
Off again, on again?
    Something like that. Better: I'm his sheep. One he
knows: old flop-ear, old crook-shank. He calls me by name.
I know his voice now, and now when he calls I know it is to
lead me in and out, to pasture, out of dangerous paths, back

to light. Mutton-head, perhaps, but his! None too wise, but safe with the Shepherd. See John 10:27f.''[28]

The reference in John reads: "My sheep hear my voice, and I know them and they follow me: and I give unto them eternal life; and they shall never perish, neither shall any man pluck them out of my hand."

William S. Caldwell drew two thumbnail sketches:

Rev. Walter Johnson was much more than just a Professor of Homiletics—one who helped us with the mechanical parts of writing and delivering a sermon. He truly showed us that just being a good speech-giver was never enough. This speech must be deeply integrated into the Word of God in contemporary terms. He would really drive us to understand the situation in which the original word was addressed. However, he never left the issue there. He forced us, through very helpful criticism, to really understand ourselves and the congregation whom we would be addressing with the truth of God's word. As a result we were not allowed to get sloppy in our interpretation of theology but allowed to see it as the main reason for sermon preparation and delivery. Walter took a great personal interest in each of us who were fortunate enough to be his students, with the result that our uniqueness was always being stressed. Walter's own life was an important witness to us. I was his student during the time that he first came down with incurable cancer. Yet through it all he always was in good spirits. He never let us think that he was any less whole because he had this dread disease. Instead he radiated the truth that wholeness is always more than a lack of physical ailment—it is oneness with God, in faith and trust. This always shone like a bright star in the many conversations that he held with us, not only in class, but in his office and many bull-sessions at his home. I am sure that I am a better preacher from having had the opportunity to have this kind of Homiletics Professor.

Dr. Stuart Currie and his tremendous intellectual ability served to really whet my mind for further knowledge. He would scare me through his great knowledge, but I always knew that this wasn't a put-down on his part. Over and again he showed us that we must have knowledge first hand if we were to communicate God's love. He wouldn't sit still if we used big words in our sermons. Instead he always reminded us that we needed to hit

[28] Ray Maxwell, "Separated, But Not From Blaze of Memory." Austin Presbyterian Theological Seminary: *The Forum,* an occasional paper in the hands of T.W.C., Jr.

people where they were with the truth in simple two syllable language. Never in my life have I ever been around another person like Dr. Currie who could tell so many interesting local stories to bring his point home. Because of his inspiration I know that I try to use much simpler language and many more illustrations. I also know that my discontent with the status quo is the result of his leading.[29]

One of the short-term teachers was a bachelor, Dr. Grover Foley, who taught theology during the sabbatical leave of J. Rodman Williams. John R. Evans commented, "Grover lived in the dormitory (single men's) but was little known and not often seen. He would rise before daybreak, characteristically walk (he did a lot of that!) to his office and study, standing up, at a desk which had been especially prepared for him. Students in the dorm could only speculate that he was reading Barth or Brunner; his sentiments and theologizing were more consistently Barthian. Rumor had it that he had asked a young girl to marry him, but reconsidered when he learned that she had not read all of Barth's theological volumes!"[30]

The matter of support for student and family was met in various ways. Sam Lanham had practiced law in Waco. When he and his family came to the Seminary, he first worked for the Texas Insurance Commission and then for five semesters taught in The University of Texas School of Law. He and his wife managed some apartments and she received a grant to complete her Master's Degree in special education. Further, he recalled

. . . the seminary represented a great turning point for me theologically. I came to the seminary out of a very conservative central Texas Baptist background. I had always been interested in biblical scholarship and had never bought the biblical literalist view of scripture. But from an ethical standpoint I was very very conservative. I was opposed to any form of social action by the church and during my first year at seminary I fought long and hard over this issue with various members of the faculty. What I found from the faculty, however, was by no means any form of condemnation but instead considerable help and legitimate disputation which no doubt laid the ground work for some things to happen later. I experienced a kind of ethical awaken-

29 William S. Caldwell letter to T.W.C., Jr., November 12, 1975, and in the hands of the latter.
30 John R. Evans letter to T.W.C., Jr., November 7, 1975, and in the hands of the latter.

ing while studying church history under Dr. E. T. Thompson. I've always been an amateur historian and I seem to respond to historical categories. Therefore, Dr. Thompson's courses were a real "aha" experience for me as I saw the development of the whole matter of church and social concern. All of a sudden the ethical dimensions of Christianity took on a completely new look for me and I look back on that as a religious experience of equal significance to some of the more dramatic ones which shifted me from the law practice to the seminary. I will always be grateful for the atmosphere of love and understanding which formed the background for the reception of Dr. Thompson's wisdom.[31]

As Michael Renquist pondered over his time at the Seminary, he wrote:

There have been times when I thought my seminary had failed me miserably in preparing me for the practice of ministry. And then I chuckle at my pretentiousness: maybe God wasn't ready for me to learn yet what was being offered to me at the time.

There have been times when I was very proud of my seminary: when some lucid learning, long ago thought forgotten, snakes its way into my consciousness or when I read of the response the seminary has made to the changing styles of ministry in the 70's.

What I think and feel about the seminary I left is generally what I think and feel about the ministry that I am still committed to. There are times when I feel damned for having said yes, and times when I unabashedly glow with confidence and self-approval. Like a kaleidoscope that waits for a nudge before shifting and changing, so too is my image of the ministry and the seminary. Change. Maybe that's the contribution that was most important. Gearing myself for change. Being comfortable with change. Being comfortable with being comfortable about change. Not having to worry about trying to keep up some image or reflection or role but letting the bits and pieces that make up the kaleidoscope that we call life—and death and life again—fall where they may.[32]

A whole generation of students watched Walter Johnson die. Kenneth D. Altfather spoke for others as well as for himself when he said:

---

31 Sam Lanham letter to T.W.C., Jr., November 25, 1975, and in the hands of the latter.
32 Michael Renquist letter to T.W.C., Jr., received December 10, 1975, and in the hands of the latter.

. . . the most poignant recollection is of Walter Johnson and his process of dying while I was there. During my three years at the seminary we all knew as did Walter that he had terminal cancer. There were weeks that we did not know whether we would have class with him or not because he might be in Houston receiving treatment. In a way we were all working through the grief process in preparation of death with him. When he died in the spring of my senior year, we all participated in the Memorial Worship Service at Westminster Church. The church was full and we all sang the great hymns of the church. I particularly remember singing "For All the Saints" and noting that there were not many dry eyes in the house. As we all bore the pain of our grief we loudly sang, and it was at this point that I realized the joy of our hope and resurrection amid the pain of death. This was a moving experience for me in my personal theological pilgrimage and one which has aided me throughout my ministry.[33]

Another who remembered circumstances attendant on Walter Johnson's death was Robert Donald Lively.

Without a doubt, the most meaningful experience for me as a seminarian occurred with the death of Dr. Walter Johnson, who was homiletics professor at the seminary. The expressions of grief to this particular death were too numerous to be recounted here, but there was a common denominator in this multitude of expression. And that common denominator was that in death, as in life, this servant of the Lord Jesus Christ strengthened the faith of the community of which he was a member. His widow offered perhaps the most profound expression in the form of a response to Dr. Rachel Henderlite in the hallway of M. D. Anderson Hospital hours, perhaps minutes, before his passing from this existence. Dr. Henderlite hugged the young widow-to-be and courageously and compassionately spoke these few words: "Keep the faith baby." The young woman returned the hug with these words: "It's the faith that is keeping me."

For weeks the seminary community had cried, had prayed formally and spontaneously, had stayed awake and had waited for the cancer to work its conspiracy against the body. And it finally happened that he quit breathing in March. We buried him in a family plot just east of the city of Austin. The leaves had just begun to burst from the branches as we stood there at his grave-

[33] Kenneth D. Altfather letter to T.W.C., Jr., November 20, 1975, and in the hands of the latter.

222

side on that cold Spring morning. The line of cars proceeded from the tiny cemetery to a standing-room-only sanctuary where Joe Cochran and John Evans led this body of believers in a liturgy which had been written just weeks before by the deceased. I wept unashamedly as I watched his daughter, who was then a fifth-grader, hang a banner in the chancel area which read "Celebrate Life." In all, it was the most glorious witness to the resurrection in which I have yet had the honor of participating.[34]

The atmosphere of the Seminary was impressive to John R. Blue: "My Seminary days are remembered by the love, concern, and compassion each person had for me. They each knew me in a different way and during a different time. I came one day saying, 'Here I am.' For four years all said, 'Good!' You cannot beat that type of love."[35]

For some the Seminary meant toil, as Neil Weatherhogg recalls, "Our three years in Austin and my three years at Austin Seminary were both the 'best of times and the worst of times.' Three years of financial and spiritual struggle tried the souls of both Janet, my wife, and me. Three years of intense work—she taught public school music and earned her Master's Degree in music at the same time; I often held down three jobs while taking a full load at the seminary. . . ."[36]

Stuart Dickson Currie had been born not far from the Seminary, raised on its campus, schooled by its teachers. He taught in its classrooms, worshipped in its chapel, died within its walls. His father had been its president. Stuart Currie loved it for what it had been, for what it was, for what it could be in the Kingdom.

As a youth he had at the Choate School shown an indication of his lifetime interests by winning prizes in Bible and German. After being graduated from The University of Texas and Austin Seminary in 1945 he served pastorates successively at Haskell and Taylor, Texas, and at Fulton, Missouri. His Ph.D. was awarded by Emory University, Atlanta, Georgia. He taught in the Bible department at Queens College, Charlotte, North Carolina, 1956–61, and came to the Seminary in the fall of 1961. First he taught Church History, but in 1964 became Professor of New Testament Languages and Exegesis.

[34] Robert Donald Lively letter to T.W.C., Jr., December 5, 1975, and in the hands of the latter.

[35] John R. Blue letter to T.W.C., Jr., December 2, 1975, and in the hands of the latter.

[36] Neil Weatherhogg letter to T.W.C., Jr., received December 21, 1975, and in the hands of the latter.

The last fourteen years of his life at the Seminary left an indelible impression on many students. Dr. Currie was, for instance, one of those before whom a student was required orally to display his mastery of the content of the New Testament. If in earlier times the faculty sermon had been a traumatic experience, this content examination, later, proved to have its own special hazards. Robert D. Lively recalls,

Perhaps my most anxious moment of that year occurred on December 11, 1969 (I still remember the date). I had to appear before Dr. Stuart D. Currie for the purpose of convincing this one-of-a-kind scholar that I had mastered the content in the Gospel narratives as well as in the book of The Acts of the Apostles. I waited nervously outside Dr. Currie's office while some colleague, unbeknownst to me, snatched victory from the jaws of failure as he mumbled through his confused recollections of the Sermon on the Mount. After four minutes, which seemed to me like four weeks, the door swung open, and a frightened student briskly walked past my station. The student mumbled something about having forgotten Matthew, but I failed to hear him exactly in that I was concentrating so intensely upon his paled facial coloration.

I tried to appear confident as I made my way into the professor's office. Dr. Currie passed me in the door, and he asked over his shoulder if I would like to have some coffee. I responded as politely as possible that I was not in need of any coffee, and Dr. Currie in turn responded with: "Well, I hope that this doesn't mean that it's going to be a dry run." I was ready to faint. Dr. Currie returned to the office. I shook almost uncontrollably in a chair just opposite his awesome desk, and Dr. Currie waited patiently for me to begin. But, not knowing where to begin, I said nothing. Again, it was probably four minutes but it seemed like four years, Dr. Currie broke the silence. "Mr. Lively, where do you propose that we begin." I had convinced myself that it was better not to gamble with this man, and consequently I meditated before that fact that if confronted with the question of what I knew and didn't know, I would be honest. And, so I was honest in my response, "Dr. Currie," I uttered on dry lips, "I'll shoot you straight. I know Mark well. I know John very well. And I know Acts extremely well, but when I start with Luke it comes out Matthew, and when I begin with Matthew, it invariably sounds like Luke." I waited in silence for the professor's response. Dr. Currie gazed down at me and said: "Mr. Lively, I don't care where it is that you begin, I just want you to con-

224

vince me that you read the book and didn't see the movie."
Somehow I passed that hour oral examination. . . .[37]

Currie had his own way of bringing commonsense to any situation
and of exposing cant no matter with what pseudo-piety it might be
clothed.

> . . . It seems that Dr. Stuart Currie was taking a walk across
> the campus of The University of Texas. This was in the early
> seventies when every major campus in this country was being
> besieged by Christian student movements which were charac-
> teristically fundamental and conservative in doctrine. And it was
> the prevalent opinion of most seminarians at this time in history
> that such movements were both shallow and temporal.
> Well, anyway Dr. Currie was enjoying his stroll through this
> state's mammoth mega-versity when he was interrupted by a
> young zealous Christian who was interested to know whether or
> not this middle-aged gentleman (Dr. Currie) knew Jesus Christ
> as his Lord and Savior. The young zealot prefaced his approach
> to the professor with these remarks: "Sir, you know, I love you
> and God loves you." Dr. Currie responded: "Well, you know,
> half of that is good news."[38]

A former Houston police officer who had much to do with organizing an inner-city congregation, the University Presbyterian Church
in Houston, Lionel Hallonquist, painted a picture of his most memorable character.

> There was a man who I knew upon first sight was "strange,"
> for he dressed like no other professor that I had ever seen (san-
> dals and off-color tie), always had a plug of tobacco in his mouth
> (or at least I assume he did, but I wonder where the juice went).
> In addition, he read in class from the Greek, Hebrew, and Latin
> original text as well as others that I didn't even know. He told
> us if we wanted to know history to go and read a book, for he
> understood his job as trying to enable the students to "feel" the
> different eras. He quoted verbatim, including page number,
> from the widest range of sources. Yes, he was a unique professor.
> I had always fancied myself as a pretty competent athlete, but
> now this "strange" man, 25 years my senior, surpassed me in
> baseball (either right or left handed), wore me to a frazzle on
> the handball court, and generally caused me to stand in awe.
> But there was another side to the man. There was a man of

[37] Robert Donald Lively, *op. cit.*
[38] *Ibid.*

tenderness who helped when I needed understanding, who ministered when I was physically ill, who always had an open door and a warm heart to support me.

That man was Stuart D. Currie whom God chose to serve and has now chosen to reign.[39]

One alumnus suggested that the seminary is a way-station where one's sense of call is taken seriously by devoted teachers who see themselves as succeeding to the degree their labors become for the student superfluous. To the degree the Seminary turns out professionals, it fails. Thomas White Currie, III brought his thoughts about the mission of the Seminary to a conclusion with the following:

Thus, the seminary trains men and women for work and not for their vocation. True, that work, as all work, is to be rendered to God in obedient service. But it is not rendered apart from the response of the whole person to the gracious calling (vocatio) of God. Indeed, in itself the work is merely that, work! It does not precede our call (we are not what we do) nor does it constitute our call (we do not appeal to it), but rather it follows from our call. This reflects, I think, the Reformers' understanding of the person and work of Jesus Christ. For we do not worship him because of what he does but rather because of who he is. His work follows from his person and we do not deduce his person from the mighty deeds which he achieved.

And yet the training which the seminary gives is always for the sake of pointing to the present reality of the living Lord. To train men and women for the gospel ministry is to train men and women to share in the ministry of Jesus Christ as it is carried out by the whole church. But this ministry, since it is his, can never attempt more than he himself attempted; nor can it attempt any less. It can "only" point to him as the Risen Christ and attest to his saving presence. It cannot then move on to point to itself as professionally competent and hence, a credible witness in the eyes of the world, a witness who should be received with proper respect.

No. Chaucer's parson suggests a different way, a way which finds "sufficiency in little things" and which seeks "no pomp or glory" in its dealings. I rather think that parson knew work when he saw it and was not tempted to elevate it by calling it anything else. And yet I think also he knew who he was and

[39] Lionel Hallonquist letter to T.W.C., Jr. dated December 17, 1975 and in the hands of the latter.

whose he was and what was required of him. Allow me to conclude with:[40]

Well ought a priest a fair example give
By his own cleanness, how his flock should live.
He set not his benefice to hire,
To leave his sheep encumbered in the mire
And run to London, to Saint Paul's
To find himself a chantry for souls,
Or with a brotherhood to dwell apart,
But rather on his flock's weal set his heart
So that the wolf might not lead them astray.
He was a shepherd and no mercenary.[41]

Currie was later to write:

Since the time that I wrote this article I have changed in my thinking somewhat. I do not disagree with anything that I said there but I would say it now very differently—not because I would wish to qualify or limit what I said there but more to underline and establish it on even firmer grounds. As I re-read the Chaucer, I was struck by the meaning of those words when applied to Jesus Christ. In the article I took them, as I think Chaucer himself probably meant them, as applying to this particular parish priest. But I wonder, when one begins to talk about faithfulness, about distinctions between shepherds and hirelings, about searching out those bogged down in the mire, about not escaping this world's needs but associating with them; when one begins to use this kind of language, are there not more biblical warrants for referring these words to God and *his* Good Shepherd? (e.g., Ezekiel 34, Jeremiah 23, and of course, John 10, Luke 15:3–7, and Psalm 23). Really, it is not the example of the parson that we want to recommend but the example of him who was *Priest*, as well as Prophet and King. To be sure, in his priesthood—a priesthood of faithfulness and unreserved commitment to God—we also have a share, but this share is granted to the whole church (1 Peter 2:9) so that the distinction between the parson and his flock is provisional and a matter of church order. It is a distinction that fades away in the face of that between Jesus Christ on the one hand and the sheep on the other. As you are aware this is really a Reformation insight. . . .[42]

---

40 Thomas W. Currie, III. *Austin Seminary Bulletin* LXXXIX, 4 (November 1973) , 54.
41 Translation from the middle English by Alison H. (Mrs. Thomas W.) Currie, Jr.
42 Letter from Thomas W. Currie, III, February 27, 1977, to T.W.C., Jr.

Field Education   18

In the early days the field work program of Austin Seminary was
a series of informal arrangements between students and congregations needing someone to preach Sunday by Sunday, with the president or one of the professors often acting as a contact person. There
was usually no shortage of needy congregations although there was
often shortage of funds. The vacant pulpits were often some distance
away. While the students were wanting experience and usually needing money that might be received as travel expense and honoraria,
there were also considerations of cost of travel and time required for
sermon preparation and travel, all of which had to be weighed
against obligations in the academic program.

The more formal organization of the field work effort, begun under C. Ellis Nelson and continued under James A. Millard,[1] was
developed more extensively by Henry W. Quinius who came to the
post August 1, 1955. The air lift occurred under the aegis of James
A. Millard. When the pilots graduated, the air lift had to be terminated, and the program resumed its more mundane character.

Considerations of distance and density of population and of concentration of Presbyterian congregations suggested that the effort
should be focused on the Austin and San Antonio areas. But transportation complications and the need to decentralize the work led
to organizing the field work program around a student's first summer
so that following his first year he would be expected to spend ten to
twelve weeks as student pastor, student assistant, as student minister
in a National Park, or in some similar work. He might be enrolled in
the Presbyterian Institute of Industrial Relations at McCormick
Theological Seminary, Chicago, or in a program at the Institute of
Religion in Houston in Clinical Pastoral Education.

In 1957 the Association of Directors of Field Work, a nationwide
organization of the American Association of Theological Schools,

[1] Henry W. Quinius letter to T.W.C., Jr., March 1, 1976, together with accompanying paper in the hands of the latter.

changed its name and its emphasis to "Field Education" with the idea that the student activities should be integrated into the curriculum of the theological school.[2] Consequently, at Austin Seminary there was inaugurated the Community Understanding Program. One Saturday night a student would ride with a taxi. Another Saturday night he would accompany a police officer. He would visit the Juvenile Detention Home, the Salvation Army Center. He would familiarize himself with the work of the Probation Officer and accompany a Public Health Nurse on her rounds. There were visits to the IBM Assembly Plant, to the Austin Council of the AFL-CIO, and to a meeting of Alcoholics Anonymous. There were opportunities to visit congregations and pastors of other races and denominations. Seminars followed the visits and speakers from the above mentioned and other segments of the community.

The summer work for students until the early sixties consisted largely of supplying in pastorless congregations. Increasingly, thereafter, the students found summer work as assistants to a pastor. The Director of Field Education visited each student during the summer for conference and counsel.

A program of internship was developed by means of which a student after his second year might spend from nine to fifteen months with a pastor or in some church agency. Usually, the intern was located within the Southwest but some were in New York, Missouri, and Florida. Some interns were at work in centers of Clinical Pastoral Education.

In 1969 the Field Education program for first-year students was revised. Students were assigned to visit and observe churches of various denominations and confer with the clergymen.

Although first-year students were still forbidden to preach in vacant churches, second- and third-year students were encouraged to go out two to three times per month. The Seminary has consistently encouraged candidates to live on campus or close by and not to try to combine their basic course with the effort to serve as even part-time pastor to a congregation. The feeling of the faculty was that the academic load ought to demand full time.

When the policy of the church was amended to allow women to be ordained, the Director of Field Education encountered no difficulty in gaining consent for women to be accepted on the circuit.[3]

---

[2] *Ibid.*, p. 3.
[3] *Ibid.*, p. 10.

The border between Field Education and Continuing Education was sometimes ill-defined. The Town and Country Pastors' Institute conducted at the Seminary from the twenties onward was changed. Still, with underwriting in part from the General Assembly and with a grant from the Hogg Foundation, Dr. Quinius annually led The Church In Community Institutes. These had a sequel, Management for the Ministry Seminars. The latter sought for the clergy the studies in conflict resolution, creative problem solving, etc., analogous to aids offered executives in industry.[4]

The consistent effort of the Field Education Department was to supply the students with the practical experience in various facets of the life and work of the church so that on graduation they would be better prepared to enter their chosen field of service.

Another side of this field work was the impact on the small churches to which the students went for one Sunday or for one semester or for an intern year, or served as part of a group for a limited time.

Perhaps the only Presbyterian Church in San Jacinto County will serve as a case in point. The church at Old Waverly is a country church off any highway. It is about ten miles east of New Waverly and about fifteen miles west of the county seat of Cold Spring. In 1950 the Waverly Presbyterian Church reported twenty-three communicants. By the end of 1975 it reported fifty-six. One of the members there, Mrs. Isabel Browder, reported: "Prior to our first contact with the Seminary we were having church services only one Sunday per month—on Sunday afternoon. We wanted to go to two Sundays per month, and try to have services at 11:00 a.m. We contacted Dr. Stitt in November, 1947 to see if it was possible to obtain student supply. He very willingly said this could be arranged, and according to our records, Earl Wiggins was the first student.

"These students (and their families if they were married) usually came to the home of one of our members on Saturday afternoon and spent the week-end. As we got to know them better, we naturally became very attached to them and prevailed on the Seminary to let them serve our church as long as possible, which in many cases was for several semesters each. The ones who really stand out in our minds because of length of service are: Earl Price, Hampton Bowman, Joel (Red) May, Bill Fogleman, Ralyn Parkhill, Charles Burton, C. Van Shaw, Meredith Bollinger, James Beverley, Norman

4 *Ibid.*, pp. 12, 13.

Honeycutt, Bob Lewis, Neil Weatherhogg, Douglas Hall, and John C. Hamby.

"Many of the students on the list were with us perhaps only a few times, so we could not really evaluate them, but our records do show that others on the list were with us numerous times, and were particularly liked as regards personality and preaching (and so advised the Seminary at the time). They were Earl Wiggins, James Mosley, Henry Freund, Bob Leslie, Theron Neese, Alan Farquhar, Geo. Fisher, Jr., J. E. Brock, John M. Brand, Cleve Wheelus, Carlton Eaton, Rodney Peacock, James F. Hardie, Jr., Martin Hager, and Tom Bailey.

"In 1966 we decided to try to have church every Sunday at 11:00 a.m., and it was necessary that we be served by many students, instead of one, or possibly two, and by this time we had become spoiled by having our favorites with us for long periods of time. Also, during the summer months it was becoming increasingly more difficult to obtain students, so we started working through the Presbytery, which in turn worked through the Seminary during the school year. In June, 1969, through Presbytery we were able to work out something full time with Mr. Bob Lewis, who took care of our services and the services of another small church or two in the area, so our connection with the Seminary ceased at that point.

"We will be forever grateful to Austin Seminary for its past efforts in our behalf, and of course, since we are such a small church and it is doubtful that we will ever be able to support a full-time pastor, there is always that chance that we may again someday be asking [the] Seminary for assistance."[5]

The growth of this congregation has not been spectacular. Hidden as it is within sight of only two or three residences, its survival is a testimony to the perseverance and fidelity of its members. But woven into the pattern of its growth has been the ministry brought to it through the only seminary that was in a position to help. This sort of field education was one of the singular ways in which the Seminary taught students the value of small things and the gallantry of devoted Christians who keep on keeping on.

[5] Mrs. Isabel Browder letter to T.W.C., Jr., September 25, 1975, and in the hands of the latter.

Development of the Curriculum
And a New President

19

When the Seminary began its work, the assumption was that the chief courses to be offered would be Church History, Systematic Theology, Old Testament Hebrew, and New Testament Greek together with Exegesis, Homiletics, Church Polity, and especially the content of the English Bible. This general format continued until the 40's.

Dr. E. R. Sims, a professor from the Spanish Department at The University of Texas, offered lectures in the Spanish-speaking area from 1925–1937. Full-time teachers in this area were Dr. O. C. Williamson, 1928–1933, and Dr. R. D. Campbell, 1933–1945. They were succeeded by The Rev. E. A. J. Seddon, Jr, 1945–1947, and the Rev. G. Wendell Crofoot, 1946–1947.

Christian Education received added emphasis with the coming of Dr. C. Ellis Nelson in 1940 whose work in the department continued until his departure to Union Theological Seminary, New York, in 1957.

Theology assumed its place as queen of the studies as it was taught by James I. McCord from 1944 until his departure to be president of Princeton Theological Seminary in 1959. In 1947 Dr. T. Watson Street came and brought new vigor to the department of Church History. His personal interest in missions and his annual spring trips with students to visit churches and missions in Mexico added a new perspective. James A. Wharton coming in 1956, John F. Jansen in 1958, Prescott H. Williams, Jr. in 1959, Stuart Currie in 1961 and W. Eugene March in 1964 gave verve to the Biblical studies. Rachel Henderlite came to the Christian Education Department in 1965 as the first woman professor. The seventies brought Edward Dixon Junkin (1970), Robert Shelton (1971) and Jack Martin Maxwell (1976), but saw the loss of David Stitt (into the pastorate in 1971), J. Rodman Williams (to the presidency of Melodyland School of Theology, Anaheim, California in 1972), Rachel Henderlite (retirement 1972), Henry W. Quinius (to the pastorate in 1975), James A.

L. Frank Moore, Board Chairman 1972–1973

Wharton (to the pastorate in 1975) and Stuart D. Currie (to death in 1975).

W. Walter Johnson came to teach homiletics in 1961 but died in 1970. George S. Heyer, Jr. came in 1964 to teach in the field of the history of doctrine. Calvin C. Klemt came as Librarian in 1966. In 1967 Ross D. Dunn came to teach Christian Ethics and to be the director of Continuing Education. In 1973 students began to be able to study pastoral care under William C. Spong. Merwyn S. Johnson began teaching Theology in 1974. The year 1975 saw the arrival of David Ng in the area of Church Program and Nurture, John E. Alsup in New Testament, J. Carter King in Supervised Practice of Ministry.

From the early years pastoral care had been taught tangentially with other subjects, but, as the demand for counselling on the part of ministers became heavier, the Seminary sought means of preparing students in this broad area. The connection with the therapy efforts at the State Hospital in Austin was established. The participation with the Institute of Religion in the Medical Center at Houston was effected. In 1972 Thomas H. Cole came to the Seminary as Visiting Professor of Pastoral Care. Furthermore, in recognition of the

234

William Speight McLean, Board Chairman
1974–1976

responsibility of the congregation in the institutional life of its community, Carl Siegenthaler came to the Seminary as Adjunct Professor of Urban Ministry in 1974.

From its beginning until 1971, the Seminary offered as its basic degree the Bachelor of Divinity. Beginning in 1948, in recognition of advanced work, the degree of Master of Theology was conferred. In the fall of 1971, the Seminary awarded its first Master of Divinity and began the next year to give this title to its basic theological degree. Then, in 1975, it began an emphasis on the "in sequence" and "in ministry" Doctor of Ministry degree. These innovations were part of the Seminary's continuing effort to offer candidates and ministers an increasing versatility and competence in the wide spectrum of demanding calls made on the clergy.

The awarding of a "Master of Divinity" grew out of the Seminary's participation in the American Association of Theological Schools, where the effort was being made to arrive at some standardization of clergy preparation. The word "bachelor" in a degree title was offensive to some who felt that three or four years study beyond a college degree merited a more imposing word than "bachelor." To some, the designation of "doctor" was a little too ponderous, and

235

besides, there was already a degree "Doctor of Theology." The basic theological degree of "Master of Divinity" and the advanced degree of "Doctor of Ministry" were the titles chosen over the light-hearted suggestion: "Wizard of Theology." The four seminaries related to the Presbyterian Church, U.S., kept in touch by means of The Southern Presbyterian Association of Theological Schools. The watchword of this S.P.A.T.S. was "and with twain he covered his feet."

The basic first degree offered by the Seminary in 1975–76, the Master of Divinity degree, entailed the prerequisites of a Bachelor's degree from some accredited university or college. As noted in the 1975–1977 catalogue, the work at the Seminary for this degree required satisfactory completion of 230 credits of required and elective work. (See chart,[1] pages 238–39).

Another degree, the Doctor of Ministry, was offered. Students could complete the requirements for this degree in an "in-sequence" fashion, adding an additional year to the study for the Master of Divinity degree. Or, if they preferred to complete the requirements "in ministry," they could matriculate after an interval while still continuing in the pastorate or other duty. Thus, they might plan to be in residence three consecutive weeks in January and/or in June, for a total of seven three-week periods in a maximum span of seven years.

Three areas of specialization were offered in the in-ministry Doctor of Ministry Program: 1) "Professional Competencies for Particular Ministries," 2) "The Bible and Proclamation in the Contemporary Church," and 3) "Ministry in the Bilingual, Multi-Cultural Southwest."[2]

The curriculum was consistently focused upon aiding students or ministers in the effort to increase their skill in serving in various facets of the life of the Church and the Kingdom.

Credit for much of the research and study eventuating in the expanded curriculum was due President Prescott H. Williams, Jr. The rapidly enlarging horizons of the task of the parish minister and the consequent need for new maps and guides led him, while he was dean, to begin inquiries which resulted in new course offerings in the basic degree and the continuing education courses leading to the Doctor of Ministry degree.

Dr. Prescott H. Williams, Jr. was inaugurated fifth President of the Seminary as a part of the proceedings of The Convention of

---

[1] *Austin Seminary Bulletin* XCI, 1 (August 1975), 37, 38, 39.
[2] *Ibid.*, p. 33.

Prescott Harrison Williams, President 1972–1976, Professor
of Old Testament Languages and Archaeology

Synod E (later, The Synod of Red River) meeting in the University
Presbyterian Church, Austin, Texas, Tuesday, September 26, 1972.[3]

Dr. Williams had given a new dimension to the Seminary curriculum through his archeological activities. These were concentrated for relatively brief periods in the years of 1962, 1964, 1966, and 1968. He was associated with Ernest Wright, with the American School of

3 1973 Minutes Synod of Red River, Presbyterian Church in the United States, *First Stated Meeting,* also Convention of Synod "E," No. II, Denton, Texas 76201, p. 89.

SCHEDULE OF REQUIRED COURSES

The courses required in the Master of Divinity program are distributed according to the following chart:

	FIRST YEAR Course	Credits	SECOND YEAR Course	Credits	THIRD YEAR Course	Credits
FALL TERM	Introduction to the History of the Christian Movement	8	The Theological Task in the Reformed Tradition	6	The Theological Task Today	6
	Introduction to the Old Testament	6	The Interpretation of New Testament Texts	4	The Church in Mission to the Community	4
	Introduction to the Theological Task	6	The Task of Teaching	6	Senior Preaching	4
	Introduction to the Church's Ministry and the Role of the Minister	6	The Church as a Worshiping Community	4	Reflections: Personal Ethics for Professional Ministry	2
	Reflections: Personal Religious Discipline	2	Reflections: Personal Responsibility to Ecclesiastical Traditions	2	SPM: The Church and its Community Setting	4
	SPM: Observations of the Minister at Work	4	SPM: The Data of the Bible	4		
		32		26		20
JANUARY TERM	Elementary Biblical Hebrew	8	The Theological Task in the Modern World	6	Denominational Christianity in its Historical Setting	4
	Introduction to Exegetical Skills	4	The Task of Pastoral Care Theory and Models of	6		
	Introduction to the New Testament	6				

SPRING TERM

Course	Credits
The Interpretation of Old Testament Texts: I & II Kings	4
The Theological Task in the Ancient and Medieval Church	4
Introduction to Christian Ethics	6
Reflections: Personal Religious Experience	2
SPM: Observations of Persons in the Helping Professions	4
	30
Church Administration	4
The Government of the Church	2
Reflections: Personal Theological Integrity	2
SPM: Leadership Skills in the Particular Church	4
	24

SUMMER TERM

Course	Credits
The Task of Preaching	6
Elementary New Testament Greek	16
Reflections: Personal Relations in the Christian Community	2
SPM: Directed Study Project	2
	26

In addition to these required courses, every candidate shall also elect:

a. at least eight additional credits in the Biblical Department (four of which shall be in Old Testament Exegesis and four of which shall be in New Testament Exegesis);

b. at least eight additional credits in the Theological-Historical Department;

c. at least eight additional credits in the Church's Ministry Department;

d. at least eighteen additional credits in the supervised practice of ministry mode.

NOTE: Courses required in the Master of Divinity program (both titles and descriptions) are subject to change by action of the Faculty.

Oriental Research in Jerusalem, and with the Department of Antiquities of Jordan. In 1968 the Seminary had been a full partner in the expedition to excavate on the site of ancient Shechem just east of the pass between Mt. Ebal and Mt. Gerizim. One of the Seminary students, Dan Hughs, was an assistant architect for that "dig" and one of the other professors, Dr. Stuart D. Currie, also participated. The 1964 expedition had discovered an idol, a baal, the image of a Syrian weather and fertility god against the worship of which the prophets of the Old Testament often warned.[4] Such excursions into the hidden relics of Bible times added interest as well as historical evidence to the Seminary curriculum.

In January of 1975 Dr. Williams decided that his chosen field was teaching and archeology rather than administration, and he announced his resignation from the office of President and returned to the chair of Old Testament Languages and Archeology effective no later than May 31, 1976.[5]

The task of Prescott Williams in succeeding Stitt in the office of President had been the more difficult because of the superlative fashion in which the Seminary had developed since 1945. Nevertheless, Williams proved to be a bridge. He presided over Seminary during a period in which it was demonstrated that the progress of the institution was far from automatic. The supporting synod learned that the time had come for more congregations and more candidates' committees and more able and generous givers to rally to the Seminary's cause. The load was too heavy for the few who had been expected to carry it.

It was in the spirit of gratitude for his efforts, of affection for him personally, of appreciation of his gifts in his field of Old Testament Languages and Archeology, and of his wisdom and courage in offering the reins of administration to a yet to be chosen successor that the Synod of Red River in Little Rock in 1975 gave Williams a standing ovation.

---

[4] *The Texas Presbyterian*, October 1964, vol. IV, no. 10, p. 6; November 1964, vol. IV, no. 11, p. 6; December 1964, vol. IV, no. 12; January 1965, vol. V, no. 1, pp. 2, 6. In the archives of Austin Seminary.

[5] Minutes of the Board, January 6, 1975.

Into the Last Quarter
Of the Twentieth Century

20

The Board of Trustees, meeting February 20, 1976, elected as the sixth President Dr. Jack Martin Maxwell. He began his work the following April 1 and was officially inaugurated at the meeting of the Synod of Red River in Dallas Tuesday, September 28, 1976.

Dr. Maxwell, a native of Morrilton, Arkansas, spent his youth in Corpus Christi, Levelland, and Andrews, Texas. He graduated from The University of Texas in Austin in 1960. From Princeton Theological Seminary he received his Master of Divinity degree in 1963 and his Doctor of Philosophy degree in Homiletics and Liturgics in 1968. After serving as an instructor in homiletics at Princeton Theological Seminary, he became pastor of the Presbyterian Church of Sewickley, Pennsylvania, a suburb of Pittsburgh.[1] His wife, the former Sandra Nagy, came from Lancaster, Pennsylvania.

Dr. Maxwell's interest in the nature of true worship led him to give special study to the struggles in the German Reformed Church of the middle 1800's concerning the liturgy, and the results of that investigation are to be found in his volume, *Worship and Reformed Theology, The Liturgical Lessons of Mercersburg.* After a careful analysis of the work of John Williamson Nevin and Philip Schaff and others, the reaction of the denomination to their efforts and other related events, Dr. Maxwell suggests the propriety of striking a new balance between Word and Sacrament in the ministry of the church, emphasizing particularly the fact that the true act of worship is corporate in nature.

In the Epilogue he remarks

> Since ours "must always be a liturgy of the tabernacle, never of the temple," that liturgy will change as God's pilgrim people continue to wander in and out of wilderness and promised land. Mercersburg was but a way station on that pilgrimage; yet if we remember those way stations in our past, we are better able to distinguish between the mirage and the oasis . . . the most im-

[1] *Austin Seminary Bulletin XCI*, 6 (March 1976), 1, 3.

Jack Martin Maxwell, President 1976–   , Professor of Homiletics
and Liturgics

portant lesson . . . is this: whatever else the liturgy may be, it is
the rhythmical heartbeat of that conglomeration of sinners who
become a community of saints when bread is broken and wine is
poured out in remembrance of Jesus Christ.

Blame us not if we value our liturgy: it embodies the anthems
of the saints; it thrills the heart with the dying songs of the
faithful; it is hallowed with the blood of the martyrs; it glows
with sacred fire.[2]

2 Jack Martin Maxwell, *Worship and Reformed Theology*. Pittsburgh Theological Monograph Series. Dikron Y. Hadidian, General Editor (Pittsburgh, Pennsylvania: The Pickwick Press, 1976), p. 413.

The Seminary to which Dr. Maxwell came differed in many respects from the institution to which his predecessors came. Dr. Sampson found a dream. Dr. Vinson found an infant. Dr. Currie found a sick waif. Dr. Stitt found an undernourished juvenile. Dr. Williams found an ambitious youth. Dr. Maxwell found a young adult ready for adventure and anxious to plunge ahead.

Dr. Robert Lewis Dabney, the first Professor of Mental and Moral Philosophy at The University of Texas and a teacher in the Austin School of Theology before the turn of the century, had been careful to avoid stepping on the rails of the new-fangled electric streetcars in Austin for fear of electrocution. Dr. Maxwell came to a Seminary located only a short way from the research center of The University of Texas where multi-million degree fusion experiments were seeking to harness the energy secrets of the sun and the stars. But the deepest needs of the children of men were the same as they were when Jesus agonized, saying "O Jerusalem, Jerusalem . . . how often would I have gathered thy children together, even as a hen gathereth her brood under her wings, but ye would not!"

The Presbyterian Church at the beginning of the final quarter of the twentieth century was not growing in numbers. The number of its missionaries abroad was diminishing and the communicant membership at home was shrinking. The flight from city to suburb and to recreation areas and second homes did not leave city churches unaffected. The sense of increasing population density where resources were limited on spaceship earth put a high premium on the pill. Women found new freedom and challenge beyond the tasks that had for so long bound them to home and child. The ordination of Rachel Henderlite, May 12, 1965, by the Presbytery of Hanover opened new vistas for women and for seminaries.

Women had taken Bible courses offered by Seminary teachers for credit in The University of Texas since 1910[3] and had audited other courses in the B.D. curriculum since the 20's. The first woman to be granted a degree (Bachelor of Religious Education) was Julia Mitchell Tarver in 1943.[4] The first alumna to be ordained was Patricia Ann McClurg, B.D., of the class of 1967 by the Presbytery of Brazos, July 9, 1967.[5] As the number of women candidates began to increase the Seminary entered the final quarter of the twentieth century as a coeducational institution.

There were all too few Mexican-Americans and Blacks in the Presbyterian Church, and this deficiency was reflected in the Seminary community. There were a number of Mexican-American congrega-

Arch McD. Tolbert, Board Chairman 1976–

tions and a number of those of Mexican-American heritage in predominantly Anglo congregations in the Synod of Red River. There were fewer than a dozen Black congregations and not many integrated congregations in the Synod. The Seminary had numbered in its student body from time to time a dozen Blacks including ecu-

---

3 "Religion at The University of Texas," a brochure published by the Association of Religious Teachers, University of Texas, May 17, 1956, n.p., pages unnumbered, in the Seminary Library.

4 *Austin Seminary Bulletin.*

5 E. D. Witherspoon, Jr., Compiler, *Ministerial Directory of the Presbyterian Church U.S. 1861–1967* (Doraville, Georgia: Foote & Davies, 1967), p. 352.

menical students. Two of these served Presbyterian congregations after Seminary days, Ellis Larry Green and David Oliver Shipley.

In a Synod within whose bounds so many reside who are not white Anglo-Saxon Protestants there is a mighty challenge for the church to mount new efforts to confront every segment of society with the grace of the living Saviour and for the Seminary to redouble its commitment to welcoming and preparing those who can be instrumental in this evangelistic enterprise to reach their optimum usefulness.

In an era when shortages of many kinds compound the erosion of inflation and when the world of plenty seems bent on becoming a world of want, in an era when cynicism, materialism, the passion for comfort and amusement gnaw at the vitals of faith, when the very miracles of modern medicine not only yield health and healing but also aggravate and prolong the agonies of what once were fatal illnesses into helpless senility or worse, in an era when man can walk on the moon but fears to walk downtown at night, in an era when an energy-hungry world is crying out for a cornucopia more nearly inexhaustible than Spindletop, the new president was called on to lead board, faculty, and students another step after Him who, bearing all the burden of sin and facing Good Friday and Golgotha, proclaimed, "Be of good cheer! I have overcome the world!"

Epilogue: A Look Ahead

Austin Presbyterian Theological Seminary has been a small seminary of a small denomination. For seventy-five years it has served a community composed largely of white, middle-class citizens of the Southwest. Although its constituency was not untouched by the sentiments of the Old South and of the Bible Belt, and while the Seminary has shown a constant loyalty to the fundamentals of the faith, there has also been a courageous openness to the developments in the critical study of scripture and to ethical imperatives of the Christ-taught conscience. The impulses have not been toward revolution, but toward constructive, creative work within the ongoing life of the fellowship of Christ.

The Seminary has been an agency to aid in training candidates to serve as ministers in Mexican-American congregations, but the number of candidates by the seventies had diminished almost to the vanishing point. Although some of the ecumenical students were Black, very few Black candidates from the Southwest studied at the Seminary. The increase in Black and Brown and Indian congregations may parallel and, perhaps, be an essential factor in the increase of candidates from these groups. This may need to be the case at least until there are widespread multi-racial components in many congregations and until there is a readiness in churches to accept ministers of various ethnic backgrounds.

The five years between the resignation of David Stitt and the calling of Jack Maxwell were marked by continual change and many difficulties of a particularly frustrating character. The unceasing battle of financing continued, taking a greater toll because of growing inflation. Efforts to enlarge the financial base, expand the library, increase the endowment met with little success, while needs became, if anything, more clamant.

Despite the financial struggles, a widespread sense of what the Seminary has been and what it can be gave evidence of its influence. Large congregations of the Presbyterian churches in Arkansas,

Louisiana, Oklahoma, and Texas could look afar for ministerial leadership; however, small and medium-sized congregations and embryonic churches were much more dependent for preachers on indigenous candidates and on a local school. In the symbiotic relation between the congregations of the Presbyterian Church, U.S., in the Southwest and the Seminary, one could readily identify the contribution of the Seminary as seminal to an authentic and faithful witness.

The early seventies saw massive changes in the faculty and administration. Then came the resignation from the office of President of Prescott Williams to take effect no later than May 31, 1976.

To these difficulties was added the general malaise of the early seventies. There was the controversy concerning the involvement of the nation in a long, undeclared war in Southeast Asia. President Richard M. Nixon who helped extricate the U.S. from Vietnam himself left the office of President Friday, August 9, 1974, a discredited man.

It was during these same early seventies that the General Assembly of the Presbyterian Church, U.S., in the process of reorganizing its boards and consolidating them in Atlanta, countenanced a repudiation of able and devoted executives, thus incurring waste of human and financial resources and loss of confidence on the part of many.

The Seminary did not escape the effects of the riptides of disillusionment with leaders. Some laymen harbored the unwarranted opinion that the Seminary was not sufficiently committed to the Bible and to the standards of the church. Others were convinced that the Seminary had not sufficiently broadened its view of the wide spectrum of theological education. Still others felt that there was too big a gap between the preparation offered at the Seminary and the realities of the parish. There was a readiness to believe that things were not going as they should at the Seminary and a temptation to look elsewhere for what the Seminary ought to be offering.

These had been tough years for all concerned, but with the coming of Jack Maxwell the opportunity for a new stability, a new mutual esteem and trust between the Seminary and its constituency in the Synod of Red River, a new base for further progress seemed to be at hand.

Seldom, if ever, has the Seminary lit the fire of faith and commitment, but frequently it has blown upon that flame and shown where fuel was to be had. If the Seminary could not heal withered hands, the Seminary could when these hands have received the touch of the

248

Master, display the choice of handles that might be seized. The Seminary could not issue a call to the ministry of the Word and sacraments, but it could light a candidate's way as he or she tried to hear and heed that call and to follow him who came not to be ministered unto, but to minister and to give his life a ransom for many. The Seminary might not be able to clean the Augean stables of pride and prejudice within the church, but it could point to a greater than Hercules who cleansed the temple and reminded us, "My house shall be called a house of prayer for all nations." The Seminary could not save mankind or nation, but it could show the heralds of God where the trumpets might be found and offer music lessons. The Seminary could never be the light of the world, but it could direct lost spelunker guides toward the mouth of the cave. The Seminary could not coerce the Holy Spirit to mount a crusade for the evangelization of the world in this generation, but it could remind that this is the only generation we'll ever have in which to bring that Good News to all mankind.

There is the tale of St. Peter tending the pearly gates. Hearing a knocking, he asked, "Who's there." The reply came, "It is I, Mary Jones." St. Peter is reported to have muttered: "O glory! here comes another English teacher!" Well, St. Peter to the contrary notwithstanding, one of the tasks of the Seminary is to deliver to the church a ministry that is at home in the mother tongue of those it seeks to serve, so the hearers are not distracted by language that is crippled, defective, incorrect. It is no accident that Presbyterian ministers— such as William Holmes McGuffey—have long distinguished themselves as teachers.

One element in the equipment of any minister of the Gospel is the "semper fidelis." It is a grievous handicap, difficult to overcome, never to have been part of a tiny, struggling congregation, a "home mission" church where survival always seemed touch and go, where it was painfully obvious that every person was of crucial importance. The character that grows, the links that are forged, the sacrifices that come to be taken for granted in such situations are often hard to come by in larger, more affluent congregations. In the latter, individual responsibility seems sometimes to be blurred, if not lost. The welfare and the potential of the congregation does not seem to be compromised quite so severely if one person is absent or one teacher is out or one offering envelope is missing. In a small struggling church there is the opportunity to develop a "sink or swim" quality of loyalty and devotion, a costly faith and faithfulness, a discipline that is close to the heart of true discipleship.

There is something to be pitied in the life of a minister whose experience lacks such training. No doubt, other settings offer the opportunity to develop such depth of sympathy, such perseverance in the faith, such winsome valor, but, at least, in retrospect, there is much a veteran of such a church has to be thankful for. There is the lesson to be learned: not to despise the day of small things, not to quench the smoking wick.

There is much about being faithful in a small, discouraging situation that can prepare a person for larger responsibilities. However, this observation is not to be taken as an over-rosy, romantic view of the town and country church. One professor[1] listened to a young minister who had ideas about the importance of serving in a rural community. Then he remarked that it should never be forgotten that the ministry of the church is to people, and in our society the places where people are concentrated are the cities.

In cities or in more pastoral settings, people high and low, rich and poor, old and young, wise or foolish, black, white, red, or brown, for their very life need the Gospel. They need those ministers of the Word, lay or otherwise, who are competent, but not professional, who are compassionate, but not condescending, who, as D. T. Niles is reported once to have said, act like one starving man telling another starving man where they can find bread.

As a community of the Word, by sitting at the feet of missionaries and evangelists, by listening to profound theologians, by watching the methods of teachers, by entering into worship and proclamation, by exposure to challenges calculated to quicken the conscience, and, most of all, by parting a veil of ignorance, the Seminary invites a student to hear a knock on the heart's door, and, if he or she will, to lift the latch and invite the Saviour himself to enter and to mount the throne of his or her life.

The Seminary can never rightly offer its students aids toward success, but it can point to a pelican who for the saving of her brood pours out her own life's blood, to a skull-shaped hill beyond the city wall, to an empty cross, an empty tomb, and to a living Saviour who calls his disciples not to be successful, but to be faithful. The Seminary can help us to hear and, by his grace, to join the chorus of "ten thousand times ten thousand, and thousands of thousands, saying with a loud voice, 'Worthy is the Lamb that was slain to receive

---

[1] Thomas W. Currie in a conversation recalled by Thomas W. Currie, Jr.

power, and riches, and wisdom, and strength, and honor, and glory, and blessing.' " And to share the conviction that he shall reign forever and ever. Hallelujah!

APPENDICES

APPENDIX I
The Faculty

THE AUSTIN SCHOOL OF THEOLOGY, 1884–1895

Accessus   *Exitus*

Professors:

1884	R. K. Smoot, D.D.—Church History and Government	1895
1884	R. L. Dabney, D.D., LL.D.—Theology	1895

Instructors, Assistant & Associate Professors:

1884	G. L. Bitzer, D.D.—Hebrew, Greek	1885
1885	Archibald Alexander Little—Hebrew, Greek	1886
1886	William Stuart Red—Hebrew, Greek	1888
1888	Thomas Cary Johnson—Hebrew, Greek	1890
1890	John McLeod Purcell—Sacred Rhetoric and Biblical History	1891
1891	William Jared Tidball—Hebrew, Greek	1895
1891	Jacob Amos Lefevre—Polemic and Didactic Theology and Exegesis	1894

AUSTIN PRESBYTERIAN THEOLOGICAL SEMINARY TO 1976

Professors:

1902	T. R. Sampson, D.D., LL.D.—President (1900–1905) Church History, Polity	1915
1902	S. A. King, D.D.—Systematic Theology, Emeritus	1914
1902	R. E. Vinson, D.D., LL.D.—Old Testament Languages and Exegesis, English Bible, Practical Theology, President (1909–1916)	1916
1903	R. K. Smoot, D.D., LL.D.—Church History, Polity	1905
1904	E. D. Brown, D.D.—Hebrew and Greek	1906
1906	Eugene C. Caldwell, D.D., LL.D.—Old Testament Languages and Exegesis	1914
1908	S. E. Chandler, D.D.—Greek	1909
1910	J. L. Bell, D.D.—New Testament Language and Exegesis	1913
1911	Thomas W. Currie, D.D.—English Bible, Church History, President (1922–1943)	1943
1913	S. M. Glasgow, D.D.—Greek, Homiletics	1914
1914	W. Angus McLeod, D.D.—Systematic Theology	1918
1915	Robert L. Jetton, D.D.—New Testament Language and Exegesis	1918
1916	Neal L. Anderson, D.D.—Acting President	1917

Accessus *Exitus*

1921 Arthur Gray Jones, D.D., LL.D.—Systematic Theology 1927
Emeritus
1923 Robert F. Gribble, D.D.—Old Testament Languages 1960
and Exegesis, Emeritus
1926 S. L. Joekel, D.D.—English Bible, Religious Education 1954
1927 George Summey, D.D., LL.D.—Systematic Theology, 1940
Pastoral Theology, Emeritus
1938 Eugene W. McLaurin, D.D., Ph.D.—Systematic 1958
Theology, New Testament Language and Exegesis,
Polity, Emeritus
1945 David L. Stitt, D.D., LL.D.—President, Pastoral 1971
Theology
1946 James I. McCord, D.D., LL.D.—Systematic Theology, 1959
Dean
1948 C. Ellis Nelson, D.D., Ph.D.—Christian Education 1957
1949 T. Watson Street, D.D., Th.D.—Church History and 1961
Missions
1952 James A. Millard, D.D., Th.D.—Homiletics 1959
1957 Henry Willard Quinius, Jr., B.B.A., Th.M., D.D.— 1975
Church Administration and Director of Field
Education
1958 J. Donald Butler, Ph.D.—Christian Education 1961
1958 John F. Jansen, Th.D.—New Testament Interpretation ——
and Acting Dean (1959–62)
1964 Stuart Dickson Currie, Ph.D.—New Testament 1975
Language and Exegesis
1964 J. Rodman Williams, Ph.D.—Systematic Theology and 1972
Philosophy of Religion
1964 Prescott Harrison Williams, Jr., Ph.D.—Old Testament ——
Languages and Archaeology; 1966, Dean of Faculty;
1971, Acting President; 1972–1976, President
1965 Rachel Henderlite, Ph.D.—Christian Education 1971
(Visiting Professor of Christian Education, Emerita,
1971–72)
1967 James Allen Wharton, Th.D.—Old Testament 1975
1973 Wallace Eugene March, Ph.D.—Old Testament ——
1975 Robert M. Shelton, Ph.D.—Homiletics ——
1976 Jack Martin Maxwell, Ph.D.—President, Homiletics ——
and Liturgics
1976 Edward Dixon Junkin, Th.D.—Dean, Church History ——

Instructors; Assistant, Adjunct, Associate and Visiting Professors:

Accessus		*Exitus*
1914	Robert F. Gribble, B.A., B.D., D.D.—Instructor in Hebrew and New Testament Greek	1918
1921	Daniel Allen Penick, Ph.D.—Instructor in New Testament Language and Exegesis	1957
1921	A. H. Perpetuo, M.A.—Instructor in Semitics, Spanish-Speaking Department	1923
1925	E. R. Sims, Ph.D.—Lecturer in Spanish-Speaking Department	1937
1925	T. Chalmers Vinson, D.D.—Instructor in Theology	1927
1925	L. H. Wharton, M.A., D.D.—Instructor in Homiletics	1937
1928	O. C. Williamson, D.D.—Instructor in Spanish-Speaking Department	1933
1933	R. D. Campbell, D.D.—Instructor in Spanish-Speaking Department	1945
1936	Julian Sleeper, D.D.—Instructor in Homiletics	1937
1937	Conway T. Wharton, D.D.—Instructor in Homiletics	1940
1940	*C. Ellis Nelson, M.A., B.D., D.D., Ph.D.—Associate Professor of Christian Education	1948
1943	Glenn Maxwell, M.A., B.D.—Instructor in Theology	1944
1944	*James I. McCord, M.A., B.D., D.D., LL.D.—Associate Professor of Systematic Theology and Dean	1946
1945	Gus J. Craven, B.A., B.D.—Director of Field Work and Instructor in Christian Education	1946
1945	E. A. J. Seddon, Jr., B.A., B.D.—Instructor in Spanish-Speaking Department	1947
1946	W. Meade Brown, Jr., B.A., B.D.—Instructor in Church History and Missions	1947
1946	G. Wendell Crofoot, B.A., B.D.—Instructor in Spanish-Speaking Department	1947
1946	Frederick Eby, Ph.D., LL.D.—Visiting Professor of Christian Education	1948
1947	Thomas B. Gallaher, M.A., D.D.—Instructor in Christian Education	1948
1947	*T. Watson Street, S.T.M., Th.D., D.D.—Associate Professor of Church History and Missions	1949
1950	Howard W. Townsend, B.S., M.A., Ph.D.—Instructor in Speech	1956
1952	Jack B. McMichael, B.D., Ed.D.—Visiting Instructor of Christian Education	1953
1953	Bernard Citron, Ph.D.—Visiting Professor of Biblical Theology	1955

*Names marked with asterisk also on list of professors.

Accessus   *Exitus*

1955 Ernest Best, Ph.D.—Visiting Professor of Biblical   1957
      Theology
1955 William Ith Boand, B.D.—Instructor in Bible   1956
1955 Norman Dressel Dow, Th.M., M.A., M.L.S.—Assistant   1965
      Professor of Bibliography, Librarian
1955 Carlyle Marney, Th.D.—Guest Professor of Homiletics   1958
1955 *Henry Willard Quinius, Jr., B.B.A., Th.M.—Associate   1957
      Professor of Church Administration and Director of
      Field Education
1956 John Robert Hendrick, B.A., B.D.—Instructor in Bible   1959
1956 *James Allen Wharton, B.A., B.D.—Assistant Professor   1967
      of Bible
1957 Edward B. Paisley, D.D., Ph.D.—Visiting Professor of   1958
      Christian Education
1957 John Rea Thomas, B.D., M.A.—Instructor in Pastoral   1962
      Counseling
1957 Grover Cleveland Wilson, Jr., B.A., B.D.—Instructor   1958
      in Biblical Theology
1958 Dietrich Ritschl, Ph.D.—Visiting Professor of Biblical   1963
      Theology; 1960, Associate Professor of History of
      Dogma
1958 Carl E. Schneider, Ph.D., LL.D., Th.D.—Visiting   1959
      Professor of Church History
1958 Earl Constantine Scott, B.S., B.D.—Assistant Professor   1964
      of New Testament
1959 Lena Lea Clausell, B.A., M.R.E.—Visiting Lecturer in   1962
      Christian Education
1959 Paul Calvin Payne, Ph.D., D.D.—Visiting Professor of   1960
      Christian Education
1959 *J. Rodman Williams, Ph.D.—Associate Professor of   1964
      Theology and Philosophy of Religion
1959 Don Marvin Williams, B.A., B.D.—Teaching Fellow in   1970
      Homiletics—1960; 1970, Visiting Professor of
      Homiletics
1959 *Prescott Harrison Williams, Jr., Ph.D.—Assistant   1964
      Professor of Old Testament Languages and Archaeol-
      ogy; 1961, Associate Professor of Old Testament
      Languages and Archaeology
1960 William J. Fogleman, B.A., B.D.—Assistant Professor   1963
      of Practical Theology and Director of Continuing
      Education
1961 Frank F. Baker, B.A., B.D., Th.D., D.D.—Visiting   1962
      Professor of Missions

256

Accessus		*Exitus*
1961	*Stuart Dickson Currie, Ph.D.—Assistant Professor of Church History; 1962, Associate Professor of Church History	1964
1961	W. Walter Johnson, B.A., B.D., Th.M., Th.D.—Assistant Professor of Homiletics; 1967, Associate Professor of Homiletics	1970
1961	Charles Leonidas King, A.B., B.D., D.D., LL.D.—Visiting Professor of Homiletics	1964
1962	Keith Renn Crim, Th.M., Th.D.—Visiting Professor of Missions	1963
1962	John Brewer Spragens, B.A., B.D., D.D.—Assistant Professor of Christian Education and Dean of Students	1968
1963	Grover Ellis Foley, B.Sc., S.T.B., Th.D.—Visiting Professor of Theology	1965
1964	William Davidson Blanks, B.A., B.D., Th.M., Th.D.—Visiting Professor of Church History	1965
1964	George Stuart Heyer, Jr., A.B., B.D., M.A., Ph.D.—Assistant Professor of the History of Doctrine and Director of Continuing Education; 1966, Associate Professor of the History of Doctrine and Director of Continuing Education; 1967, Associate Professor of the History of Doctrine	——
1964	John Marshall Guthrie, B.A., B.D., Th.M.—Visiting Professor of Missions	1964
1964	Jorge Lara-Braud, B.A., B.D.—Visiting Professor of Missions; 1965, Assistant Professor of Missions; 1966, Visiting Professor of Missions	1968
1964	*Wallace Eugene March, B.A., B.D., Th.D.—Instructor of Old Testament Languages; 1966, Assistant Professor of Old Testament; 1969, Associate Professor of Old Testament	1973
1965	Ernest Trice Thompson, B.A., B.D., M.A., Th.M., D.D. Litt. D.—Visiting Professor of Church History	1970
1966	Calvin C. Klemt, B.A., B.D., M.L.S.—Librarian	——
1967	Ross Denison Dunn, B.A., B.D.—Assistant Professor of Christian Ethics and Director of Continuing Education	——
1967	Stanley F. Hogle, B.A., B.D., S.T.M.—Visiting Professor of Pastoral Care	1968
1968	Ian F. McIntosh, M.A., B.D., Th.M., Th.D.—Assistant Professor of Pastoral Theology	1971
1969	Houston Hodges, B.D.—Visiting Professor in the Department of the Church's Ministry	1971

Accessus   *Exitus*

1970 *Edward Dixon Junkin, B.A., B.D., Th.D.—Assistant   1976
      Professor of Church History; 1973, Associate Professor
      of Church History; 1974–76, Assistant to the Dean
1971 Alfred Frederick Swearingen, B.A., S.T.B.—Visiting   1971
      Professor of Worship
1971 J. Randall Nichols, Th.D.—Visiting Professor in   1971
      Homiletics
1971 Thomas F. Torrance—Visiting Lecturer in Theology   1971
1971 *Robert M. Shelton, B.A., B.D., Th.M., Ph.D.—   1975
      Associate Professor of Homiletics
1972 Thomas H. Cole—Visiting Professor of Pastoral Care   1972
1972 David Jacques Ernsberger, B.A., B.D., S.T.M.—Visiting 1975
      Professor of Christian Education
1972 Dietrich Ritschl, Ph.D.—Visiting Lecturer in Theology 1972
1972 Jorge Lara-Braud, B.D.—Visiting Professor of Theology 1972
1973 William Conwell Spong, B.A., M.Div., Th.M.—Adjunct   ——
      Professor of Pastoral Care
1974 Merwyn S. Johnson, Ph.D.—Assistant Professor of   ——
      Theology
1974 Carl Siegenthaler, B.A., M.Div., M.S.W.—Adjunct   ——
      Professor of Urban Ministry
1975 Robert Russell Ball, B.A., B.D., S.T.M.—Teaching   1975
      Fellow in the Department of the Church's Ministry
1975 David Ng, B.A., M.Div., D.D.—Associate Professor of   ——
      Church Program and Nurture
1975 John Edward Alsup, B.A., M.Div., Th.D.—Visiting   ——
      Professor of New Testament, 1975–76; June 1, 1976,
      Assistant Professor of New Testament
1975 J. Carter King, III, B.A., M.Div.—Visiting Professor ——
      of Ministry, 1975–76; June 1, 1976, Assistant Professor
      of Ministry and Director of Supervised Practice of
      Ministry
1975 Hilmer Charles Krause, Jr., B.A., B.D., S.T.M.—   ——
      Adjunct Professor of Hispanic Ministry
1975 Jack L. Whitehead, Ph.D.—Adjunct Professor of   ——
      Speech Communication
1975 Rubén Pacillas Armendáriz, B.A., M.Div.—Adjunct   1976
      Professor of Hispanic Ministry
1976 Ralph Erb Person, B.A., B.D.—Visiting Professor of   ——
      Church History

APPENDIX II

Roster of Members of The Board of Trustees

Accessus		*Exitus*
1899	Rev. S. B. Campbell (Chairman 1899–1905), Lancaster, Texas	1905
1899	Dr. T. J. Bell, Tyler, Texas	1903
1899	Judge G. H. Gould, Palestine, Texas	1906
1899	Judge S. P. Greene, Fort Worth, Texas	1904
1899	Rev. A. G. Jones (Chairman 1907–1920), San Antonio, Texas	1920
1899	Rev. S. A. King, Waco, Texas	1903
1899	Rev. W. H. Leavell (Chairman 1906–1907), Houston, Texas	1907
1899	Rev. B. T. McClelland, Brownwood, Texas	1901
1899	Rev. J. S. Moore, Sherman, Texas	1903
1899	Rev. C. J. Ralston, Oklahoma Territory	1903
1899	Rev. W. N. Scott, Galveston, Texas	1901
1899	Rev. R. K. Smoot, Austin Texas	1904
1901	Mr. J. A. Austin, Brownwood, Texas	1905
		1907–1910
1901	Mr. H. M. Trueheart, Galveston, Texas	1913
1902	Mr. J. M. Brownson, Victoria, Texas	1906
1902	Mr. A. P. Moore, Tyler, Texas	1906
1903	Rev. H. S. Davidson, Mangum, Oklahoma Territory	1910
1903	Rev. J. O. Reavis, Dallas, Texas	1907
1904	Mr. M. M. Johnson, Austin, Texas	1908
1904	Rev. John V. McCall, Gainesville, Texas	1918
1906	Rev. J. E. Green, Arkadelphia, Arkansas	1908
1906	Rev. C. R. Hyde, Little Rock, Arkansas	1911
1906	Rev. C. H. Maury, Conway, Arkansas	1913
1906	Mr. Henry Moore, Texarkana, Arkansas	1908
1907	Rev. J. P. Robertson, Paris, Texas	1921
1907	Rev. Thornton Whaling, Dallas, Texas	1911
1908	Mr. C. A. Bridewell, Hope, Arkansas	1910
1908	Mr. T. W. Gregory, Austin, Texas	1913
1908	Rev. E. P. Kennedy, Monticello, Arkansas	1908
1909	Rev. J. L. Read, Junction City, Arkansas	1917
1910	Rev. E. Brantley, Antlers, Oklahoma	1931
1910	Rev. T. S. Clyce, Sherman, Texas	1916
1910	Rev. W. M. Lewis, Clifton, Texas	1913

Accessus   *Exitus*

1910	Mr. E. R. Long, Batesville, Arkansas	1913
1911	Mr. Rhodes S. Baker, Dallas, Texas	1913
1911	Rev. A. H. P. McCurdy, Brownwood, Texas	1913
1911	Mr. R. W. Porter, Little Rock, Arkansas	1918
1912	Rev. J. M. Clark, Shawnee, Oklahoma	1916
1913	Mr. A. N. McCallum, Austin, Texas	1937
1913	Mr. Lauch McLaurin, Austin, Texas	1919
1913	Rev. James I. Norris, Pine Bluff, Arkansas	1913
		1920–1920
1914	Mr. R. F. Gribble, Waco, Texas	1916
1914	Rev. W. S. Jacobs, Houston, Texas	1916
1914	Dr. T. P. Junkin, Brownwood, Texas	1918
1914	Mr. T. H. Williams, Austin, Texas	1921
1916	Mr. G. E. McCelvey, Temple, Texas	1916
1916	Rev. C. C. Weaver, Oklahoma City, Oklahoma	1919
1917	Rev. E. T. Drake, Orange, Texas	1944
1917	Mr. L. L. McInnis, Bryan, Texas	1920
1917	Mr. J. A. Thompson, Taylor, Texas	1927
1919	Rev. C. H. H. Branch (Chairman 1921–1922), Texarkana, Arkansas	1923
1919	Mr. Ben Clayton, Houston, Texas	1921
1919	Rev. J. P. Kidd, North Little Rock, Arkansas	1921
1919	Mr. B. C. Powell, Little Rock, Arkansas	1920
1919	Mr. J. H. Rogers, Austin, Texas	1920
1919	Rev. E. W. Williams, Bonham, Texas	1919
1920	Rev. C. T. Caldwell (Chairman 1923–1945), Waco, Texas	1950
1920	Rev. J. E. Latham, Oklahoma City, Oklahoma	1928
1921	Rev. J. E. James, Gonzales, Texas	1927
1921	Rev. W. R. Minter, Austin, Texas	1940
1922	Mr. J. E. Jarratt, San Antonio, Texas	1941
1922	Rev. Samuel L. Joekel, Waxahachie, Texas	1925
1922	Mr. Robert Adger Law, Austin, Texas	1958
1923	Mr. V. O. Alexander, Pine Bluff, Arkansas	1932
1923	Rev. R. L. Jetton, Jonesboro, Arkansas	1928
1923	Rev. John Van Lear, Little Rock, Arkansas	1932
1925	Rev. James V. Johnson, Camden, Arkansas	1925
1926	Rev. Julian S. Sleeper, Texarkana, Arkansas	1941
1926	Mr. H. L. Ponder, Walnut Ridge, Arkansas	1928
1927	Rev. T. M. Hunter, Beaumont, Texas	1936
1928	Rev. R. L. Owen, Big Spring, Texas	1944
1928	Rev. B. O. Wood (Chairman 1946–1950), San Angelo, Texas	1957

Accessus		Exitus
1928	Rev. H. L. Paisley, Fayetteville, Arkansas	1932
1929	Rev. W. McF. Alexander, New Orleans, Louisiana	1941
1929	Rev. R. M. Firebaugh, Goodland, Oklahoma	1938
1929	Rev. H. H. Thompson, Baton Rouge, Louisiana	1932
1931	Rev. J. W. Moseley, Duncan, Oklahoma	1937
1932	Rev. B. C. Bell, Shreveport, Louisiana	1933
1932	Rev. J. H. Christian, Baton Rouge, Louisiana	1945
1932	Mr. Mack H. Long, Little Rock, Arkansas	1948
1933	Mr. D. L. McRae, Prescott, Arkansas	1933
1933	Rev. C. E. Newton, Pine Bluff, Arkansas	1947
1934	Mr. W. C. Brown, Hot Springs, Arkansas	1970
1935	Rev. S. D. Bartle, Fordyce, Arkansas	1935
1935	Rev. S. E. McFadden, Ruston, Louisiana	1937
1937	Rev. Charles L. King (Chairman 1951–1960), Houston, Texas	1963
1938	Rev. Wade H. Boggs, Shreveport, Louisiana	1943
1938	Rev. C. M. Campbell, Gonzales, Texas	1938
1938	Rev. B. W. Downing, Wewoka, Oklahoma	1942
1938	Mr. Joe E. Lawther, Dallas, Texas	1938
1939	Rev. Fred I. Cairns, Conway, Arkansas	1941
1939	Mr. M. B. Hughey, Charlotte, Texas	1943
1940	Rev. John Knox Bowling, Duncan, Oklahoma	1944
1942	Rev. R. Guy Davis, Wynne, Arkansas	1944
1942	Mr. J. Adair Lyon, New Orleans, Louisiana	1946
1942	Mr. J. S. Pulliam, Dallas, Texas	1945
1943	Rev. M. E. Melvin, Oklahoma City, Oklahoma	1946
1943	Mr. Arch Underwood, Lubbock, Texas	1952
1944	Rev. Frank C. Brown, Dallas, Texas	1945
1944	Rev. Hugh E. Bradshaw, Belcher, Louisiana	1948
1945	Rev. S. C. Guthrie (Chairman 1961–1962), Kilgore, Texas	1962
1945	Rev. L. Allen Holley, Wewoka, Oklahoma	1945
1945	Rev. C. L. Power, Shreveport, Louisiana	1947
1945	Mr. Glenn A. Railsback, Pine Bluff, Arkansas	1973
1946	Rev. H. Grady James, Wewoka, Oklahoma	1952
1946	Mr. D. D. McIver, Baton Rouge, Louisiana	1948
1946	Rev. James E. Moore, Big Spring, Texas	1946
1946	Mr. J. R. Scott, Jr., Falfurrias, Texas	1956
1947	Mr. Roy L. Klein, Dallas, Texas	1961
1948	Rev. W. L. McColgan, Pine Bluff, Arkansas	1951
1948	Rev. Patrick D. Miller, San Antonio, Texas	1948
1948	Mr. Marion R. Wellford, New Orleans, Louisiana	1948
1949	Mr. Barton W. Freeland, Crowley, Louisiana	1974

Accessus   *Exitus*

1949	Mr. Sam B. Hicks, Shreveport, Louisiana	1967
1950	Mr. Tom A. Cutting, Fort Smith, Arkansas	1959
1950	Mr. Earl Rawlins, Duncan, Oklahoma	1950
1950	Mr. Tom Sealy, Midland, Texas	1952
1950	Mr. W. J. Stebbins, Garyville, Louisiana	1951
1951	Rev. H. A. Anderson, San Antonio, Texas	1958
		1964–1964
1951	Rev. Walter A. Bennett, Oklahoma City, Oklahoma	1954
1951	Rev. Marion A. Boggs, Little Rock, Arkansas	1963
1951	Mr. Henry H. Bryant, San Antonio, Texas	1963
1951	Mr. Franklin Flato, Corpus Christi, Texas	1961
		1963–1973
1951	Rev. Ernest D. Holloway, Monroe, Louisiana	1951
1951	Rev. W. L. McLeod, Lake Charles, Louisiana	1957
1951	Mr. B. W. Trull, Palacios, Texas	1957
1952	Mr. Tom G. Clark, Arkadelphia, Arkansas	1963
1953	Mr. William J. Murray, Jr., Austin, Texas	1961
		1963–
1953	Mr. Myron Turfitt, New Orleans, Louisiana	1956
1953	Rev. Claude D. Wardlaw, Lake Charles, Louisiana	1964
1954	Mr. W. H. Gilmore, Midland, Texas	1962
1954	Mr. J. W. Logan, Durant, Oklahoma	1956
1955	Rev. J. Martin Singleton, Oklahoma City, Oklahoma	1964
		1966–1971
1957	Mr. R. P. Gregory, Houston, Texas	1963
		1966–1968
1957	Mr. O. L. Parsons, Lawton, Oklahoma	1965
1957	Mr. Morgan L. Shaw, New Orleans, Louisiana	1957
1958	Mr. David Crow, Shreveport, Louisiana	1959
		1965–1967
1958	Rev. William M. Elliott, Jr., Dallas, Texas	1963
1958	Rev. Albert B. Link, New Orleans, Louisiana	1967
1958	Mr. Hamilton E. McRae, Jr., Midland, Texas	1965
1959	Mr. Vannie E. Cook, McAllen, Texas	1961
1959	Rev. John William Lancaster (Chairman 1962–1972),	1965
	Austin, Texas	1967–1973
1960	Rev. William A. Benfield, Shreveport, Louisiana	1964
1960	Mr. Raymond Orr, Fort Smith, Arkansas	1962
1962	Rev. Robert P. Douglass, Dallas, Texas	1967
1962	Mr. James W. Hargrove, Houston, Texas	1969
1962	Mr. Walter B. Howard, Texas City, Texas	1967
1962	Mr. Robert B. Trull, Palacios, Texas	1970
		1972–

Accessus		*Exitus*
1964	Mr. Allen H. Carruth, Houston, Texas	1971
1964	Mr. Jack East, Jr., Little Rock, Arkansas	1967
		1973–
1964	Mr. Clarence L. Norsworthy, Jr., Dallas, Texas	1971
1964	Rev. H. Edwin Pickard, Beaumont, Texas	1967
1964	Mr. Leon Stone, Austin, Texas	1972
1964	Mr. Gaston Williamson, Little Rock, Arkansas	1971
1965	Rev. T. Chalmers Henderson, Arkadelphia, Arkansas	1967
1965	Rev. James P. McCrary, Oklahoma City, Oklahoma	1965
1965	Rev. Arch McD. Tolbert (Chairman 1976–), Baton Rouge, Louisiana	1973 / 1975–
1966	Rev. C. Ellis Nelson, New York, New York	1974
1968	Rev. Joe M. Brown, Odessa, Texas	1975
1968	Rev. William W. Hatcher, New Orleans, Louisiana	
1968	Mr. William G. Hazen, New Orleans, Louisiana	1975
1968	Rev. Robert F. Jones, Fort Worth, Texas	1970
1968	Rev. William S. McLean (Chairman 1974–1976), Little Rock, Arkansas	
1968	Mr. Morrell F. Trimble, New Orleans, Louisiana	1973
1969	Mr. Roy E. Glass, San Angelo, Texas	
1969	Mr. L. Frank Moore (Chairman 1972–1973), Shreveport, Louisiana	1973
1970	Mr. Weldon H. Smith, Houston, Texas	
1971	Mrs. Jack Boyd (Ruth), Sweetwater, Texas	1972
1971	Rev. Patricia Ann McClurg, Pasadena, Texas	
1972	Rev. Carlos S. Buck, Houston, Texas	1973
1972	Rev. Walter M. Crofton, Fort Smith, Arkansas	
1972	Mr. G. R. Hollingsworth, Dallas, Texas	
1972	Mr. Robert S. Lindsey, Little Rock, Arkansas	
1972	Mr. Collier Wenderoth, Jr., Fort Smith, Arkansas	1976
1974	Mr. Emanuel M. Harrison, Baton Rouge, Louisiana	1975
1974	Mr. Harold C. Harsh, New Orleans, Louisiana	1976
1974	Ms. Patricia S. Huntress, Oklahoma City, Oklahoma	
1974	Miss Cora V. Sylestine, Livingston, Texas	
1974	Rev. William H. Tiemann, Dallas, Texas	
1974	Rev. William Newton Todd, Hot Springs, Arkansas	1975
1974	Mr. David M. Vigness, Lubbock, Texas	
1975	Mr. Joseph H. Culver, Austin, Texas	
1975	Mr. Clarence N. Frierson, Shreveport, Louisiana	
1975	Rev. Ben Gutierrez, New York, New York	
1975	Rev. David L. Jones, Shreveport, Louisiana	
1975	Rev. Thomas H. Schmid, New Orleans, Louisiana	
1975	Rev. Don G. Shepherd, Amarillo, Texas	

1975 Rev. Robert B. Smith, Midland, Texas
1977 Mrs. William T. (Millie) Dabe, New Orleans, Louisiana
1977 Mr. Ed D. Vickery, Houston, Texas

The location of each member of the Board is that from which he was first elected.

APPENDIX III

Austin Seminary
Present Campus and Housing Properties,
Listed Chronologically

1907 Board authorized purchase of present Seminary site of 5¼ acres on 27th Street, at cost of $5,029.00.

1908 Lubbock Hall and Sampson Hall constructed (at cost of $8,159.00 and $37,504.28 respectively).

1909 Four faculty residences (#1–4) constructed on 27th Street at cost of $25,626.15.

1913 Faculty residence #5 and land (2621 Speedway) acquired at cost of $11,449.85.

1924–25 Property east of campus purchased for $4500 and five four-room cottages erected at cost of $5770.73. This property on Wooldridge Street (married student housing known as the courts) was expanded through the years (to $15,497.34 in 1930, and to $21,259.22 in 1937).

1941–42 Chapel constructed (cost, with furnishings $53,000).

1946–47 2903–5 University Ave. ("Faculty duplex") purchased. (N 84' of Lots 9 and 10, Block 4) (Cost $18,000).

1947–48 Whitis land, apartments and equipment acquired. ($27,-053.90) (On 27th Street, adjoining campus, to west).

1949–50 Library constructed ($190,602.68).

1949–50 Park property purchased from City of Austin ($35,216.50). (Bounded by 29th, 30th, University Ave. and Cedar St.).

1951–52 2904–6 University Avenue married student apartments constructed.

1951–52 1617 Westover Road purchased for a faculty home (C. Ellis Nelson).

1951–52 2529 Spring Lane—land purchased for President's Home.   264

1952–53	Spring Lane—President's Home constructed.
1952–53	108 Laurel Lane purchased for a faculty home (T. Watson Street).
1953–54	Wynne House and land acquired. (On 27th Street, adjoining campus, to west).
1953–54	115 West 29th Street purchased (S 66' of Lots 9 & 10, Block 4). ($8,000+).
1953–54	101 East 30th Street purchased (Lot 13, Block 4) ($7,000+).
1955	Single Students Dormitory constructed ($240,764).
1955–56	4800 Parkcrest (Later Balcones Drive) purchased for a faculty home (Quinius).
1956–57	5707 Trailridge purchased for a faculty home (Millard).
1957–58	101–103 West 30th, 2910 University—Married Student Apartments constructed.
1957–58	"Archer Property" including 3108 Grooms and 209 E. 32nd purchased.
1958–59	110 West 29th Street purchased (Lot 11, Block 4).
"	106 West 29th Street purchased (Lot 14, Block 4).
"	104 West 29th Street purchased (Lot 15, Block 4).
"	2900–02 Speedway purchased (Lot Res. 14, Block 4).
"	2912 Speedway purchased (N.116' Lot 1, Block 4).
"	205 East 30th Street purchased (Lot 2, Block 4).
1959–60	200 East 30th Street purchased (Lot 13, Block 2).
"	107 East 30th Street purchased (Lot 6, Block 4).
"	6003 Bullard Drive purchased for a faculty home (W.Fogleman).
"	Four old faculty residences on 27th Street razed.
1960–61	4609 Horseshoe Bend purchased for a faculty home (J. Wharton).
1962	Trull Memorial Administration Building constructed.
"	McMillan Memorial Classroom Building constructed.
1962–63	Sampson Hall demolished.
"	Wynne House demolished, after severe damage by fire.
1963–64	203 East 30th Street purchased (Lot 3, Block 4).
1963–64	2904 Speedway purchased (S.34' Lot 1, Block 4).
1964–65	Old buildings at 2900–02 Speedway removed.

1965–66   Dean of Students Residence constructed at 2900 Speedway.

"   105 East 30th Street purchased (Lot 7, Block 4).

"   109 East 30th Street purchased (Lot 5, Block 4).

"   201 East 30th Street purchased (Lot 4, Block 4).

1966–67   Property east of Speedway sold to University of Texas (under threat of use of powers of eminent domain). This included 2621 Speedway and 2617–34 Wooldridge Street.

1968–69   Old building at 2912 Speedway demolished.

1969–70   6003 Bullard Drive sold (to Professor Johnson).

1969–70   1517 Westover Road sold (formerly used as faculty home).

1970   108 West 29th Street purchased (Lot 12, Block 4).

1971   4800 Parkcrest (Balcones Drive) sold (to Professor Quinius).

1973   5707 Trailridge sold (formerly used as faculty home).

1973   2529 Spring Lane sold (formerly President's home).

1974   Title to "Mission Ranch" property at 507 and 607 Bellevue was transferred to the Seminary by Synod of Red River.

1975   4609 Horseshoe Bend sold (formerly used as faculty home).

Bibliography

BOOKS

Baker, William M. *The Life and Labors of the Rev. Daniel Baker, D.D., Pastor and Evangelist.* Philadelphia: William S. & Alfred Martien, 1858.

Bunyan, John, *The Pilgrim's Progress.* New York, Chicago, Toronto: Fleming H. Revell Company, 158 Fifth Avenue, New York, N.Y., 1903.

Caldwell, C. T. *Historical Sketch of The First Presbyterian Church, Waco, Texas.* Waco, Texas: Methodist Home Press, 1937.

Clark, James and Halbouty, Mike. *Spindletop.* New York: Random House, 1952.

Currie, Stuart D. *The Beginnings of the Church.* Richmond, Virginia: The CLC Press, 1966.

————. *Good News in Samaria, The Simon Magus Episode.* Montreal: The Presbyterian College, McGill University, 1972.

Glasgow, Samuel McPheeters. *Border Trails.* N.p., no publisher, n.d. in Library at Union Theological Seminary, Richmond, Virginia.

Hamilton, E. H., *Afraid? Of What?.* Bristol, Tenn. 37620: Mallicote Printing, Inc., copyright 1968 by E. H. Hamilton.

Harriman, W. Averell and Abel, Elie. *Special Envoy to Churchill and Stalin 1941-1946.* New York: Random House, 1975.

Joekel, Samuel L. *Fitly Framed Together.* Richmond, Virginia: John Knox Press, 1948.

Johnson, Thomas Cary. *The Life and Letters of Robert Lewis Dabney.* Richmond, Virginia: The Presbyterian Committee of Publication, 1903.

Jones, Arthur Gray. *Calvin: The Times: The Man: The Historic Significance.* N.d. (ca. 1909), in the Library of Austin Seminary.

————. *Temple Builders and Other Sermons.* New York: Fleming H. Revell Company, 1929.

————. *Thornton Rogers Sampson.* Richmond, Virginia: Richmond Press, Inc., Printers, 1917.

King, Samuel A. *A Sermon on Thanksgiving,* November 29, 1894. Columbia, Missouri: E. W. Stephens Printer, 1895.

————. *The System of Doctrines of the Westminster Standards.* Richmond, Virginia: The Presbyterian Committee of Publication, ca. 1905.

Kotker, Norman, Editor. *Texas.* New York, N.Y.: Charles Scribner & Sons, n.d.

Mathews, Basil. *John R. Mott World Citizen.* New York and London: Harper and Brothers, 1934.

McLeod, William A. *The Story of the First Southern Presbyterian Church.* Austin, Texas: n.p., ca. 1939.

Mott, John R. *Five Decades and a Forward View.* New York and London: Harper and Brothers, 1939.

The Plan Providing for the Reunion of the Presbyterian Church in the United States of America and the Presbyterian Church in the United States as the Presbyterian Church of the United States, May 1943. Printed for the use of The General Assembly of The Presbyterian

Church in the United States.

Pulsifer, Harold Trowbridge. *Mothers and Men.* Cambridge: Houghton Mifflin Co., The Riverside Press, 1916.

Purcell, Mabelle. *Two Texas Female Seminaries.* Wichita Falls, Texas: The University Press, Midwestern University, 1951.

Red, William Stuart. *A History of the Presbyterian Church in Texas.* Austin, Texas: The Steck Company, 1936.

Thompson, Ernest Trice, *Presbyterians in the South.* Vol. I, John Knox Press, 1963; Vols. II and III, John Knox Press, 1973.

Webber, F. R. *Church Symbolism.* Cleveland, Ohio: J. H. Jansen Publisher, 1938.

Wiggin, Kate Douglas and Smith, Nora Archibald. *Golden Numbers*, Children's Crimson Series. New York: Grosset & Dunlap Publishers, 1902. Copyright, Doubleday & Co., Inc.

Works, George A. *Report of a Survey of the Colleges and Theological Seminaries of the Presbyterian Church in the United States.* Louisville, Kentucky: n.p. 1942.

BOOKS: PARTS OF SERIES

Ministerial Directory of the Presbyterian Church, U.S. 1861–1967. Rev. E. D. Witherspoon, Jr., Compiler. Doraville, Georgia: Foote & Davies. Published by order of the General Assembly, 1967.

Pittsburgh Theological Monograph Series. Dikron Y. Hadidian, General Editor. Book 10. Pittsburgh, Pennsylvania, 15213: The Pickwick Press, 5001 Baum Boulevard, 1976. Maxwell, Jack Martin. *Worship and Reformed Theology.*

Texas Almanac and State Industrial Guide, 1974–1975. Dallas, Texas: A. H. Belo Corporation.

The World Almanac and Book of Facts, 1973 Edition. New York, N.Y.: The World Almanac, 230 Park Avenue, 10017.

OCCASIONAL PUBLICATIONS

Acknowledgment card from the family of Thomas White Currie in the hands of T.W.C., Jr.

Currie, Thomas W. "The Life and Teachings of Jesus," Bible 301. Austin, Texas: Extension Teaching and Field Service Bureau, The University of Texas, n.d. (mimeographed).

Order of Worship, 5:00 p.m., May 12, 1943, The University Presbyterian Church, Austin, Texas, in the file of T.W.C., Jr.

"Religion at The University of Texas." Austin, Texas: The Association of Religious Teachers, University of Texas. May 17, 1956. Seminary Library.

Smoot, R. K. *The Austin Presbyterian Theological Seminary, A Statement of Facts.* Austin, Texas: n.p., October 19, 1904. In the safe in the business office of the Seminary.

PERIODICALS

Black, Malcolm. The Austin School of Theology. Austin, Texas: n.p., n.d. ca. 1889. This leaflet was in the Seminary Library at one time in the early 1950's but could not be located in 1976.

Bulletins of Austin Presbyterian Theological Seminary. Student *Bulletin* and *Theolog* 1925–1957.

268

Caldwell, Eugene C. "The Millenium." *The Union Seminary Review* XXXI, 3 (April 1920), 207–234.

Catalogues, Announcements, and Bulletins of Austin Presbyterian Theological Seminary, Austin, Texas. Bound in volumes at the Seminary Library. Vol. I (ca. April 1902–1909), II (1910–1922), III (1922–1933), IV (1934–1947), V (1948–1952), VI (1953–1958), VII (1957–1961), VIII (1961–1965), IX (1965–1972). Catalogues for succeeding years not bound as yet.

Currie, Thomas W. "Theological Education Today." *The Union Seminary Review* XL, 1 (October, 1928), 58–73.

Gribble, R. F. "When Is a Christian Not a Christian?" *The Southern Presbyterian Journal* I, 5 (September 1942), 13.

Lee, Lawrence. "Madison Lane Part V." *American Mercury*, P. O. Box 1306, Torrance, Ca. 90505, vol. 30, no. 119 (November 1933).

Minutes of the General Assembly of the Cumberland Presbyterian Church, Nashville, Tennessee: Board of Publication, Cumberland Presbyterian Publishing House.
> Fiftieth General Assembly 1880—Austin Seminary Library
> Sixtieth General Assembly 1890—Austin Seminary Library
> Seventieth General Assembly 1900—Austin Seminary Library
> Eightieth General Assembly 1910—Memphis Theological Seminary, Memphis, Tennessee

Minutes of the General Assembly of the Presbyterian Church in the United States with an Appendix.

1880	1930	1944
1890	1936	1965
1900	1938	
1910	1941	

Minutes of the General Assembly of the Presbyterian Church in the United States of America with an Appendix.
> New Series, Vol. VI, A.D. 1880, New York: Presbyterian Board of Publication
> New Series, Vol. XIII, A.D. 1890, Philadelphia: By the Stated Clerk
> New Series, Vol. XXIII, A.D. 1900, Philadelphia: By the Stated Clerk
> New Series, Vol. X, No. 2, 1910, Philadelphia: Office of the General Assembly

Minutes of the Synod of Louisiana, Presbyterian Church in the U.S., Seventieth Stated Meeting, Broadmoor Presbyterian Church, Shreveport, Louisiana, May 18, 19, 1971. Vol. 8, No. 6, 1971.

Minutes of the Synod of Red River, Presbyterian Church in the United States, First Stated Meeting, also Convention of Synod "E," No. II, Denton, Texas 76201. 1973.

Minutes of the Synod of Texas of the Presbyterian Church in the United States.

1894	1899	1904	1910	1914	1919	1933
1895	1901	1905	1911	1915	1921	1942
1896	1902	1908	1912	1916	1923	1971
1897	1903	1909	1913	1917	1930	

The Texas Presbyterian

October 1964, vol. IV, no. 10.
November 1964, vol. IV, no. 11.
December 1964, vol. IV, no. 12.
January 1965, vol. V, no. 1.
In the archives of Austin Seminary.

Vinson, R. E. "The Old Testament in the Light of Its Own Times," *The Presbyterian Quarterly* XVII, 64 (October 1903), 161–188.

ESSAYS AND ARTICLES IN COLLECTIONS

Joekel, Samuel L. "The Eternalness of the Christ." In *The American Pulpit Series, Book One*, pp. 78–91. New York and Nashville: Abingdon-Cokesbury Press, 1945.

UNPUBLISHED MATERIALS

1. *Official Seminary Records*

Audit Report, Austin Presbyterian Theological Seminary, Austin, Texas, April 30, 1946, by R. A. Moore Company, Certified Public Accountants, Fort Worth, Texas. In the hands of the Business Manager of the Seminary.

Minutes of the Faculty of Austin Presbyterian Theological Seminary in the Office of the President.

1902–1914	1951–1959
1914–1927	1960–1967
1928–1939	1968– Unbound
1940–1950	

Minutes of the Trustees of the Austin School of Theology, Nov. 13, 1889–Feb. 25, 1930, T. W. Gregory, Secretary, in the Seminary vault.

2. *Theses*

Currie, Thomas White, Jr., "A History of Austin Presbyterian Theological Seminary, Austin, Texas 1884–1943." Doctor of Theology dissertation, Austin Presbyterian Theological Seminary.

Sharpe, Dwight A. "Arthur Gray Jones, Nobleman of God." Minor paper for Master's degree. Austin Presbyterian Theological Seminary, Austin, Texas, 1952.

3. *Private Letters and Papers*

Akers, Homer C. Letter to T.W.C., Jr. dated December 1, 1955 and in the hands of the latter.

Altfather, Kenneth D. Letter to T.W.C., Jr., dated November 20, 1975 and in the hands of the latter.

Ames, Mrs. Jessie Daniel. Letter to Samuel L. Joekel dated October 26, 1943 and in the Seminary Library Archives.

Arnold, William H. Letter to T.W.C., Jr. dated December 23, 1975 and in the hands of the latter.

Austin Presbyterian Theological Seminary Chapel Service Order of Worship, September 4, 1974 in the hands of T.W.C., Jr.

Bailey, Henry M. Letter to T.W.C., Jr. dated November 3, 1955, in the hands of the latter.

Barnett, Prentice H. Letter to T.W.C., Jr. dated December 17, 1975 and in the hands of the latter.

Bennett, Jack K. Letter to T.W.C., Jr. dated December 2, 1975 and in the hands of the latter.

Beverley, James Andrew. Letter to T.W.C., Jr., dated December 2, 1975 and in the hands of the latter.

Blue, John R. Letter to T.W.C., Jr. dated December 2, 1975 and in the hands of the latter.

Boand, William I. Letter to T.W.C., Jr. received December 11, 1975 and in the hands of the latter.

Boggs, Marion A. Letter to T.W.C., Jr. dated August 18, 1975 and in the hands of the latter.

Boggs, Wade H. Letter to T.W.C., Jr. dated November 2, 1955. In the hands of the latter.

Branch, Mary E. Letter to Samuel L. Joekel dated October 27, 1943 and in the Seminary Library Archives.

Browder, Mrs. Isabel. Letter to T.W.C., Jr. dated September 25, 1975 and in the hands of the latter.

Burch, Harry H. Letter to T.W.C., Jr. dated November 29, 1955 and in the hands of the latter.

Caldwell, William S. Letter to T.W.C., Jr. dated November 12, 1975 and in the hands of the latter.

Campbell, Fred L. Letter to T.W.C., Jr. dated November 20, 1975 and in the hands of the latter.

Correu, Larry M. Letter to T.W.C., Jr. dated December 29, 1975 and in the hands of the latter.

Crofoot, Wendell. Paper, n.d., in the hands of T.W.C., Jr.

Cruz-Antonio, José. Letter to T.W.C., Jr. dated December 17, 1975 and in the hands of the latter.

Currie, David M. Letter to T.W.C., Jr. dated November 4, 1975 and in the hands of the latter.

Currie, Thomas White, III. Letter to T.W.C., Jr. dated February 27, 1977 and in the hands of the latter.

Dodson, S. K. Letter to Rev. Stuart Currie dated Hamburg, Arkansas, October 15, 1975 and in the hands of T.W.C., Jr.

Dodson, S. K. Letter to T.W.C., Jr. dated Hamburg, Arkansas, November 11, 1975 and in the hands of the latter.

Evans, John R. Letter to T.W.C., Jr. dated November 7, 1975 and in the hands of the latter.

Farquhar, D. Alan. Letter to T.W.C., Jr. dated December 3, 1975 and in the hands of the latter.

Freeland, Barton W. Letter to T.W.C., Jr. dated October 13, 1975 and in the hands of the latter.

Gardner, David C. M. Letter to T.W.C., Jr. dated November 21, 1975 and in the hands of the latter.

Gardner, Oscar. Letter to T.W.C., Jr. undated and in the hands of the latter.

Gillies, John. Letter to T.W.C., Jr. dated November 23, 1975 and in the hands of the latter.

Gray, Katherine. Letter to Samuel L. Joekel, October 14, 1943. In the Archives of the Seminary Library.

Guthrie, Shirley C. Letter to T.W.C., Jr. dated December 22, 1975 and in the hands of the latter.

Gutierrez, Ben F. Letter to T.W.C., Jr. dated January 8, 1976 and in the hands of the latter.

Hallonquist, Lionel. Letter to T.W.C., Jr. dated December 17, 1975 and in the hands of the latter.

Hamilton, E. H. "I Am Not Afraid!" The Story of John W. Vinson, Christian Martyr of North Kiangsu, China. Paper received by T. Watson Street from Ethel (Mrs. C. T.) Wharton with covering letter dated September 19, 1957. In the hands of Dr. Street.

Hardie, James F. Letter to T.W.C., Jr., September 20, 1955. In the hands of the latter.

Hardie, James F. Paper received by T.W.C., Jr. August 23, 1957. In the hands of the latter.

Henderlite, Rachel. Letter with enclosure to T.W.C., Jr. received January 7, 1976 and in the hands of the latter.

Henderson, P. F. Letter to Samuel L. Joekel, n.d. In the Seminary Library Archives.

Janda, Clement H. Letter to T.W.C., Jr. dated December 4, 1975 and in the hands of the latter.

Jansen, John F. Letter to T.W.C., Jr. dated October 19, 1975 and in the hands of the latter.

Jarvis, William R. Letter to T.W.C., Jr. dated December 12, 1975 and in the hands of the latter.

Johnson, John C. Letter to T.W.C., Jr. dated November 29, 1955 and in the hands of the latter.

King, Charles L. Letter to T.W.C., Jr. dated October 14, 1975 and in the hands of the latter.

Lang, Cecil H. Letter to T.W.C., Jr. November 3, 1955. In the hands of the latter.

Lanham, Sam. Letter to T.W.C., Jr. dated November 25, 1975 and in the hands of the latter.

Lively, Robert Donald. Letter to T.W.C., Jr. dated December 5, 1975 and in the hands of the latter.

Lloyd, R. Gage. Paper, n.d. in the hands of T.W.C., Jr.

Love, Edgar. Letter to Samuel L. Joekel dated October 28, 1943 and in the Seminary Library Archives.

Lowe, Girard. Letter to Samuel L. Joekel dated October 5, 1943 and in the Seminary Library Archives.

March, W. Eugene. Letter to T.W.C., Jr. dated October 1, 1975 and in the hands of the latter.

Marney, Carlyle. Letter to T.W.C., Jr. received November 21, 1975 and in the hands of the latter.

Maxwell, Ray, *Separated, But Not from the Blaze of Memory.* Austin, Texas: Austin Presbyterian Theological Seminary: *The Forum,* an occasional paper in the hands of T.W.C., Jr. (mimeographed). Special Edition, April 17, 1975.

McCall, George A. Letter to T.W.C., Jr. dated December 3, 1975 and in the hands of the latter.

McCord, James I. Paper received by T.W.C., Jr. February 17, 1956 and in the hands of the latter.

McCord, John H. Letter to T.W.C., Jr. received December 4, 1975 and in the hands of the latter.

McLaurin, Eugene W. Letter to T.W.C., Jr., December 7, 1955. In the hands of the latter.

McLaurin, Eugene W. (Secretary). Records of General Assembly's Committee on the Revision of the Confession of Faith and Catechisms. In the Archives of the Seminary Library.

Miller, M. M. Letter to T.W.C., Jr. dated November 25, 1955 and in the hands of the latter.

Mimeographed paper on twelve theses, dated Austin, Texas, October 25, 1959, placed in the hands of T.W.C., Jr. October 24, 1975 by Dean E. Dixon Junkin.

Montgomery, G. R. M. (Bob). Letter to T.W.C., Jr. received December 6, 1975 and in the hands of the latter.

Mosley, Ellis G. Letter to T.W.C., Jr., n.d. in the hands of the latter.

Murray, Michael F. Letter to T.W.C., Jr. dated December 23, 1975 and in the hands of the latter.

Nelson, C. Ellis. Letter to T.W.C., Jr. dated February 23, 1956 and in the hands of the latter.

Newton, James W. Letter to T.W.C., Jr. dated December 30, 1975 and in the hands of the latter.

Owens, John E. Letter to Sam L. Joekel dated October 13, 1943 and in the Library of the Seminary, Archives.

Paisley, E. B. Letter to T.W.C., Jr. dated November 3, 1957 and in the hands of the latter.

Parkhill, Ralyn C. Letter to T.W.C., Jr. dated November 11, 1975 and in the hands of the latter.

Penick, D. A. Letter to T.W.C., Jr., April 22, 1956. In the hands of the latter.

Penick, D. A., Conversation recorded by T.W.C., Jr., July 17, 1957. In the hands of the latter.

Pryor, William E. Letter to T.W.C., Jr. dated December 10, 1975 and in the hands of the latter.

Purcell, Malcolm L., "Reminiscences of Austin Seminary," n.d. Received by T.W.C., Jr., June 26, 1956. In the hands of the latter.

Purcell, Malcolm L. Letter to T.W.C., Jr., September 16, 1975. In the hands of the latter.

Quinius, Henry W. Letter and paper to T.W.C., Jr. dated March 1, 1976. Paper. 15 pp. In the hands of the latter.

Railsback, Glenn A. Letter to T.W.C., Jr. dated October 3, 1975 and in the hands of the latter.

Renquist, Michael. Letter to T.W.C., Jr., received December 10, 1975 and in the hands of the latter.

Riccobene, S. P. Letter to T.W.C., Jr., dated November 29, 1955 and in the hands of the latter.

Sanden, O. E. Letter to Samuel L. Joekel, October 10, 1943 and in Seminary Library Archives.

Sealy, Tom. Letter to T.W.C., Jr. dated December 22, 1975 and in the hands of the latter.

Seddon, E. A. J. Letter and paper to T.W.C., Jr. dated November 26, 1955 and in the hands of the latter.

Sharpe, Dwight A. Letter to T.W.C., Jr. dated December 23, 1955 and in the hands of the latter.

Shelton, Robert M. Letter to T.W.C., Jr. dated December 18, 1975 and in the hands of the latter.

Shepherd, Don G. Letter to T.W.C., Jr. dated December 19, 1975 and in the hands of the latter.

Singleton, J. Martin. Letter to T.W.C., Jr. received December 1, 1955 and in the hands of the latter.

Singleton, Nell (Mrs. J. Martin). Letter to T.W.C., Jr. dated August 2, 1975 and in the hands of the latter.

Slusser, Gerald H. Letter to T.W.C., Jr. dated December 2, 1975 and in the hands of the latter.

Smiley, John W. Letter to Board of Trustees dated August 16, 1971. Copy in the hands of T.W.C., Jr.

Smith, J. Allen. Letter received by T.W.C., Jr. December 26, 1975 and in the hands of the latter.

Solomon, John C. Letter to T.W.C., Jr. received November 30, 1955 and in the hands of the latter.

Spragens, John B. Letter to T.W.C., Jr. dated September 3, 1975 and in the hands of the latter.

Sprague, Minna (Mrs. Geo. A.) Letter (and accompanying tribute) to Samuel L. Joekel dated October 9, 1943 and in the Seminary Library Archives. Mrs. Sprague was a former President of the Women of the Church of the Synod of Texas, U.S.

Stitt, David L. Letter to T.W.C., Jr., August 30, 1957. In the hands of the latter.

Street, T. Watson. Paper. Unsigned, n.d. Received by T.W.C., Jr. March 23, 1976 and in the hands of the latter.

Swinney, Leonard R. Letter to T.W.C., Jr. dated November 23, 1975 and in the hands of the latter.

Thompson, Ernest Trice. Letter to T.W.C., Jr. dated February 28, 1976 and in the hands of the latter.

Trull, R. B. Letter to T.W.C., Jr. dated October 13, 1975 and in the hands of the latter.

Turner, Joseph L. Letter to T.W.C., Jr. dated December 11, 1975 and in the hands of the latter.

Tyler, Fred. Letter to T.W.C., Jr. dated November 30, 1955 and in the hands of the latter.

Vinson, T. C. Letter to T.W.C., Jr. received November 5, 1955. In the hands of the latter.

Weatherhogg, Neil. Letter to T.W.C., Jr. received December 21, 1975 and in the hands of the latter.

Wharton, James A. Letter to T.W.C., Jr. dated October 13, 1975 and in the hands of the latter.

Wiggins, Earl B. Letter to T.W.C., Jr. dated December 16, 1975 and in the hands of the latter.

Wood, B. O. Letter to T.W.C., Jr. dated October 8, 1975 and in the hands of the latter.

Works, Geo. A. "A Report on the Colleges and Seminaries of the Presbyterian Church in the United States made to the Executive Committee of Christian Education and Ministerial Relief," Section IV, The Seminaries of the Presbyterian Church in the United States. (Mimeographed). In the Library of Union Theological Seminary, Richmond, Virginia.

Yeargan, Maurice C. Letter to T.W.C., Jr. dated November 4, 1955 and in the hands of the latter.

Minutes of the Board of Trustees of Austin Presbyterian Theological Seminary in the keeping of the Business Manager.

1900–1908 Book "A"	1940–1949
1900–1919	1950–1959
1920–1929	1960–1969
1930–1939	1970– Unbound

Index

Akers, Homer Clifford, 99–101
Albrecht, John Frederick, Jr., 216
Allen, J. W., 41
Alliance of the Reformed Churches Holding the Presbyterian System (World), 66, 167, 187
Alston, Wallace McPherson, 179
Alsup, John E., 164, 234
Altfather, Kenneth Dale, 221, 222
American Association of Theological Schools, 117, 229, 235
American Pulpit Series, The, 97
American School of Oriental Research, 237, 238
Ames, Jessie Daniel, 109
Anderson, Harvard Arthur, 89
Anderson, Neal Larkin, 48–52, 64
Anderson, William Madison, Jr., 64
Andre, Mukeba, 179
Archeology, 163, 240
Arkansas College, 57
Armendariz, Ruben Pacillas, 167
Arnold, William Henry, 199
Association of Religious Teachers, 135
Auburn Affirmation, 59
Austin College, Sherman, Texas, 1, 7, 22, 23, 26, 47, 58, 60, 76, 77, 96, 97, 99, 137, 201
Austin Presbyterian Theological Seminary, Austin, Texas, 10, 12, 15–22, 26, 47, 58, 59
  Alumni, 131, 136 (Alumni Bulletin), 180 (Alumni Association), 199–227
  Board, 11–13, 15, 29, 31, 41, 48–53, 55, 58, 111, 113, 115, 117, 119–121, 129, 131, 139, 143, 151, 157, 158, 162, 163, 172, 173, 191–198, 208, 241
  Bulletin, 66 (Student Edition), 68, 74, 76, 77, 109 (Student Edition), 136 (Alumni), 180 (Faculty), 181 (Faculty), 184–190 (Faculty)
  Chapel, 104, 119 (services in Sampson Hall), 119–130, 213
  Curriculum, 114–118, 233–239
  Early rules, 24
  Endowment, 16, 17, 26, 31, 47–54, 65, 71, 118, 119, 131, 142–149, 151–153, 173
  Faculty, 29, 41, 42, 76, 111, 112, 115–117, 119–121, 142
  Fellowships, 131:
    Alumni Fellowship (first post B.D.)
    David L. Stitt Fellowship
    Board of Trustees Fellowship
    W. P. Newell Fellowship
    Janie Maxwell Morris Fellowship
  First graduates, 27
  First students, 23, 24
  Growth of (Report of C. Ellis Nelson), 158
  Lecture Series:
    Mid-Winter Lectures, or Mid-Winter Colloquium, 132, 177, 180
    E. C. Westervelt Lectures, 133
    Robert F. Jones Lectures, 133
    Settles Lectures in Missions and Evangelism, 133
    Thomas W. Currie Lectures, 132
  Lecturers:
    1925, 64
    1927–1928, 64
    1928–1929, 64
    1932–1933, 109
    1945, 177, 178
  Library, 6, 9, 10, 62–65, 114, 115, 117, 119, 131, 137, 142, 151, 154, 155, 175, 176
  Location:
    Stuart Seminary, 8–12
    Permanent Austin, Speedway at 27th, 29, 30
    Need for, 17–22
  Property additions, 10–12, 29–31, 65
  Proposal to merge, 114, 117
  Scholarships, 131
    Mr. and Mrs. Sam B. Hicks Scholarship
    Martin G. Miller Scholarship
  Student body, 48, 121, 183
  Student housing:
    Leper Colony, 151, 152
    Married, 155, 157
    Single, 157
Austin School of Theology, 4, 6–10, 12, 21, 29, 41, 58, 93

Bachelor of Divinity, 235
Bailey, Henry McClelland, 44, 45
Bailey, Thomas Jefferson, Jr., 232
Baker, Daniel, 1, 116
Ball, Sarah C. (Mrs. George), 17, 18, 26
Barnett, Prentice Harmon, 200, 201
Barr, James, x
Battle, W. J., 55, 86, 134–135

Beach, Waldo, 178
Begg, Edleen, 45
Bell, James Lewis, 41
Bell, T. J., 11
Belleville, Alice (Mrs. H. J.), vii
Benedict, Harry Yandell, 73
Benfield, William Avery, Jr., 177
Bennett, Jack Karlyle, 208, 209
Benson, George A., 179
Best, Ernest, 165, 206, 210
Beverley, James Andrew, 212, 213, 231
Biblical Theology, 163
Bitzer, George Leese, 5, 8
Blain, Robert Waller, 42
Blois Camp Meeting, 59, 97
Blue, John Rayner, 223
Boand, William Ith, 206
Bobb, Donald Frederick, 179
Boggs, Marion A., 198
Boggs, Wade Hamilton, 37–38
Bollinger, Meredith, 231
Book of Church Order, 111 (proposed change)
Book of Confessions (PCUS), 189
Bowman, Benjamin Hampton, 231
Boyd, George, 182
Branch, Charles Henry Hardin, 56
Branch, Mary E., 110–111
Brand, John Michael, III, 232
Bright, John, 178
Broadway Presbyterian Church, Fort Worth (later: St. Stephen Presbyterian Church), 139
Brock, J. E., 232
Brooks, Fred, 122
Browder, Isabel, 231, 232
Brown, Jean, 121
Brown, Josephine, 121
Brown, Robert McAfee, x, 178
Brown, W. C., Jr., 121
Bunyan, John, iv
Burch, Harry Homer, 101–102
Burton, Charles Gerald, 231
Business League of Austin, 29
Butler, J. Donald, 170
Buttrick, George Arthur, 179

Caldwell, Charles Turner, 122–123
Caldwell, Eugene Craighead, 35–39, 41, 107
Caldwell, William Stone, 219
Camargo, G. Baez, 177
Campbell, Charles Milton, 65, 66
Campbell, Frederick Lee, 209
Campbell, Robert Douglas, 55, 65, 94–95, 161, 233
Campbell, Samuel Blair, 8–13, 15
Carrick, Malcolm, 179
Centenary College, Shreveport, La., 169
Chaney, Barbara (Mrs. Don), vii
Chester, Samuel Hall, 64
"Child Tax," 20
Choctaw Indians, 81, 83
Christian Education, 133, 157, 159, 161–163
Church Extension, Board of (PCUS), 201
Church History and Polity, 22, 26, 44, 86, 100, 107, 133, 162–164, 173, 223, 233
Church Program and Nurture, 164, 234
Clausell, Lena Lea, 163
Cleland, James T., 179
Cocke, Alonzo Rice, 6
Cole, Thomas H., 234
College of Wooster, Wooster, Ohio, 58
Columbia Presbyterian Theological Seminary, 114
Community Church, Natalia, Texas, 99
Community Understanding Program, 230
Confession of Faith, 111
Congregational Church, 81, 110
Continuing Education, 64, 231, 234
Cornelius, E. T., 177
Correu, Lawrence M., 98
Coulter, L. A., 64
Counselling, 234
Covenant Life Curriculum, 186
Craven, Gus John, 161
Crofoot, George Wendell, 62, 63, 67, 233
Cruz-Antonio, José, 215
Cumberland Presbyterian Church, 4, 170
Currie, Alison (Mrs. T. W., Jr.), viii
Currie, David Mitchell, v, 104–106
Currie, Elizabeth Jeannette (Bettie), v
Currie, James Stuart, v
Currie, Jeannette Roe (Mrs. Thomas W.), 62, 103, 130
Currie, Sara Files (Mrs. S. D.), vii
Currie, Stuart Dickson, v, 163–166, 168, 171, 172, 185, 186, 188, 189, 217–220, 223–226, 233, 234, 240
Currie, Thomas White, v, ix, 32, 42, 48, 51, 53–55, 57, 60–63, 65–69, 71–74, 84–88, 91, 95, 99–107, 109–111, 113, 117, 119–130, 135, 164, 172, 243
Currie Lectures, The Thomas White,

278

iv, ix, x, 178
Currie, Thomas White, III, v, 226, 227

Dabney, Robert Lewis, 1, 2, 5–8, 24, 93,
    107, 112, 116, 243
Daniel Baker College, 17, 26, 47, 65, 98
Daniel, Eugene Lewis, Jr., 179
Daniel, Tshisungu, 179
Davidson College, Davidson N.C., 59
Declaration of Faith (PCUS), 189
Depression, The Great, of the 1930's,
    71, 81, 85, 88
Deutsch, Ernest Frank, 120, 161
Dickerson, M. S., 179
Dickey, Brooks Irving, 64
Dillenberger, John, x
Dispensationalism, 37, 111
Docherty, George M., 179
Doctor of Ministry, 235, 236
Dodson, Samuel Kendrick, 25, 26
Doggett, Marshall Wellington, 42
Douglass, Robert Perry, 131
Dow, Norman Dressel, Jr., vii
DuBose, Henry Wade, 115
Dunn, Ross Denison, 163, 168, 189, 234

Eaton, Carlton Oliver, 232
Eden Theological Seminary, Webster
    Groves, Mo., 201–203
Eickenroht, Marvin, 120
El Buen Pastor Presbyterian Church,
    Austin, Texas, 65
Elliott, William Marion, Jr., 179
English Bible, 41, 42, 55, 62, 102, 107–
    108, 114–115, 162, 233
Episcopal Seminary of the Southwest,
    167, 168
Ethics, Christian, 163, 165, 234
Evans, John Ronald, 220

Faculty, 53, 54
Faculty Preaching (students preaching
    before the faculty), 87
Farmer, H. H., 179
Farquhar, Don Alan, 211, 232
Federal Theology, 24, 25
Field, John Wesley, 65
Field Work, 161, 229–231
Firebaugh, Robert McElwee, 81
First Presbyterian Church, Fort Worth,
    Texas (Women of the Church), 178
First Presbyterian Church, Galveston,
    Texas, 208
First Presbyterian Church, Haskell,
    Texas, 139

First Presbyterian Church, Houston,
    Texas 173, 191
First Presbyterian Church, Lott, Texas,
    60
First Presbyterian Church, Memphis,
    Tennessee, 72
First Presbyterian Church, San An-
    tonio, Texas, 49, 55, 57
First Presbyterian Church, Taylor,
    Texas, 55
First Presbyterian Church, Waco, Tex-
    as, 23, 55
First Presbyterian Church, Waxahach-
    ie, Texas, 59
First Southern Presbyterian Church,
    Austin, Texas (formerly The Free
    Presbyterian Church), 2, 5, 6, 22, 26,
    29, 55, 59
Fisher, George, Jr., 232
Flato, Mr. and Mrs. Edwin, 133, 178
Fogleman, William Jethro, 231
Foley, Grover, 220
Freeland, Barton W., 191–193
Freibelmann, Julius, 125
Freund, Henry Otto, 232
Frye, Roland Mushat, 178
Fulton, Charles Darby, 64

Gardner, D. C. M., 215
Gardner, Oscar, 81–92
Gear, Felix Bayard, 177
General Assembly of The Presbyterian
    Church, U.S., The, 2, 4, 23, 37, 50,
    55, 60, 63, 69, 106, 111–113, 118, 163,
    188, 216, 231, 248
General Assembly, UPUSA, 186
General Education Board of New York,
    114
Gildersleeve, Basil, 93
Gill, Leonard Thurston, 23, 27
Gillies, John, 206, 207
Glasgow, Samuel McPheeters, 42–43
Glosse, James, 178
Glossolalia, 188, 189
Goodland Indian Home, 81
Gospel Airlift, 201–204
Gould, G. H., 11
Grand Avenue Presbyterian Church,
    Sherman, Texas, 60
Grant, Edward D., 75
Gray, Katherine, 62
Green, Ellis Larry, 245
Green, Emma (Mrs. Thomas L.), 89,
    205
Greene, S. P., 11, 15, 26

Gregory, Thomas Watt, 17, 34, 52
Gribble, Robert Francis, 43, 44, 48, 53, 58, 66, 85–87, 94, 96–99, 123, 125, 129, 131, 161, 162, 164, 195, 199, 210
Guerrero, Jose de la Luz, 63
Guthrie, Shirley Caperton, 193, 194
Gutierrez, Ben Felan, 207, 208

Hadden, David and Monica, 214
Hager, William Martin, 232
Hall, Douglas, 232
Hall, Warner Leander, 179
Hallonquist, Frank Lionel, Jr., 225
Hamby, John Charles, 232
Hamilton, Evelyn Harrison, 77–79
Hancock, Charles Frederick, 23, 24, 27
Hardie, James Finley, 23, 25, 33, 38, 44, 98, 177
Hardie, James Finley, Jr., 232
Harren, Herman, vii
Hazel, William John, 85, 88
Hemphill, C. R., 64
Henderlite, Rachel, 159, 163, 179, 183, 184, 188, 189, 222, 233, 244
Henderson, P. F., 113–114
Hendrick, John Robert, 163, 178
Hendry, George S., ix
Herrscher, George Conway, 182
Heyer, George Stuart, Jr., 163, 168, 189, 234
Highland Park Presbyterian Church, Dallas, Texas, ix, 71, 73, 74, 91, 133, 178
   Tom Currie Men's Bible Class: ix, 71, 133, 178
Hispanic American Institute, 167
Hodge, Charles, 24
Hodges, Jack, 168
Hogg Foundation, 231
Holt, Brian, vii
Homiletics, 41, 42, 44, 91, 162–165, 172, 233, 241
Honeycutt, Norman, 232
Hromadka, Joseph Lukl, 177
Hudson, John Black, 24, 27
Hughs, Dan Terrell, 240
Hyde Park Presbyterian Church, Austin, Texas, 85, 199

Institute of Religion, Houston, Texas, 167, 229, 234
International Missionary Council, 181

James, Harrell Grady, 81–83, 86–89
Janda, Clement H., 215, 216

Jansen, John Frederick, 163, 164, 166–168, 170, 184, 188, 189, 212, 213, 215, 216, 233
Jarvis, William Robert, 208
Jetton, Robert Lawson, 43, 44, 48
Jewett, Frank L., 134–135
Joekel, Samuel Levinson, 44, 59, 84, 85, 87, 97–99, 105, 117, 118, 125, 135, 161, 162, 164, 200, 204, 208
John Bulow Campbell Foundation of Atlanta, 114
Johns Hopkins University, 93
Johnson, Charles, 178
Johnson, John Cadien, 102
Johnson, Josephus J., 29, 30, 41
Johnson, Merwyn Stratford, 164, 189, 215, 234
Johnson, Thomas Cary, 8
Johnson, William Walter, 163, 169, 170, 188, 219, 221–223, 234
Jones, Arthur Gray, 10, 11, 49, 51, 54, 55, 57, 60, 107
Jones, E. Stanley, 109, 125
Jones, Robert Franklin, 90
Jones (Robert F.) Lectures, 178
Joplin, Robert Ware, 62
Junkin, Edward Dixon, viii, 164, 173, 182, 183, 189, 214, 215, 233

Keeton, W. Page, 179
Kelly, Balmer, 178
Kennedy, William Bean, 179
Kerney, Leroy G., 179
Kidd, John Philip, 44, 68
Kieft, Joseph V., 161
King, Charles Leonidas, 105, 120, 131, 163, 173, 191, 192, 215
King, J. Carter, III, 164, 234
King, Samuel Alexander, 11, 23–26, 29, 43, 45, 112
Klemt, Calvin Carl, vii, 163, 164, 234

Lancaster, John William, 197
Lang, Cecil Herbert, 37, 39, 43, 48
Lanham, Samuel Willis Tucker, III, 133, 220, 221
Lara-Braud, Jorge, 163, 167
Latourette, Kenneth Scott, 177
Law, Robert Adger, 131
Leake, Mrs. C. S., 89, 90
Leavell, William Hayne, 10, 11, 30
Lefevre, Jacob Amos, 8
Lehmann, Paul, x
Leper Colony, 85, 199, 213–215
Leslie, John Douglas, 64

Leslie, Robert Homer, Jr., 232
Lewis, Robert Barron, 232
Little, Archibald Alexander, 8, 64
Little, Sara P., 179
Liturgics, 241, 242
Lively, Robert Donald, 222–224
Lloyd, Robert Gage, 101
Logan, William Malcom, 134
Louisville Presbyterian Theological
Seminary, Louisville, Ky., 114, 163,
177
Love, Edgar, 109
Lowe, Girard, 72
Lowrance, Eugene Stewart, 7
Lowrance, William Lee, 11
Lubbock, Gov. Frank R., 30
Lubbock Hall, 31, 53, 65, 121

McCall, George Alexander, 213, 216,
217
McCall, John Vallandingham, 7, 60, 62
McClelland, Brainard Taylor, 11
McClendon, Charles Jackson, 179
McClurg, Patricia Ann, 244
McCord, James Iley, 93, 94, 98, 99, 103–
106, 133, 161–166, 169, 179, 200, 206–
208, 210, 211, 233
McCord, John Hulan, 209, 210
McCormick Presbyterian Seminary,
Chicago, Illinois, 65, 229
McCurdy, Andrew Howlett Porter, 10
McDonald, William G., 6
McLaughlin, Henry W., 64
McLaurin, Eugene William, 32, 37, 93,
98, 99, 111, 125, 133, 161–164, 169,
185, 200, 205, 209–211
McLean, William Speight, 235
McLeod, William Angus, 7, 23, 27, 43,
44, 48, 107
McMillan Classroom Building, 159
McMurry, Stonewall Jackson, 6, 7

Mackay, John A., ix, 179
Mahaffy, J. P., 33, 34
Malloy, Lawrence Milton, 88
March, Wallace Eugene, 163, 164, 168,
169, 185, 188, 214, 215, 233
Marney, Carlyle, 164–166, 178
Martin, Motte, 64
Mar-Yosip, Michael, 128
Master of Divinity, 235, 236
Master of Theology, 161, 235
Maxwell, Jack Martin, vii, x, 233, 241–
243, 247, 248
Maxwell, Ray, 217–219

Maxwell, Sandra Nagy (Mrs. J. M.), 241
May, Joel Edwin (Red), 231
Melvin, Marion Edmund, 64
Memphis Theological Seminary, Mem-
phis, Tenn., 170
Millard, James Abia, Jr., 162–164, 207,
208, 210, 229
Millenium, 36, 37
Miller, Maynard Michael, 67
Missionary Inquiry, Society of, 179
Missions, 162, 163
Mollegaen, A. T., 178
Monroe, Noble, 90, 91, 204
Montgomery, George Robert Martin,
Jr., 214, 215
Montgomery, James Alves, 7
Moore, John Silliman, 11, 15
Moore, L. Frank, 234
Moore, R. A., Audit Report, 143–149
Mosley, Ellis Greenlee, 67, 68
Mosley, James Wiley, 232
Mott, John R., 15
Muilenburg, James, 178
Munroe, Edmund Marshall, 105
Murray, Glenn William, 89
Murray, Michael Fielding, 182, 216

Neal, James Kelly, 161
Neese, Theron, 232
Nelson, Carl Ellis, 105, 118, 125, 133,
157, 161–164, 179, 200, 202, 210, 229,
233
Nevin, John Williamson, 241
New Testament Interpretation, 163
New Testament Language and Exege-
sis, 5, 39, 42–44, 48, 55, 83, 86, 93, 98,
114, 115, 117, 133, 161, 162, 223, 233,
234
Greek in Seminary Curriculum, 5
Newell, Samuel William, 128
Newton, James William, 201
Ng, David, 164, 234
Nichols, James Hastings, x
Niebuhr, H. Richard, 165, 178
Northridge Presbyterian Church, Dal-
las, Texas, 169

Oak Cliff Presbyterian Church, Dallas,
Texas, vii
Oates, Wayne E., 179
O'Connor, Leslie Lee, 161
Old Testament Languages and Exege-
sis, 5, 7, 17, 26, 35, 36, 38–41, 43, 44,
55, 58, 83, 85, 86, 111, 114, 115, 117,
162, 163, 233

Hebrew in Seminary Curriculum, 5, 7, 38, 44
Osborne Property, 196
Outler, Albert, 178
Owen, Jan William, 105
Owens, John E., 72

Paisley, Edward Bland, 106, 108, 163
Pan-American School, Kingsville, Texas (formerly Tex-Mex Industrial Institute, Kingsville, Texas, and Pres-Mex School for Girls, Taft, Texas), 73
Panic of 1894, 7
Park Avenue Cumberland Presbyterian Church, Memphis, Tenn., 170
Parkhill, Ralyn Clayton, 203, 204, 231
Parsons, David Vibert, Jr., 205
Parsons, Michael Leonard, 182
Paschall, Harry Owen, 182
Pastoral Theology, 161, 234
Payne, Paul Calvin, 163
Peacock, Rodney, 232
Penick, Daniel Allen, 6, 7, 48, 55, 58, 93, 117, 161, 200
Perkins School of Theology, 185
Perpetuo, Antonio Horatio, 55, 58
Pierre, Bakatushika, 179
Population, growth in Arkansas, Louisiana, Oklahoma and Texas, 1840–1910, 3
Prairie View College, Texas, 109
Pres-Mex (Taft, Texas), 94
Presbyterian Church in the U.S., 1, 4, 8, 22, 42, 63, 94 (Board of Home Missions), 113, 114 (Executive Committee of Christian Education) (Advisory Committee on Christian Education), 159
Presbyterian Church in the U.S.A., The (UPUSA), 4, 58, 63, 106 (Board of Christian Education), 112 (Synod of Texas), 166, 170
Presbyterian Church of Sewickley, Pennsylvania, 241
Presbyterian Education Association of the South, 114
Presbyterian Historical Foundation, Montreat, N.C., 63
Presbyterian Institute of Industrial Relations, Chicago, Illinois, 229
Presbyterian School of Christian Education, Richmond, Virginia (formerly Assembly's Training School), 60
Presbyterian Survey, The, 77
Presbytery of Brazos, Presbyterian

Church, U.S., 64, 98
Presbytery of Brownwood, Presbyterian Church, U.S., 64
Presbytery of Central Texas, Presbyterian Church, U.S., 5–7, 64, 69, 71
Presbytery of the Covenant, Presbyterian Church, U.S., 201
Presbytery of Dallas, Presbyterian Church, U.S., 64
Presbytery of Eastern Texas, Presbyterian Church, U.S., 64
Presbytery of El Paso, Presbyterian Church, U.S., 64
Presbytery of Fort Worth, Presbyterian Church, U.S., 64
Presbytery, Indian, Presbyterian Church, U.S., 83
Presbytery of Paris, Presbyterian Church, U.S., 64
Presbytery of Western Texas, Presbyterian Church, U.S., 64
Price, Robert Earl, 231
Prince, Clarence, 179
Princeton Theological Seminary, Princeton, N.J., 58, 163, 177, 233, 241
Pruitt, William Franklin, 85, 86, 90, 91
Pryor, William Edgar, 210, 211
Purcell, A. L., 10
Purcell, John Edwin, 64
Purcell, John McLeod, 7, 8, 12
Purcell, Malcolm Lee, 39

Quanbeck, Warren A., 178
Queen's College, Charlotte, N.C., 223
Quinius, Henry Willard, 106, 161, 163, 164, 173, 189, 208, 216, 217, 229, 231, 233

Race relations, 6, 187
Railsback, Glenn A., 142, 143, 149, 151, 152, 195
Rainey, Homer Price, 104, 121, 177
Raitt, Earl, 161
Ralston, Calvin J., 11
Ranson, Charles W., 181
Read, David H. C., 179
Read, John Leighton, 23, 24, 27
Red, G. C., 12
Red, Mrs. R. K., 9, 10, 12
Red, William Stuart, 8, 65
Redhead, John Agrippa, Jr., 179
Regional Synods, 113
Renquist, Michael George, 221
Riccobene, Samuel Peter, 101

Ritschl, Dietrich, x, 163, 169, 170, 178, 212, 216
Robbins, Fred S., 120, 121, 123
Robertson, Edward Dale, 205, 206
Robertson, Jerome Pillow, 7
Ross, William, 179
Rugh, Arthur, 64
Rundell, Frank R., 121

St. Luke United Presbyterian Church, Amarillo, Texas, 195
St. Paul Presbyterian Church, Houston, Texas, vii
Sampson, Frank, 34
Sampson Hall, 31, 53, 59, 63, 65, 81, 84, 88, 119, 158, 159
Sampson, Thornton Rogers, 16, 17, 22, 26, 29–35, 44, 47, 107, 116, 134, 135, 243
Samuel Huston College, Austin, Texas, 109
Sanden, Oscar Emanuel, 73
Sanders, James A., 178
Sautter, Cathy (Mrs. Marvin), vii, 167, 168, 172
Schaff, Philip, 32, 103, 241
Schaller, Lyle, 178
Scherer, Paul, 178
Scofield Bible, 111
Scott, Marshal L., 178
Scott, Walter S., 65
Scott, William Nelson, 11, 15
Sealy, Tom, 195
Second Presbyterian Church, Memphis, Tenn., 177
Seddon, Ernest Alfred Joseph, Jr., 92, 94–96, 161, 233
Selfridge, Lawrence Elmer, 7
Settles Lectures, 177, 179, 180, 185
Settles, Mrs. W. R., 133, 177
Sexton, James Wittin, 9, 10
Sharpe, Dwight Alfred, 67
Shaw, Charles Van Dyke, 231
Shelton, Robert M., 164, 170–172, 188, 189, 233
Shepherd, Don Glen, 195, 196
Sheppard, William Henry, 61
Sherrill, Lewis Joseph, 179
Sherrill, Richard Ellis, 6, 62
Shipley, David Oliver, 245
Shriver, Donald, 179
Siegenthaler, Carl Edward, 164, 189, 235
Sims, E. R., 60, 233

Singleton, James Martin, 96, 97, 102
Singleton, Nell (Mrs. J. Martin), 60, 97
Skinner, James William, 64
Skinner, Julia Lake, 64
Sleeper, Mr. and Mrs. John, 118
Slicker, Joseph Allen, 202
Siusser, Gerald Herbert, 201–203
Smiley, John, vii, 152, 153, 156, 195
Smith, Cecil Hiawatha, 44
Smith, H. Shelton, 179
Smith, Harry Edmund, 179
Smith, James Allen, 204–206
Smith, John Coventry, 178
Smith, Seymour A., 179
Smith, Wade Cothran, 64
Smoot, Richmond Kelley, 1–3, 5–8, 11, 26, 58, 107, 112, 116
Solomon, John Calvin, 101
Southern Presbyterian Association of Theological Schools, 236
Southwestern Presbyterian University, Memphis, Tennessee (formerly at Clarksville, Tennessee), 59, 98
Southwestern Regional Interseminary Organization, 109
Spanish-Speaking Department, 20, 55, 60, 65, 94, 161
Spindletop, 14
Spong, William C., 164, 234
Spragens, John Brewer, 168
Sprague, Minna (Mrs. George A.), 109
Stafford, W., 6
Staples, C. M., 6
Steere, Douglas, 178
Steimle, Edmund A., 179
Stendahl, Krister, 165
Stitt, David Leander, vii, 51, 89, 105–106, 134, 139–143, 151, 152, 161, 162, 164, 165, 167, 169–177, 179, 180, 193, 195–197, 200, 204, 208, 210, 212, 231, 233, 240, 243, 247
Stitt (David L.) Fellowship, 176
Stitt, Jane Wilkinson Dupuy (Mrs. David L.), 139, 176, 195
Stitt, William S., 139
Stone, John Timothy, 65
Stout, John, 179
Street, Thomas Watson, 77, 105, 162–164, 169, 173–175, 185, 200, 206, 208, 212, 215, 233
Strickland, James Arthur, 202
Stuart Seminary, Austin, Texas, 9, 11, 12, 17, 29
Student Volunteer Movement, 15
Sullivan, George Monroe, 161

Summey, George, 59, 69, 82–84, 87, 90, 98, 107, 111
Sunday, Carroll Rodney, 91
Supervised Practice of Ministry, 164, 234
Sweet, William Warren, 154
Swinney, Leonard Robert, 199, 200
Synod of Arkansas, Presbyterian Church, U.S., 8, 20, 64, 115
Synod of Louisiana, Presbyterian Church, U.S., 64, 65, 115
Synod of Missouri, Presbyterian Church, U.S., 139
Synod of Oklahoma, Presbyterian Church, U.S., 8, 20–21 (Indian Territory), 64, 115
Synod of Red River, Presbyterian Church, U.S., 237, 240, 241, 248
Synod of Texas, Presbyterian Church, U.S., 1, 5–11, 15, 18, 19, 23, 26, 42, 47, 48, 52, 53, 55, 64, 65, 96–98, 109 (Women of), 112, 115, 151
Synod of Texas, UPUSA, 185
Synod of Virginia, Presbyterian Church, U.S., 20
Systematic Theology, 17, 23, 43, 44, 55, 57, 59, 98, 107, 133, 162–164, 206, 233

Tarver, Julia Mitchell, 244
Taylor, Charles Allen, 182
Taylor, John Randolph, 189
Tenney, Benjamin Kingsbury, 64
Tenney, Samuel Mills, 63
Testa, Michael, 179
Texas-Mexican Presbytery, 94
Tex-Mex (Kingsville, Texas), 94
Texas Presbyterian College, Milford, Texas, 47
Theses, Twelve, 182, 183, 212
Third Presbyterian Church, New Orleans, Louisiana, 60
Thomas, John Rea, 212
Thompson, Ernest Trice, vii, 105, 163, 164, 172, 173, 177, 187, 221
Thompson (Hoxie) Lectures, 178
Thornton, Edward E., 179
Tidball, William Jared, 7, 8
Tiemann, William Harold, viii
Tillotson College, Austin, Texas, 110
Tolbert, Archibald McDuffie, 244
Tolliver, Ed., 43
Tompkins, Jerry Robert, vii
Town and Country Pastors' Institute, 231
Trainum, William H., 23

Trevino, Elias, 65
Trinity University, San Antonio, Texas (formerly at Waxahachie, Texas), 59, 97
Trueblood, D. Elton, 178
Trull Administration Building, 158, 159
Trull, Robert B., 196
Turner, Joseph Lee, 211, 212
Tyler, Frederick William, 96–98

Union between Presbyterian denominations, 6, 22, 112–113 (Estab. Permanent Committee on Cooperation and Union), 128
Union of PCUS and Reformed Church of America, 188, 189
Union of PCUS and UPUSA, 113, 189
Union Theological Seminary, New York, N.Y., 162
Union Theological Seminary, Richmond, Virginia (formerly at Hampden-Sydney, Va.), vii, 2, 5, 23, 36, 57, 59, 73, 163, 169, 191
United Presbyterian Church in the U.S.A., 207
United Urban Council of Austin, Texas, 167
University of Chicago, The, Chicago, Illinois, 58
University of Glasgow, Glasgow, Scotland, 206
University of Texas, The, Austin, Texas, 1, 5, 9, 21, 29, 39, 48, 55, 58–61, 63, 68, 71, 73, 81, 86, 92, 93, 98, 103, 104, 115–117, 135–137, 135 (Division of Extension - Bible Correspondence Course), 139, 157, 161, 168, 177, 180, 220, 223, 241, 243
University Presbyterian Church, Austin, Texas (formerly Highland Presbyterian Church), 6, 55, 60, 62, 84, 91, 93, 129, 139, 162, 237
Urban Ministry, 164, 235

Vanderlass, Clara Caswell Dismukes, 62
Van Dusen, Henry Pitney, 179
Vigness, Dr. David M., viii
Vinson, Jeanie de Forest Junkin (Mrs. J. W.), 77
Vinson, John Walker, 74–79
Vinson, Robert Ernest, 23, 30, 31, 38, 39–44, 47–50, 74, 107, 133–135, 243
Vinson, Thomas Chalmers, 32, 37, 43, 44, 60, 74

Wager, Herbert Franklin, 44
Walls, Guillermo Alexander, 65
Waverly Presbyterian Church, Old Waverly, Texas, 231
Weatherhogg, Neil Marvin, 223, 232
Webb, Leslie Everett, Jr., 201, 202
Wedel, Theodore, 178
Wehrli, A. G., 178
West, James Robertson, 23, 27
Westberg, Granger E., 179
Westerhoff, John H., 179
Westervelt (E. C.) Lectures, 178
Westminster Encampment, Kerrville, Texas, 64, 120
Westminster Presbyterian Church, St. Louis, Mo., 139
Wharton, Conway Taliaferro, 123
Wharton, James Allen, 163–165, 167, 169, 172, 188, 189, 206, 211, 233, 234
Wharton, Lawrence Hay, 60, 62, 91
Wharton, Turner Ashby, 64
Wheelus, Cleveland C., 232
Whitis House, 157
Whitten, J. G., 131
Wiggins, Earl Bernon, 200, 231, 232
Wilkins, Lewis Langley, Jr., 182
Williams, Don Marvin, 163
Williams, Edward Charles, 125
Williams, John Rodman, Jr., 163, 187, 188, 220, 233
Williams, Prescott Harrison, Jr., vii, 163, 164, 168, 169, 184–186, 233, 236, 237, 240, 243, 248

Williams, T. H., 53
Williams, Mr. and Mrs. Thomas Flint, Jr., viii
Williamson, Orin Conway, 60, 94, 233
Wilson, Woodrow, 34, 52
Winn, Albert Curry, 189
Womeldorf, Carlyle Ramsey, 55
Women in APTS, 42, 244
Wood, Bertram Oliver, 131, 132 (picture), 173, 196–198
Works, George A., 114–118
Works Report, 114–118, 151
World Conference on the Life and Work of the Churches, 66
World Council of Churches, 185
World Missions, Board of (PCUS), 74–79, 163, 175
World Student Christian Federation, 15
World War I, 53, 54
Wright, Ernest, 178, 237
Wroe, H. A., 53, 54
Wynne House, 159
Wynne, Toddie Lee, 106, 157, 216

Yale Divinity School, 177
Yeargan, Maurice Clark, 68
Y.M.C.A.
  Overseas, 53, 59
  Texas State, 53, 58
  University of Texas, The, 53–55, 62, 71

About the Author

Thomas White Currie, Jr., the oldest son of the third President of Austin Presbyterian Theological Seminary, has been serving congregations of the Presbyterian Church, U.S. in Texas since the summer of 1939 when he preached at Brandon and Blum in Hill County. He was ordained and installed at Eliasville August 24, 1941. His earned degrees are from The University of Texas, Austin, Union Theological Seminary, New York, N.Y., Austin Presbyterian Theological Seminary, and Union Theological Seminary of Virginia at Richmond, Virginia. In 1953 Austin College, Sherman, Texas conferred on him the Doctor of Divinity degree.

Dr. Currie has served as pastor at Ridglea Presbyterian Church, Fort Worth, and St. Paul Presbyterian Church, Houston, in addition to his present pastorate at Oak Cliff Presbyterian Church, Dallas. He was elected Moderator of the Synod of Texas, Presbyterian Church, U.S., in 1963. From 1963 to 1967 he was executive for church extension in the Presbytery of Brazos. One brother, David, is pastor at Seguin, Texas; another, Stuart, was a professor at Austin Presbyterian Theological Seminary until his death in 1975; a sister, Bettie, was on the staff of the Board of Christian Education of the Presbyterian Church, U.S. before becoming executive of the Joint Education Development Committee, a cooperative effort of nine denominations, a post from which she retired in 1977.

Mrs. Currie is the former Anne Alison Harrison of Waco, Texas, a graduate of Baylor University, Waco, and of The University of Texas at Austin. Dr. and Mrs. Currie have three daughters, Elizabeth (Mrs. Gregory L.) Williams of Jonesboro, Arkansas, Alison (Mrs. Dieter) Meier of Wiedenbrück, West Germany, and Margaret, an attorney in Austin, Texas. Their older son, Thomas White Currie, III, is pastor of Brenham Presbyterian Church, Brenham, Texas; the younger, James Stuart Currie, is a student at Austin Presbyterian Theological Seminary.

Dr. and Mrs. Currie collaborated as authors of a study book for the Women of the Church, *Great Protestant Leaders*, and Dr. Currie wrote a Church Extension study book, *Our Cities for Christ*. These were published in 1951 and 1954 respectively.